FABRICS

Today we are not only faced with a bewilderingly wide range of fabrics, but also all kinds of questions about their qualities: will they wash or dry clean; are they natural, man-made or a mixture of both; will they wear well, or shrink, fray or stretch; will they drape and hang well; are they shower- or flame-proof; are they easy to sew, handle and look after? The very basis of success in home dress-making and working on furnishings and upholstery lies in the correct choice of fabric — a mistake could prove costly.

In this very practical, straightforward book, Ann Ladbury moves from Abbot Cloth to Zibelene in more than one thousand entries, describing the important specific qualities of all the fabrics that are generally available, as well as some that come and go as fashion dictates. She also gives a simple description of the origin of each fibre and explains the distinction between the various types of fabric construction. Finally she gives a list of the different trade names, to overcome the confusion that frequently arises over the difference between them and other textile terms.

This will prove invaluable to all who make and buy their own clothes and furnishings.

THE AUTHOR

Ann Ladbury comes from a family of tailors, stretching back to her great-great-grandmother, who worked at the Court of the Emperor Franz Josef in Vienna. She has become a household name in dressmaking, with her very successful television broadcasts. Her two most recent series for BBC, *Dressmaker* and *Children's Wardrobe*, were complemented by best-selling books. On Independent Television she presented *Making Things Do* and *Making Things Fit*, as well as appearing regularly as a guest on *House Party*. Her very successful books include *The Craft of Dressmaking*, *Dressmaking for Beginners*, *Improve your Dressmaking* and *Sewing*, and she contributes a monthly column to *Pins and Needles*. Each year she travels thousands of miles, presenting her own fashion shows to capacity audiences. As a tribute to her 'outstanding leadership in the home dressmaking field', she was presented with a major international award at the first International Trade Conference and Exhibition on Home Sewing — Intersew '78 — held in Monte Carlo in October 1978.

FABRICS

Ann Ladbury

SIDGWICK & JACKSON
LONDON

First published in Great Britain in 1979
by Sidgwick and Jackson Limited

ISBN 0 283 98514 3

Line drawings by Jil Shipley

Set by Aberdeen University Press and
Printed in Great Britain by
A. Wheaton & Co, Exeter
for Sidgwick and Jackson Limited
1 Tavistock Chambers, Bloomsbury Way
London WC1A 2SG

Acknowledgements

The author and publishers would like to thank the following for their help in providing information for this book:

Allan's, Duke Street

Association of British Launderers and Dry Cleaners

J & P Coats

Courtaulds

Gomshall Associated Tanneries

I.C.I. Fibres Division

International Wool Secretariat

Jackson Brothers

John Lewis Partnership

Linton Tweeds

Selectus Limited

Tootal Fabrics

Vilene Limited

Viyella

Contents

Introduction

In this book we are concerned only with those textiles produced for clothes and furnishing and sold as piece-goods, i.e. by the metre. But fabrics are made from fibres, sometimes one fibre, often a mixture of anything from two to six, and the fabrics are then finished to make them acceptable for their specific purposes. So for choosing and making up fabrics, it helps to know something about the properties of all the fibres that are used in their manufacture as well as the properties of the resulting fabrics. And if, in addition, you want to know a little about the way the raw materials are treated in the production of the initial fibre, that section comes at the end of the book.

Since fibre-content labelling became compulsory, some totally unfamiliar words have come to the notice of the home-sewer. Sometimes she has no idea what type of fibre is being described, and the list of fibres with their percentages simply confuses her. In addition, numerous trade names are used for man-made fibres and it is often difficult to know which is the trade name and which the general term.

The purpose of this book is to explain what all these names and terms mean, and how a knowledge of them can help you when you are choosing fabrics for sewing. It attempts to define simply what each fabric is and how it will handle when it is sewn.

Part One

Choosing Fabrics

Choosing a fabric that is unsuitable for its purpose will always mean disappointment. Often the making up will prove so difficult that it is never completed, and even if it is, the result may be unsatisfactory in wear. For example, if a pleated skirt were made in a fine springy crêpe, attempts to press in pleats would probably cause iron marks, and the pleats would be unlikely to remain flat in wear. If you cover a chair or a stool in a thin crease-prone fabric, that cover will always look creased.

It is always worth while to note the fibre content of the fabric, because the percentages of the various fibres will give you an indication of how the fabric will wear and whether it will be warm, cool, etc. But there are, of course, many other points to consider.

1 Weight

Lift up approximately the quantity you will be using and see how heavy it is. This is particularly important if the fabric is heavy, i.e. coating, but it is also important if a large amount is to be used, e.g. for an evening dress, or jacket and trousers. Many people now prefer lightweight clothing, perhaps in several layers. And recent trends in manufacture have also led to much lighter fabrics for clothes; even bulky fabrics are not as heavy as they once were. But when choosing curtain fabric, your considerations may be different; heavy fabric will conserve heat in the room.

2 Weave

Examine the weave as this will affect the sewing processes and the draping qualities. For example, open lacy weave will be warm, but double hems will be visible and interfacing will show. This type of construction is excellent for light and heavier vision curtains but not for loose covers. It can be used for cushion covers, but only if a lining is added. A close twill-weave fabric is often springy and not particularly comfortable to wear.

3 Texture

Feel the fabric to see if the texture is agreeable; this is particularly important with clothes and chair covers, less so with curtains. It is not only soft, smooth textures that are attractive; rougher ones such as slub silk are nice to feel, too. Some people cannot wear panne velvet or simulated suedes because the texture is unacceptable to them.

4 Colour

There will often be a choice of colours in the same fabric. In larger fabric departments, amongst popular fabrics there may be six or eight colours to choose from. Select one or two possibilities and remove them from the distraction of the rest of the display. When buying for clothes, consider the remainder of your wardrobe and your general colour scheme. The same consideration applies even more to furnishing fabrics, because the article will be constantly on view. Impulsive colour choices are forgiveable in clothes but much less so in furnishings.

5 Price

This may be your final point of consideration, or it may be the first, depending entirely on what you are buying for and your own circumstances. If it is possible to compare two similar fabrics, then look at the price of each in conjunction with the fibre content, remembering that some fibres are cheaper than others.

6 Width

Note the width of the fabric in conjunction with the price. A high-price fabric that is wide often works out cheaper than a narrow one that is less expensive. If your design requires fabric of a certain width in order to avoid joins or to accommodate pattern pieces, then the width is the first point to consider.

Fabric Widths

The following table shows the widths of fabrics generally available. The most popular width is now 112–115cm (45in), and this seems to be because the majority of fabrics in Japan and the United States are made on looms this width.

90cm (36in)	Cottons, viscose, pure silk, some wool. Dress fabrics, nightwear, lining fabrics.

112–115cm (45in)	Cottons, viscose, polyester, acrylics, some wool. Dress fabrics, light outer wear, linings, furnishings.
140cm (54in)	Wool, some cottons. Coatings, suitings, linings, some furnishings.
160cm plus (60in) plus	Knits of all kinds. Special fabrics such as ciré and plastic. Some furnishings.
(28in)	Hand-wovens such as some silk, Welsh wool, Harris Tweed.
82cm (32in)	Interfacings.

This is only a general guide to the more popular widths. There are many exceptions. For example, silk may be 85cm, 90cm, 100cm, 102cm, 112cm, or 125cm. Lace may be 90cm, 110cm, 112cm, 115cm, 120cm, 140cm. These examples were taken from one shop.

Calculating the Quantity

You can see from the above that it is impossible for paper pattern companies to quote a quantity of fabric for each width of fabric. Most will give two or three widths to include the two most common, i.e. 115cm and 160cm. If the fabric you have found is in a width not mentioned on your pattern, you must make your own calculation. There are two ways of doing this.

1

If you are in the shop and anxious to buy on the spot, remember these points.

(a) 90cm fabric is narrow and will only take one main piece of pattern. You will therefore need to add together the lengths of all the pieces, i.e. sleeve plus front plus back, allowing more for larger sizes.

(b) 115cm is slightly wider. If the style is full, you have the extra needed for pleats, gathers, etc., so calculate as for 90cm fabric. If the pattern pieces are small, there may be room to place them side by side.

(c) 140cm fabric is wide enough to place two main pieces side by side, e.g. front and back, adding extra for the sleeve length. Trousers, too, can be cut from one length, but extra should be added for larger sizes if the total measurement of both thighs comes to more than 145 cm.

(d) 160cm fabric is wide enough to place main pieces side by side, plus the sleeve, so normally only one length of fabric is needed, unless the style is very full and requires, say, two widths in the skirt.

(e) Hand-woven fabrics are very narrow indeed, taking only one pattern piece on the width. A panelled style may have to be made and this will require additional fabric.

Note the following points when calculating:

(a) Patterned fabrics need matching or placing carefully, and this includes large florals as well as checks. Additional length is needed on the same lines as for wallpaper; you need one extra pattern for each pattern piece laid end to end on the fabric. This will generally mean three extra repeats on narrow fabrics and one or two on wide ones.

(b) Napped or one-way fabrics, including all pile fabrics, simulated suede, one-way florals, one-way checks and stripes, have to be cut with the pattern pieces laid in one direction. You cannot economize by dovetailing, so buy extra to be sure you have enough.

(c) Cuffs, facings, pockets and small collars can be cut from the fabric left between the main pieces, but allow extra fabric for elaborate styles, big collars, double wing cuffs, frills, neck flounces, circular sleeves, etc.

(d) Any pattern piece cut on the cross will take about one and a half times its length. If a pattern piece is on the cross in addition to being cut in check or patterned fabric, then allow extra for matching plus extra for the bias direction.

If crossway strips are to be cut, allow extra fabric.

(e) Always allow extra for border prints for any garment other than a plain or gathered skirt.

2

If you want to be certain to the nearest 10cm that you are not buying too much fabric, you will have to go home and lay out the pattern. If you make a habit of buying fabrics of unusual width, perhaps from market stalls, then it may be worth marking up an old sheet with various fabric widths. Prepare the sheet by marking the length, with felt pen, along one edge, marking every 10cms up to a metre and on to two metres, etc. Across the width of the sheet, mark off in various coloured pens, the widths of fabric.

To calculate the quantity of fabric needed, lay out the pattern pieces on the sheet, dovetailing where possible for economy. Read off on the edge of the sheet how much fabric of each width would be required.

Remember to add extra for matching patterns. Remember to lay the pattern pieces in one direction only for a one-way or napped fabric.

Buying the Fabric

Having narrowed your choice to perhaps two or three fabrics, and having decided how much you will need, apply the following final tests.

(a) Hold the fabric up, exposing roughly the quantity that will show when it is made up. Look at the effect in a mirror. A blouse under a jacket or pinafore dress will expose only a small area, so the fabric can be bright and it can be a print of almost any size or type. Look at a large area of the same fabric for, say, a long dress or matching jacket and trousers and the effect will be very different. Similarly with furnishings, cushion covers could be made from a bright colour or large print, but you would not decide on that fabric for curtains and loose covers — particularly if choosing a matching wallpaper, too.

(b) When buying fabric for clothes for yourself, hold the fabric against you as it will be in wear. For a skirt, hold it with the cut edge level with the skirt you are wearing and look down to see the effect; look in the mirror, and see what effect it has on your hips. Do the same thing when buying fabrics for trousers, look at the total length on yourself. If the fabric will be near your face, hold it up under your chin and look in the mirror — if you do this with several colours you will soon see which one suits you best.

(c) Drape the fabric as you intend to make it up, i.e. gathered, pleated, flat, etc., to see the effect. This is particularly important with patterned fabrics, as it will show you whether or not the design will be spoiled by breaking it up — many are in fact improved by it. This treatment will also help you to see whether the fabric will still hang properly if gathered or draped, a point that is very important if you intend to use the fabric sideways, i.e. with the selvedge horizontally. You may be doing this for economy or because of the design on the fabric.

(d) Test the fabric for creasing by crushing a piece in your hand. If it remains crumpled it is likely to behave like this in wear. If it springs up quickly when you release it, then you will have to cope with that tendency when sewing it.

(e) Examine the cut edge of the fabric. See whether it frays readily or whether pieces of pile, loops of towelling etc., detach themselves easily. If you decide to buy it, be prepared to control the fraying.

Finally, resist the temptation to use furnishing fabrics for clothes, though some dress fabrics, such as printed cotton, are suitable for curtains and cushion covers.

Flaws

It is almost impossible for a roll of fabric to be manufactured without any flaws or irregularities in the weave. Some top quality expensive fabrics are examined and repaired before they leave the mill. In other cases, especially if it is not possible to repair it, or if the additional expense would be too great, the position of the flaws is indicated by a piece of sticky tape or coloured thread attached to the selvedge. However, many flaws are missed and it is up to you to watch carefully as the fabric is being unrolled.

After pointing out a flaw, you can refuse the piece (in rare instances a specialist shop with a good reputation will refuse to sell it to you); or you can ask for additional fabric to make up for it, but pay the price of the original length; or you can accept the piece at a reduced price. Remember that if it is plain fabric and you are using small pattern pieces, you can easily place the pattern to avoid the flaws, but if it is patterned, and particularly if the pattern is something like a large check, you will need at least one additional repeat of the pattern in order to avoid it.

Try to visualize where the flaw comes in relation to the pattern pieces. For instance, if it falls in the centre of a wide fabric you are buying for trousers, you could easily arrange for it to be out of sight at the inside leg. If you are buying narrow fabric for a garment with sleeves and the flaw is near the end of the piece, make sure you will be able to cut the sleeves before hitting the flaw. Provided you can place the main larger pattern pieces safely, it is usually possible to work round one flaw.

When buying fabric for curtains you obviously cannot cut round flaws, so whether or not you accept the flaw will depend on how noticeable it is. If a garment length of fabric contains more than one flaw, reject it altogether.

When buying fabric for loose covers, cushions etc., follow the same principle as for clothes.

Choosing Interfacings

Interfacings should support any part of a garment that will be given excessive wear or that has to appear crisp. Collars, cuffs, waistbands, button fronts must always be interfaced, but there are other areas that can be interfaced to improve the appearance and life of the garment. These include yokes, pocket flaps, patch pockets, complete coat fronts, hemlines.

Choose the type and weight of interfacing according to the weight and character of the fabric. Never alter the outward appearance of the fabric by the addition of an interfacing that is too heavy.

Woven interfacings, whether iron-on or sew-in, should be cut with the straight grain in the same direction as the fabric piece. Vilene is non-woven, so it can be cut in any direction, with the exception of Superdrape which should be cut with the grain.

Sew-in interfacing must be attached to the garment, either by inclusion in the seams (lightweight fabrics) or by catch stitching round the edges after trimming off the seam allowances (heavy fabrics).

Press iron-on interfacings in position on wrong side of fabric with a firm pressing movement, not a sliding action. Use a dry iron only. Always try out iron-on interfacing on your fabric to make sure it does not stiffen too much.

Decide where to use other interfacings, such as Fold-a-Band, Wundaweb and Bondaweb, after you have started constructing the article.

GRADES OF VILENE

(Sold in pre-packs and by the metre — 82cm wide)

Sew-In

Light. White. Washes and dry cleans.	Use in lightweight fabrics, such as voile, lawn, crêpe de Chine, bouclé.
Soft. White. Washes and dry cleans.	Use in cottons, dress weights synthetics, knits, etc.
Medium. White and charcoal. Washes and dry cleans.	Use in wool, firm dress fabrics such as linen, shirts.
Heavy. White. Washes and dry cleans.	Use in coatings, suitings.

Iron-On

Soft. White and charcoal. Do not dry clean unless all edges are sewn in.	Use in cottons, polyester blends, acrylics, viscose.
Firm. White. Wash, do not dry clean unless all edges are sewn in.	Medium to heavy cottons and crisp fabrics, shirts.
Transparent. White. Warm wash and dry clean.	Use in georgette, chiffon, voile and all fine fabrics.
Superdrape. White. Washes and dry cleans.	For all jersey, except very light, and other fabrics with 'give'. Cut with the 'give' in the Vilene in the direction required.
Heavy. White. Washes and dry cleans.	For coating and all heavy fabrics.

Sew-In

Pelmet. White. Washes and dry cleans. In 82cm and 25cm width.	For pelmets and waistbands.

Iron-On

Fold-a-Band. White. Washes and dry cleans. 6cm wide. Pre-pack.	Strip slits in centre. Reinforce waistbands, pleats, cuffs, sharp openings, pocket tops.
Bondaweb. White. Washes and dry cleans. Pre-pack sheet.	Paper-backed adhesive for cutting to shape. Use for appliqué, buttonholes, to repair fraying areas. Apply with hot iron and damp cloth. Peel off paper.
Wundaweb. White. Washes and dry cleans. 3cm wide. Pre-packs in three sizes.	Adhesive web in strip form for hems, fraying areas, curtains, buttonholes, etc. Place between layers of fabric. Apply with hot iron and damp cloth.

Pressing

After choosing a suitable fabric for your purpose, success is in sight but by no means guaranteed. Fabric is manufactured flat, indeed, great emphasis is placed on the initial finishing to ensure that it is flat, and when special finishes are applied, care is taken to see that these cannot be impaired later in the life of the fabric. In some cases, for example, when applying minimum-iron and non-crease finishes, the manufacturer is trying even harder to keep the fabric flat and so it seems almost deliberately to be working against the sewer and presenting her with problems additional to those of construction.

The moment after cutting out, you are trying to convert this very flat piece of fabric into something shaped. Pressing is vital at every stage of construction in order to achieve good results. It is a time-consuming skill that has to be learnt in depth by continual practice on different types of cloth. These will vary in construction as well as in fibre content and there are always surprises in store for even the more experienced and knowledgeable presser. It is possible to be happily confident about pressing a familiar-looking fabric of known content, only to find it does not react as expected and experiments have to be conducted on spare pieces. Unfortunately, because of the wide variety of fabrics available, it is only possible to give an indication of the general method of pressing required. For example, one important point to watch when pressing is how long it is necessary to keep the iron in position, and how heavily to place it. In the absence of actual pieces of fabric these things cannot be indicated in detail, but only as, for example, 'light pressure', 'sharp movements', etc. Having noted these together with other instructions, test all fabrics first to discover the most effective time and pressure.

Pressing is the most important single activity involved in construction. Some sewing processes can be glossed over, stitching can be below standard, some things can be avoided completely by the unenthusiastic or those lacking confidence, but pressing cannot be avoided or skimped, or carried out at the wrong moment, because the resulting item will proclaim it very noticeably.

Before elaborating on all the elements necessary for successful results, I would like to emphasize that one ingredient is always vital. That ingredient is time. Pressing is a slow, time-consuming job and it must never be hurried. There are two ways of approaching the problem of fitting it into your schedule. Either have the iron set up, plugged in and hot, for the whole period of your sewing (the iron does not use much electricity if it has a thermostat control), or complete the initial sewing movements on a variety of separate pieces of fabric, even on several garments, pile them up ready for pressing and then when you have sufficient time launch into a pressing session. Your choice of method may well depend on what you are making and how close your iron is to your working area.

A combination of several factors has to be achieved if you are to press successfully; the aim is to persuade the fabric to lie permanently in its new position at various points.

1 Heat

This is, of course, provided by the iron. Most irons have a dial on which is indicated the standard settings decided upon by the Home Laundering Consultative Council. These settings are cool, warm, medium hot, hot, very hot. Suggestions for temperatures at which various fibres should be pressed are made using these descriptions. Each description appears within a sector on the dial and the temperature can be adjusted within the sector. The settings are only a guide; it is always up to the individual to decide on the correct setting.

The temperature relating to the settings are laid down as follows:

Cool (1)	*Warm* (2)	*Medium Hot*	*Hot*	*Very Hot*
110°C (230°F)	150°C (302°F)	180°C (356°F)	200°C (392°F)	Above 200°C (392°F)

But irons do vary tremendously. Everyone knows of an iron that gets much too hot and is permanently set on cool, or one that remains at very hot but produces a barely warm result.

As far as ironing after laundering is concerned, the recommendations for various fibres are as follows:

Fibres	Setting
Nylon, Elastofibres, Acrylic	Cool
Acetate, Triacetate, Polyester, Silk, Wool, Cupro	Warm
Viscose, Modified viscose, Modal	Medium Hot
Cotton Linen	Hot or Very Hot

This information does not include all the fibres, nor does it take any account of the widest area of fabrics, that is, those that contain a mixture of fibres. Surprisingly a blend is often best ironed at a hotter setting than for the original fibres. Another factor that cannot be taken into consideration by such a table is the weave, thickness and any surface interest in the fabric, any one of which may be affected by the iron temperature.

When using the iron directly on the fabric be guided by the settings indicated on the iron, but when pressing with a damp cloth, the cloth cools the base of the iron and so the iron should be used at a higher setting. If this is not done, the amount of heat actually reaching the fabric is incorrect, and the amount actually penetrating it is very little. The result is that the pressing is ineffective, as the heat is insufficient to put the fabric in position permanently. And worse than this is the possibility of harming some fabrics with too little heat combined with moisture. At best this makes the fabric warm and damp, at worst it leaves a permanent imprint of the iron.

Ironing after laundering is usually done by placing the iron directly on the fabric and sliding it. Pressing after sewing is done with the iron held in position until it has pressed the sewing process in position, and, as in nearly all cases the addition of steam is vital, the iron is used slightly hotter than when laundering.

2 Pressure

The process has literally to be pressed and to do it you use the weight of the iron. The amount of pressure needed varies with the type of fabric and is largely a matter for experiment. For example, too much pressure exerted on a pile fabric will flatten the pile, but too little on a twill weave polyester will have no effect at all. The iron, therefore, can be used lightly, even holding it just above the surface in some cases, or more heavily, while if you add the weight of your arm and body by leaning over and pressing hard, you exert the maximum pressure necessary for springy fibres and stubborn weaves.

Whatever you decide about the amount of pressure required, the iron should be used in short, sharp dabbing movements. Do not slide it when using a damp cloth. If using the iron directly on the fabric, make sure you press the process adequately with sharp movements, then finish off by sliding the iron if necessary.

3 Steam

With a few exceptions it is impossible forcibly to change the position of the fabric without applying steam. The best way to provide steam is by the use of a dampened cloth. It requires quite a lot of skill to use it properly, but it is well worth learning the techniques in order to produce good results. The cloth is squeezed out in water, leaving just enough moisture in the cloth for the fabric being pressed. The quantity is governed by the type of fibres involved as well as the absorbency of the weave, i.e. whether close or open. The cloth is placed over the process, the iron applied and the heat immediately converts the water to steam and it is the steam which is pressed into the fabric. The cloth must be removed immediately. Failure to have the iron hot enough to convert the water to steam will result in soggy fabric, possibly stretched or out of shape, and iron marks. In addition, the process will not be adequately pressed.

With many fine fabrics the steam issuing from a steam iron may be sufficient, but with all others it is not. A steam iron is fine for use after laundering, but in that instance you are only removing creases, not inducing fibres to turn sharp corners. Because a steam iron makes laundering so easy, there is a tendency to use it for pressing when sewing, but with most fabrics the iron has to be held in position for too long, to allow sufficient steam to escape, and the result is an impression of the sole plate on the fabric, and possibly shine, too.

Good professional pressing while sewing is a combination of heat, pressure and moisture, all applied together but in varying amounts according to the fibres, weave, texture and finish of the fabric. Although, in the fabric section, recommendations are made as to the best method of pressing, it is still essential to try pressing a small scrap of the fabric first to be absolutely confident of good results. Your fabric may appear to conform in every respect to the one I have described, but it may have a particular surface finish which is invisible to you and which I do not know about.

One final point for emphasis. It is very important indeed to press each process before proceeding to the next stage in construction. This is something that is always mentioned in sewing books but often foolishly ignored, through idleness or the inconvenient situation of the iron, or a lack of appreciation as to why it is necessary. I cannot emphasize too strongly that the persuasion of the fibres to take on a new direction must be done immediately the permanent stitching of that process has been completed. Poor and amateurish-looking sewing is always the result of trying to press only on completion.

PRESSING EQUIPMENT

1 Iron

Dry Iron. The heaviest you can find will be the most effective and the easiest to use. Lightweight irons affect the fabric so little that a lot of body pressure has to be added, and this makes it tiring work. An iron with a small base and sharply pointed nose is best for pressing as it covers only a small area at a time and the nose makes it easy to penetrate confined places.

Steam Iron. Buy one with steam holes distributed over the entire area of the sole plate. Those with small holed sections emit very little steam. It is a great advantage if the iron has the facility of an additional spurt of steam so that you can increase the amount.

Note that the button that sprays drops of water directly on to the surface of the fabric should only be used when laundering.

If you can only have one iron and feel a steam iron is more useful for general purposes, use it set on 'dry' when sewing, in conjunction with a damp cloth.

2 Cloth

A piece of butter muslin about one-metre square is best. It can be wrung out so that very little water remains, or left damper. It can also be folded to produce twice the amount of moisture for stubborn fabrics. It is very dangerous to use calico and other plain cotton fabrics, because even when wrung out tightly these contain too much water and therefore produce too much steam for some fibres, especially the softer synthetic fibres, such as acrylic and viscose. Other substitutes, such as a linen tea towel or a lawn handkerchief, are equally dangerous.

On many occasions it is necessary to press on the damp muslin, remove it quickly, and then press again without it, to settle the fabric before it springs up again. Obviously the bare iron cannot be used — it is too hot and anyway may well produce shine — but it is necessary to protect the fabric. For these occasions, it is useful to keep a spare piece of muslin — it can be quite small — to be used dry.

3 Sleeveboard

It would prove practically impossible to press correctly the processes involved in making clothes without a sleeveboard. This is not used for pressing completed sleeves as they would wrinkle, but the four rounded ends of different sizes are used for inserting in small shaped areas; an end is used level with the end of darts to prevent shaping being flattened, and the length of the board is used for pressing all seams, pleats and flat processes. The sleeveboard is used standing on another surface, preferably a table or bench covered with a layer of blanket or, if this is not available, on the ironing board. The sleeveboard raises the work to a more comfortable level, it ensures that only a small area of fabric is exposed for pressing so the likelihood is that you will spend more time on it, but most important of all, the sleeve-board supports the process while the table or board below takes the weight of the garment. This eliminates any danger of the fabric stretching when it becomes warm and damp under the iron.

4 Pressing Block

This is a smoothed block of wood: sophisticated types have a raised section that acts as a handle, and it is used for banging the steam into fabric after the damp cloth has been removed. It is not necessary to use it on fine fabrics and it should never be used on pile fabrics or those with raised surface interest, but it is essential for getting a good finish on seams, hems, pleats, etc., on springy fabrics and closely woven ones that are difficult to penetrate with steam.

5 Pressing Pad

This is less vital than the items already mentioned, but is a useful addition. When pressing armholes with set-in sleeves, push the pad into the armhole to support the shoulder and sleeve head, hold it in one hand and use the iron and cloth with the other. The pad can also be placed on the end of the sleeveboard to provide additional shape to the board. You can buy or make a variety of pressing pads of different shapes and sizes, but the one of most general use is probably the big oval pad with a pocket on the side to put your hand in.

6 Point Presser

After acquiring the other items of pressing equipment and upon becoming proficient, you will find a wooden point presser useful. As its name suggests, pointed areas such as collars will slide on to it, the point of the tool will force its way into the collar and you can press over it. To extend the use of the presser, cover one long edge with a single layer of blanket and make a cotton cover and it can be used for pressing seams on fabrics where there is a danger of imprints of turnings appearing.

Fibres

Yarns are made up of a number of filaments and referred to when necessary as multi-filament yarns. The length of the filament varies with each type of fibre. It may be quite short, e.g. cotton

1–5cm; or it may be very long, e.g. silk, several miles; or it may be endless, e.g. continuous until deliberately broken, as in the production of man-made filaments.

The reason for making the yarn multi-filament is that this gives it greater strength, more flexibility, and elasticity.

The number of filaments in a yarn varies. Some single- or mono-filament yarn is produced for special purposes. One example is the transparent invisible thread that can be bought in haberdashery departments. This is often used in the construction of ready-made clothes because no colour-matching is required, but it is rather harsh and slippery, has a distinctly synthetic feel, cannot be flattened for threading through the eye of a needle and is rather springy and lacking in elasticity. Try it and you will appreciate why multi-filament yarns are necessary.

Most yarns are twisted to strengthen them and protect them from breakage during weaving or knitting. This also produces a harder-wearing yarn. For example, worsted cloth is made from high-twist yarn and although fine, the cloth is exceedingly hard-wearing. The twist is either like an S or a Z. By unravelling a yarn you can discover which.

Many fibres are converted into staple before being spun and then woven into fabric; that is, they are cut up into short lengths. The reasons for this are many, depending upon the type of fabric to be produced. One reason might be to make a more fuzzy, less smooth yarn, another to give a fibre that can be blended successfully with another before spinning and weaving.

Tow fibre is similar to staple but it is cut up at a later stage in production than staple.

We have, therefore, fabrics being made from filament yarns, continuous filament yarns and staple yarns. In order to distinguish between them, unravel your fabric, tease out to a single filament and see how long it is.

THICKNESS OF YARN

The coarseness of yarn is calculated in a number of ways, with different terms of description. Cotton-count is the number of hanks of cotton that total 1lb in weight. A hank is taken as a length of 840 yards. Worsted-count is the number of hanks of worsted that weigh 1lb. A hank of worsted is taken as 560 yards. Denier is the description used for silk and man-made fibres. One denier is the weight in grams of 9,000 metres of yarn. Because the word denier is used to describe the fineness of tights and stockings, it has become well known in the household. All yarns can be described in deniers for easier understanding. To do this, convert the yards into metres, multiply that up to 9,000 and convert the 1lb into grams.

Tex is another term used to describe yarn coarseness. It is an international unit for all fibres, both natural and man-made. It is the weight in grams of 1,000 metres, or the weight of the yarn in milligrams per metre.

PROPERTIES

Some fibres are weak, some are strong, some are cool, some are warm. The properties of each differ and what can be a disadvantage in one may be an advantage in another according to its eventual use.

All fibres are thin compared with their length and all have the following properties in measurable degree:

Strength, both when dry and, equally as important, when wet.

Elasticity, the amount by which a fibre will stretch under strain and return. This is an important consideration where clothing is concerned; obviously it is better if the fibre returns to its original length after stretching, not so good if it does not. Also interesting to manufacturers is the point during stretch at which the fibre actually breaks.

Regain. This term, or moisture regain, is used to describe the amount of moisture present in the fibre per specific weight when dry. All fibres absorb moisture from the atmosphere and the regain level is important to know when choosing fabric for specific purposes. For instance, it has always been a source of surprise, and indeed a point greatly in its favour, that wool can absorb a great deal of water without feeling wet, and while still feeling warm. The constant variation in the weight of wool as a result can be of concern to manufacturers buying wool by weight, so specific conditions have to be adhered to.

Wool and other fibres that pick up moisture readily are described as hygroscopic. Some fibres, such as glass and nylon, have a comparatively low moisture regain level.

BASIC FIBRES

(Generic Names)

Some fibres are from entirely natural sources and no chemical change is undergone during the conversion to fabric. Some fibres are regenerated, that is they are man-made but from natural sources and are chemically altered. The others are entirely synthetic and derive from chemicals.

Usually the natural fibres are listed first and darkly hinted to be superior to those in the other two groups. It certainly cannot be assumed that these fibres are superior. It depends entirely on what properties you are looking for. And surely if man-made and synthetic fibres were indeed inferior, their development would not have been so rapid, and their popularity for clothing and furnishing would hardly have been so easily won. Many fabrics in any case are now mixtures or blends of fibres from either two or all three groups. So what properties have these fibres that interest us?

Man-made fibres have been with us for a long time and have earned their place in textiles. I think it is time they were accepted as equals alongside the old natural ones, so I have listed alphabetically *all* fibres used in the production of fabrics.

MAIN FIBRES		MINORITY FIBRES
Acetate		Alpaca
Acrylic		Camel
Cotton		Cashmere goat
Cupro		Elastomer
Flax		Glass
Modacrylic		Goathair
Modal		Hemp
Polyamide		Jute
Polyester		Metal
Sheep's Wool	Worsted	Mohair
	Woollen	Polyvinyl chloride (PVC)
Silk		Rabbit and Angora Rabbit
Triacetate		Ramie
Viscose		Vicuna

BLENDS AND MIXTURES

Blends

Quantities of two or more staple fibres are mixed as early as possible in processing. The amounts of each fibre are carefully measured to ensure correct results. The fibres will often possess different dye-absorption qualities, so that the earlier the blending takes place, the more evenly the dye will take at a later stage.

The advantages of blending include the possibility of reducing the price by introducing a cheaper fibre; the combining of a weak fibre with a strong one; the chance that the strength of the blend will be greater than either of the two individual fibres (this is not always so but undoubtedly a very small percentage of strong fibre will markedly improve the strength of a weak one); improving results of spinning and weaving.

After blending, the fibre is spun and woven. Blending enables poor qualities to be less obvious, but it emphasizes the good points of the component fibres.

Mixtures

A mixture is a combination of yarns of different colour and fibre content. A mixture often has one fibre in the warp and another in the weft. Mixtures of fancy yarns in woven and knitted fabrics produce attractive novel effects. And as different fibres absorb dye differently, interesting effects are often produced when mixtures are piece-dyed.

YARNS

Plain Yarns

Twist. When the yarns are twisted the direction of twist is either Z or S. The amount of twist required varies with the type of yarn and the use to which it will be put.

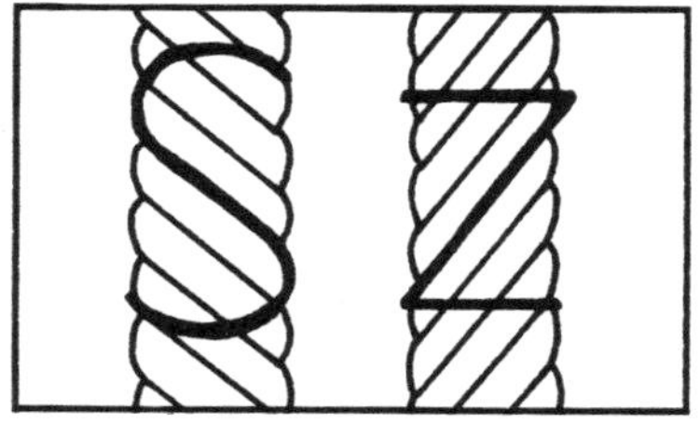

S and Z twists

Low Twist. Filament yarns are given a low twist, i.e. about 2–3 twists per inch.

Filling or weft yarns are also given a low twist of about 6–8 per inch if they are to be used in a fabric that will be brushed or napped. This low twist enables the machine to tease out the fibre more easily.

Average Twist. Most yarns from staple fibres are given an average twist, i.e. about 20–25 twists per inch. This does not destroy the softness induced by cutting into staple in the first instance.

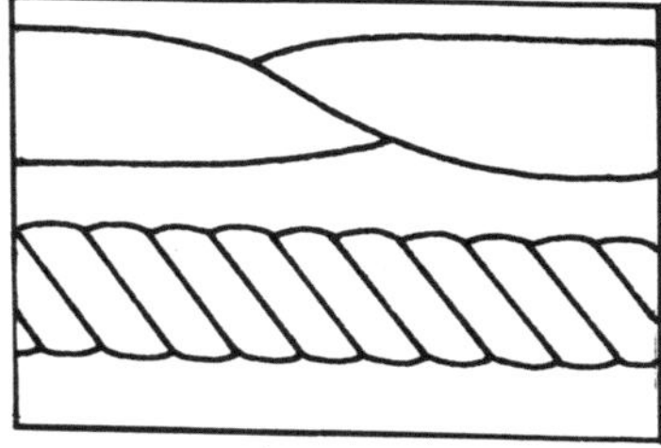

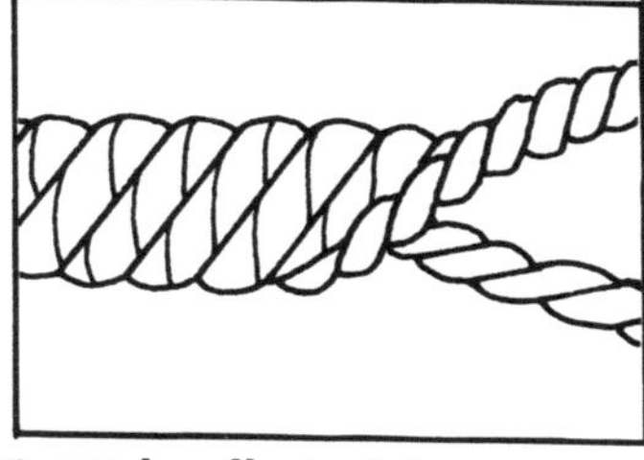

Low twist, high twist, and voile twist

High Twist. Sometimes called a hard twist, these yarns are twisted 35–40 times per inch. This makes them very compact and strong.

Two high twist yarns can be twisted yet again, keeping the spiral of both yarns running in the same direction. This is referred to as a *Voile Twist.*

Single Yarn

A single yarn is produced in the spinning process.

Ply Yarn

Two or more single yarns are twisted together to make a thicker, stronger yarn. Most ply yarns are twisted together with the spiral running in the opposite direction from the twist in the separate original yarns.

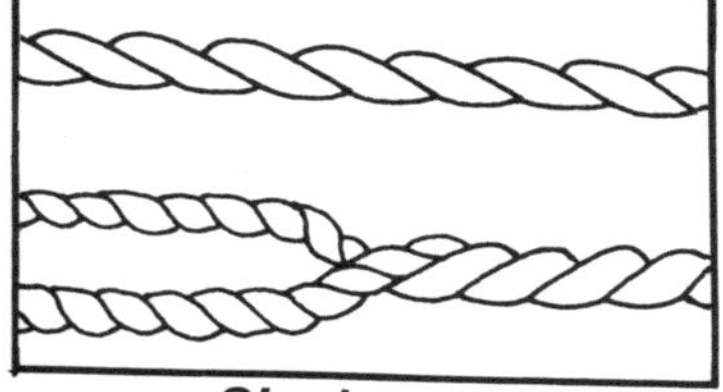

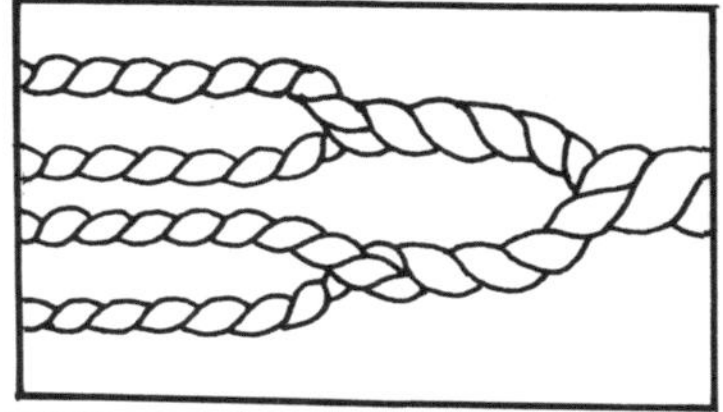

Single yarn, two-ply yarn, and cord yarn

Cord Yarn

Ply yarns twisted together form a cord. This is not often used in the production of fabric but is mainly confined to some types of sewing thread.

Textured or Fancy Yarns

1 Crêpe

The yarn is given a very high twist, as much as 70 turns per inch if it is very fine, less for thicker yarns. The crêpe is often used as the weft in the fabric, using a plain warp. After the fabric has been wet-finished the crêpe yarn snarls and produces the characteristic pebbled effect of crêpe fabric.

2 Corkscrew

A thin yarn is used as the core and a thicker yarn is wound slackly round it. Two colours may be used to produce a fancy effect. More basic yarns are produced by completely covering the core, as in some sewing threads such as gimp, and in some rubber yarns. The latter are covered with another fibre such as cotton, producing latex yarns, elastic, etc.

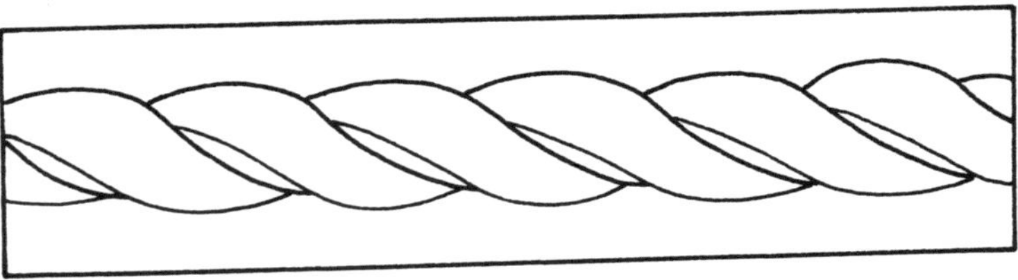

Corkscrew

3 Slub

Slub yarn is one which is irregular in thickness and produces an attractive uneven surface in the fabric. Slub in silk may be a feature of the fibre in its natural state. With other fibres the slub is introduced either by adding additional tufts of fibre or by loosening the twist, which then leaves a flat, softer section.

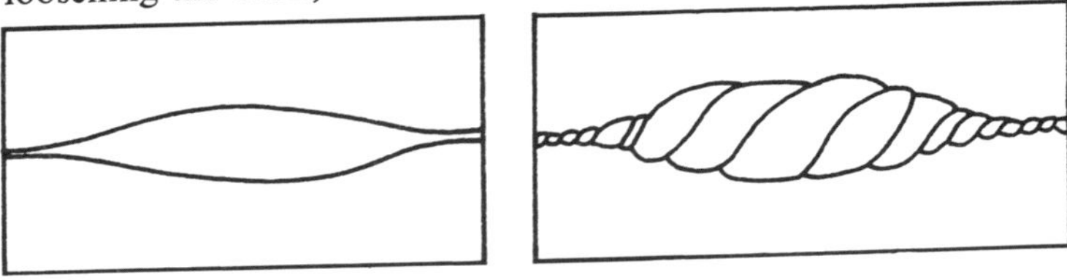

Slub

4 Nub

Lumps of yarn are introduced at regular intervals to produce a novelty effect. As two or more yarns are plied together, one is twisted many times in one place to produce the lump. The yarns, and therefore the nubs, may be various colours.

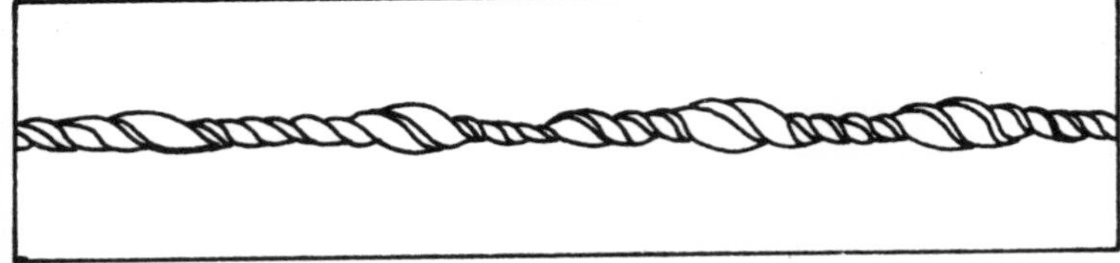

Nub

5 Bouclé

When the yarns are plied together one yarn remains slack, causing it to twist again in the same place.

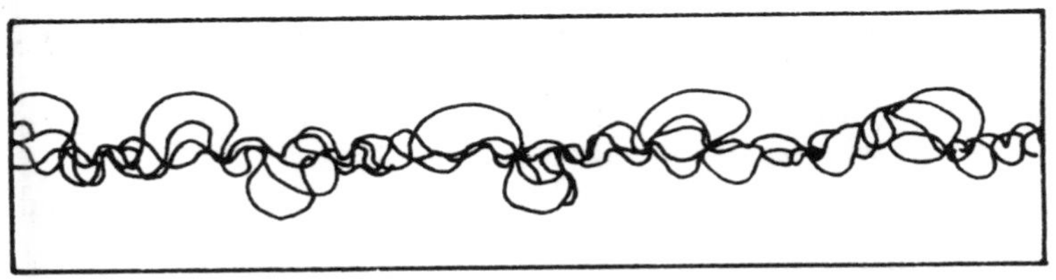

Bouclé

6 Loop

Thicker yarns are normally used because loop yarns are popular for coatings, astrakhan cloth and other fabrics with a thick loop-pile effect. A thick and thin yarn are twisted, the thicker one being overfed by the machine and causing loops at regular intervals. Woollen loop yarns can be brushed to give a mohair effect.

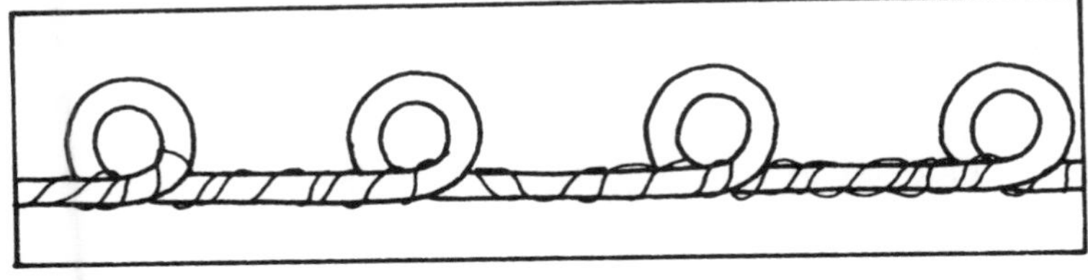

Loop

7 Ratine

An outer yarn is wound round a core yarn and at intervals the outer yarn throws out a longer loop so creating small close loops all round the core yarn.

Ratine

ACETATE

Type of fibre: Man-made cellulosic.
Source: Cotton linters (waste) or wood.
Processing:

1 The cotton or wood is converted into cellulose sheets.
2 The sheets are soaked in acetic acid (referred to as 'ageing').
3 The substance is mixed with acetic anhydride and sulphuric acid is added to act as a catalyst.
4 The resulting solution of cellulose acetate is aged again then mixed with water to cause it to precipitate.
5 The precipitated white flakes are dissolved in acetone and filtered.
6 The final solution is a clear liquid that is forced through the holes of spinnerets and spun ready for weaving or knitting.

Properties:

1 A weak fibre.
2 Fairly wrinkle resistant.
3 Has considerable elasticity.
4 Does not conduct heat.
5 Not absorbent so it sheds dirt easily in washing.
6 Little shrinkage.
7 Takes special dyes.
8 Fibre remains white.
9 Thermoplastic which means it can be heat set into pleats, creases, shaped garments etc.

Uses: Produced in staple and filament form and made into fabrics of all types for clothing and furnishing.

Also mixed and blended with other fibres including viscose and wool.

ACRYLICS

Type of Fibre: Man-made.
Source: Petroleum.
Processing:

1 Ethylene is derived from petroleum and this is followed by chemical processing that finally produces acrylonitrile.
2 Acrylonitrile is converted to resin.
3 The resin is dissolved in a solvent and extruded through a spinneret.
4 The filament is coagulated and then spun and stretched ready for weaving or knitting.

Precise manufacturing details vary from company to company.

Properties:

1 Warm, does not conduct heat well.
2 Can be heat set, i.e. is thermoplastic and can be set to a shape which it retains. It can also be permanently creased with the application of heat.
3 The fibre is not particularly strong.
4 Little stretch.
5 Little absorbency.
6 Shrinks in processing but not after fabric is finished.
7 Dyes in specific dyes only.

Uses: Produced in filament and staple form and made into a wide variety of knitted and woven fabrics for clothing of all types and furnishing fabrics.

Acrylics mix and blend very well with other fibres including wool and cotton. The yarn can also be bulked very successfully.

COTTON

Type of fibre: Natural cellulosic.
Source: The soft white hairy padding inside the ball or seed box of the cotton plant. Only available after flowers have died. Quality varies.
Processing:

1 Cleaned and baled for transporting.
2 Bales opened and contents blended with the use of a variety of beaters and spiked rollers. Cotton fibre is formed into sheets or laps.
3 Carded and combed to straighten fibres. Cotton emerges as a thick rope or sliver.

4 Drawing. The combing of several slivers which are pulled between rollers and drawn to one finer sliver. This is drawn and twisted and wound on to large bobbins.
5 Roving. Two further stages of drawing; the yarn is becoming finer.
6 Spinning. Cotton is drawn out into a thread and twisted as it is wound on to bobbins.

Properties:

1 Stronger when wet than dry.
2 Shrinks.
3 Loses strength in sunlight.
4 Soft but strong.
5 Good conductor of heat.
6 Absorbs moisture easily.
7 Dyes easily.

Uses: Can be woven or knitted. Used on its own, or mixed, or blended with other fibres, such as wool, viscose, polyester. Made into a very wide variety of fabrics for clothes, household linen and furnishings.

CUPRO

(Once called Cuprammonium Rayon)

Type of fibre: Regenerated cellulose.
Source: Cotton linters (waste). Wood is used if cotton is not available.
Processing:

1 Cotton is purified in caustic soda.
2 Dissolved in copper and ammonia (bright blue solution). May be stored.
3 Solution pumped into spinneret and extruded through holes into funnel.
4 Running water introduced to remove some ammonia and copper.
5 Cellulose is precipitated in soft condition, is stretched and spun on to rollers.
6 Filament passes from roller through acid bath which coagulates the cellulose.
7 Yarn wound, washed and dried ready for weaving or knitting.

Properties:

1 Similar to viscose but a stronger fibre.

2 Can be produced as a finer yarn than viscose.
3 Expensive.
4 Dyes easily.
5 Not a strong fibre.

Uses: Filament yarn is used for good lining fabrics.

Cupro otherwise used mainly in mixtures and blends with other fibres such as cotton.

FLAX

Type of fibre: Natural cellulosic bast fibre used to make linen fabrics.

Source: Bundles of fibre within the stalk of the flax plant.

Processing:

1 Retting. Bacterial rotting of the fibres to release the outer covering of stalk. Stalks made into bundles and dried. Seeds removed.
2 Scutching. Breaking up stems by passing between rollers in order to remove outer stem.
3 Combing. Bundles pass through series of combs which separate short fibres that are used for cheaper fabrics.
4 Spinning ready for weaving.

Properties:

1 Very absorbent.
2 Withstands high temperatures.
3 Very strong both wet and dry.
4 Uneven thickness of fibre lends typical feature to yarn.
5 Creases easily.
6 Expensive.

Uses: Made into linen and used for household furnishings, teacloths, tablecloths, etc. Flax is used in small quantities and mixed or blended with many other fibres, often to add texture or strength. Often added to cotton, wool, silk, polyester.

Small amounts are made into strong sewing threads.

MODACRYLICS

Type of fibre: Man-made.

Source: Acrylonitrile.

Processing:

1 The acrylic fibre process is used to produce the basic liquid which is then combined, under heat, with the gas vinyl chloride.

2 The resulting powder is dissolved in acetone producing a thick solution.
3 The solution is forced through a spinneret into water.
4 The resulting filament is stretched, spun and stabilized, and made ready for weaving or knitting.

Properties:
1 Stronger than acrylic.
2 High shrinkage in hot water.
3 Soft and warm.
4 Easily washed.
5 Very resilient and hard-wearing.
6 Little elasticity or loss of shape.

Uses: Modacrylics are produced mainly in staple form and mixed or blended with many other fibres either to improve performance or to decrease cost. Used in furnishing and clothing fabrics that are woven or knitted, including pile fabrics, and mixed with wool, nylon, cotton, acrylic, acetate fibres.

MODAL

Type of yarn: Polynosic (cellulose). Known also as modified rayon.
Source: Cotton waste (linters) or wood.
Processing: Similar to viscose but a shorter process.
1 Cotton or wood treated and made into sheets of cellulose. Soaked in caustic soda.
2 Sheets are broken into crumbs.
3 Crumbs are dissolved in water.
4 The resulting liquid is forced through the holes in a spinneret and into a bath of weak acid. The fibre is then stretched and spun to three times its length.
5 Wound on to bobbins for weaving.

Properties: The closest fibre to cotton.
1 Strong wet and dry.
2 Soft and absorbent.
3 Greater stability than viscose.
4 Can be mercerized.
5 Elastic.
6 Absorbs dye easily.
7 Inexpensive.

Uses: A limited range of 100 per cent modal fabrics is produced for clothing.

The fibre is used extensively in blends and mixtures with other fibres such as polyester and cotton.

POLYAMIDES

Type of yarn: Man-made. Nylon is the generic term used to describe the different polyamides in the group.
Source: Hydrogen, nitrogen, oxygen, carbon.
Processing:

1. Production methods vary, but basically processing starts with a series of chemical changes in the component elements producing adipic acid and hexamethylene diamene which combine to form a salt.
2. The salt is dissolved in water and, when ready for spinning, it is heated and reduced to a concentrated solution.
3. In another heating process the molecules combine in a long chain.
4. Still in liquid form, the molten polymer is sprayed on to a revolving wheel where it is hardened to a hard white substance.
5. Chipping breaks the substance into flakes.
6. Polymer flakes are poured on to a hot grid to melt them. The substance is pumped to a spinneret where it is extruded through holes.
7. The filaments cool and harden before being softened slightly in order to combine several filaments.
8. Filaments are drawn out to several times their length by transferring on to fast-moving reels during which process they are twisted ready for weaving or knitting.

Properties:

1. Non-absorbent.
2. A good conductor of heat unless fibre is spun.
3. Very hard-wearing and resilient.
4. Dirt cannot adhere, so easy to wash.
5. Very strong.
6. Very elastic.
7. Does not shrink.
8. White or pale colours may become grey if washed with other articles.
9. A thermoplastic fibre, so it can be permanently pleated, creased, embossed.

Uses: In filament or staple form it is made into a wide variety of fabrics for furnishing and clothes. Polyamide also mixes and blends well with other fibres such as wool, viscose. Its elasticity makes polyamide excellent for knitted fabrics.

POLYESTER

Type of fibre: Man-made.
Source: Petroleum.
Processing:
1 The basic component is converted and polyester production begins by feeding terephthalic acid and ethylene glycol into a container.
2 The two are stirred and kept at a constant temperature, after which the manufacture of the fibre is very similar to that of the polyamides, although methods vary slightly between manufacturers.

Polyester and polyamides are similar; even under a microscope it is not easy to distinguish between them.
Properties:
1 Very strong and resists abrasion.
2 Very resilient and after creasing it soon recovers.
3 Not very elastic.
4 Not absorbent.
5 Dirt does not cling to the fibre, so it washes easily.
6 Fibre shrinks but finished fabrics do not.
7 Special dyes are required.
8 Liable to 'pill', i.e. the fibre ends work up into little balls.
9 Builds up 'static' in wear which causes clinging, some people are affected more than others. Anti-static fabrics can be produced.
10 Thermoplastic fibre, so can be heat set into pleats, creases, embossing.

Uses: Made into a very wide variety of furnishing and clothing fabrics. The yarn is easily textured and crimped. Knits very well.

Also mixes or blends with other fibres such as cotton and wool.

SHEEP'S WOOL

Type of fibre: Natural, animal.
Source: The coats of sheep.

Processing:
1 Raw wool is sorted and graded to put wools of same quality together.
2 Scouring. Washing thoroughly in an alkaline solution.
3 Sulphuric acid burns out any remaining waste matter.
4 The wool is partially dried and oiled to lubricate it ready for spinning.
5 The wool is then carded, combed and drawn in a similar manner to cotton fibre. It subsequently undergoes roving and spinning.

Properties:
1 Very warm, warmer when damp.
2 Highly absorbent after water has penetrated the scales on the surface of the fibre, but repels water initially.
3 Fibre does not conduct heat.
4 Highly resilient, returns to shape easily.
5 Very weak.
6 Liable to excessive shrinkage because scales will easily overlap and lock, especially in hot water.
7 Liable to 'felt' and harden in hot water.
8 Vulnerable to moths, unless treated.
9 Absorbs dirt easily so should be kept clean with careful washing or cleaning.
10 Expensive.

Uses: Wool and worsted yarns are woven into a variety of fabrics of all types and weights, from voile to suiting, at all prices. Wool also knits well. Used for clothing and furnishing fabrics.

Wool often has other fibres mixed or blended with it to reduce the price or to add decoration.

SILK

Type of fibre: Natural.

Source: The cocoon that the silkworm spins round itself prior to emerging as a moth. Sericulture is the production of cultivated silk; the worms are fed on mulberry leaves in order to produce fine silk. Tussah or wild silk is taken from worms fed on oak leaves and it is coarser and less even.

Processing:
1 Reeling. Unwinding the silk filament from cocoon on to a reel.
2 Bunching. Making filaments into loosely twisted hanks.
3 Soaking to soften, and drying.

4 Re-winding on to bobbins.
5 Throwing. Transferring filament from the bobbins, either singly or in pairs, twisting as it is transferred. The process is similar to the spinning process used on other natural yarns.
6 Yarn is transferred to cones ready for weaving or knitting.
7 Silk may legally be 'weighted' by the addition of metallic salts in order to replace that lost when the gum or seracin is removed. Weighting may be done after throwing or during dyeing.

Properties:
1 Soft and luxurious.
2 Expensive.
3 Affected by perspiration.
4 Accepts dye readily.
5 Difficult to launder.
6 Very strong.
7 Very elastic and resilient.
8 Does not conduct heat, so it feels warm in winter.
9 Very absorbent.

Uses: Made into a wide variety of fabrics for furnishing and clothing for adults. Used in small quantities to mix and blend with other fibres, for example, wool.

TRIACETATE

Type of fibre: Man-made cellulosic.
Source: Cellulose acetate.
Processing:
1 The initial processing is similar to that of cellulose acetate, but the white flakes are dissolved in methyl chloride and alcohol.
2 The resulting solution is forced through the holes in a spinneret and spun and cooled ready for use.

Properties:
1 A weak fibre.
2 Limited elasticity.
3 Very resilient and fairly hard-wearing.
4 Very flexible.
5 Not absorbent.
6 Does not conduct heat.
7 Does not dye readily except in special dyes.
8 Thermoplastic and can be heat set into pleats and creases.

Uses: Produced in filament and staple form to make a variety of fabrics for clothing and furnishing. Also mixed and blended with other fibres such as nylon, wool, cotton and viscose.

VISCOSE

Type of fibre: Regenerated cellulose.
Source: Wood pulp or cotton waste (linters).
Processing:

1 Treated and made into sheets of cellulose, which are soaked in caustic soda.
2 Flaking. The sheets are dried and broken into flakes.
3 The flakes or crumbs are converted into cellulose xanthate; after 'ageing', the crumbs are dissolved in caustic soda solution. The result is a thick, light brown liquid.
4 The liquid is forced through the holes of a spinneret. Sulphuric acid coagulates the emerging liquid.
5 The liquid is stored for several days to allow it to degrade and then regenerate.
6 The filament is spun and wound on to spools or cones ready for weaving.

Properties:

1 Not very strong.
2 Soft.
3 Very absorbent.
4 Weaker when wet than when dry.
5 Very elastic.
6 Sheds dirt easily, so washes well.
7 A good conductor of heat.
8 Liable to shrinkage.
9 Absorbs dye easily.
10 Inexpensive.

Uses: Made as filament or staple yarn and used on its own to make a wide variety of woven fabrics.

Also mixes and blends well with other fibres such as cotton, wool, acrylics.

MINORITY FIBRES

Alpaca, Camel, Cashmere goat, Goathair, Hemp, Jute, Mohair, Rabbit, Angora Rabbit, Ramie and Vicuna are all from natural sources, as referred to in the A–Z section.

The others in common use are:

Metal

Filaments of aluminium coated with a thin film of plastic to prevent rusting. Used in small amounts as decoration in knitted and woven fabric of all fibres.

Glass

Made from silica, sand and limestone, produced in filament and staple form. Cold and non-absorbent, unaffected by heat or fire, difficult to dye. Used in furnishing fabrics, fire blankets, etc.

Polyvinyl Chloride

The basic compound was discovered in the last century, but successful conversion to a spinning material suitable for use as clothing and furnishing fabrics is comparatively recent. Waterproof, non-absorbent, a very low melting point, the range of fabrics is limited.

Elastomer

A soft polyurethane substance with tremendous elasticity, low absorbency, and thermoplastic if carefully controlled. The fibre is made in varying forms depending upon its ultimate use, but it may be used on its own in corsetry and elastics, or it may be mixed with other fibres to produce stretch fabrics.

THE EFFECT OF HEAT ON FIBRES

It is very important to be aware of the effect of heat on fibres. The temperature at which fibres are affected adversely affects not only how they are washed and the most effective method of pressing while sewing, but, most important, it affects the choice of fabric for various purposes, e.g. nightwear for children.

Acetate

Acetate softens and will stick to the iron at a fairly low temperature; at a higher temperature it will melt and leave a hole.

On burning in a flame, acetate shrinks from the flame as it burns. A black bead is formed which is easily crushed. An acrid smell results.

Acrylic

Acrylics can be pressed at a fairly high temperature without melting and sticking to the iron.

The fibre burns in a flame leaving a soft black bead.

Cotton

Cotton can be scorched with a very hot iron.

When flame is applied, it burns easily with considerable flame, leaving papery ash.

Cupro

Cupro melts and sticks to the iron at a fairly low temperature. In flame, it burns easily, leaving ash.

Flax

Linen fabrics will scorch if a very hot iron is applied to dry fabric.

When placed in flame, flax fibres are slower than cotton to ignite but then burn readily, leaving ash.

Modacrylics

These fibres will melt and stick to the iron at high temperature.

When flame is applied, they do not burn. If applied persistently they will eventually smoulder a little.

Modal

Fibre will scorch under a hot iron.

If flame is applied, it catches fire and burns readily leaving a papery ash.

Polyamide

Fibre will melt at a fairly low temperature and stick to the iron; at a higher temperature it will melt and leave a hole.

In a flame, the fibre shrinks from the flame as it burns, forming a very hard smooth bead. These beads retain the heat and can cause small burns. White smoky vapour is produced.

Polyester

Most polyesters melt and stick to the iron at a fairly low temperature. The surface of the fabric can be impaired at very low temperature.

When flame is applied, polyesters melt and withdraw from the flame as a hard black bead is formed. The beads are very hot and can cause severe burns. Black smoke accompanies melting.

Sheep's Wool

A hot iron will scorch wool; a warm iron will impair the surface but fail to affect the fabric; moisture is always needed. Wool burns hesitantly, smouldering up to quite a high temperature before it burns. A lumpy, crushable ash is left. An animal smell is given off.

Silk

Will scorch easily under a very hot iron.

When flame is applied, the fibre burns easily leaving ash. An animal smell is given off.

Triacetate

As Acetate.

Viscose

Some viscose fabrics scorch under the iron at fairly low temperatures. When put in a flame, viscose catches fire easily and burns in a similar way to cotton, leaving papery ash.

Woven Fabrics

A SIMPLE EXPLANATION OF WEAVING

A loom is a weaving machine.

A heddle is a wire with a central hole through which a warp passes. Each warp has its own heddle.

A harness is the framework surrounding the heddles.

A shed is the area formed by using the harness to raise alternate warps in order that the weft yarn may be inserted.

A reed is a framework which pushes each weft firmly against its predecessor before the shuttle returns to place another warp. This is necessary to produce an even weave, and is called beating up.

Picking is the passing back and forth of the weft shuttle. Weft yarns are sometimes called picks or picking yarns.

Warp

Warp yarns are set up on the weaving loom to run in a lengthwise direction on the fabric. These yarns are as long as can be produced conveniently to avoid weakening joins. The length of the piece of cloth is determined beforehand, and varies with design, the fibre, the colour and the demand. The warp yarns are usually stronger and sometimes thicker than the weft as they have to withstand strain. This is an important point to remember when cutting out garment pieces.

Weft

The weft yarns are those which pass across the width of the fabric and interlace with the warp. The width of the fabric varies according to the size of the loom. Weft yarns are also referred to as filling yarns because they literally fill the spaces in the warp and complete the weave. The filling yarn is carried across the warp on a shuttle. The length of yarn is limited by the amount a shuttle will hold. The shuttle passes back and forth, creating a finished edge each side. This is the selvedge and is usually of slightly closer weave than the rest of the fabric. The width of this tight edge varies between 5 and 10mm, and it should not be used in a garment because of its lack of 'give', in some fabrics there is even a 'tightness', which makes it unusable.

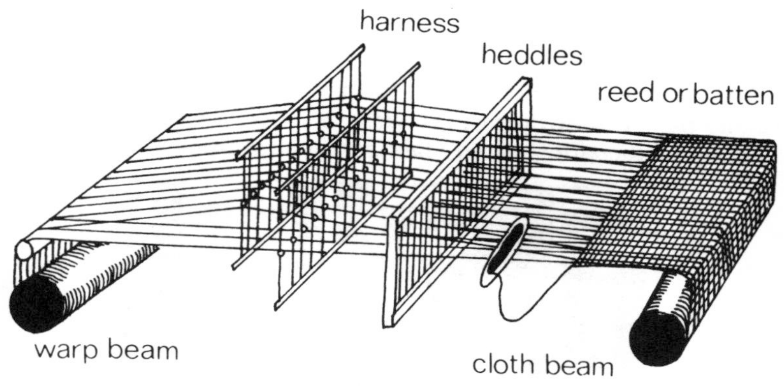

WEAVES

It is important to be able to recognize the basic weave, because this often affects the way fabric will react when handled. It also provides an indication as to how the fabric will drape when worn, and, in addition, wearing qualities are affected. For example, no matter how strong the basic fibre, a loose, open-weave fabric will not withstand hard wear.

All weaves are illustrated with plain yarns, but they may also be fancy yarns, which can make the weave even more difficult to identify. See Weave, page 12. The warp and weft yarns are illustrated as being of equal thickness but they may not be in the fabric.

1 Plain

The weft or filling yarns interweave alternately under and over each warp yarn.

2 Hopsack

Also known as basket weave, two filling yarns weave over and under pairs of warp yarns, producing a looser weave than plain, and often, therefore, a softer fabric with more drape.

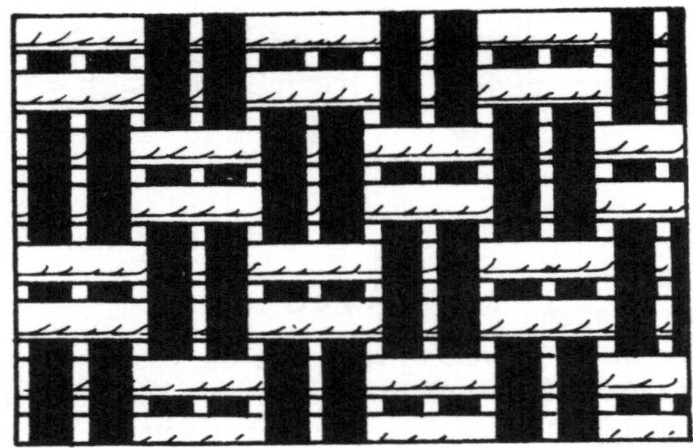

3 Satin

A diagonal weave in which each warp yarn crosses over four filling or weft yarns and then passes under the fifth. It comes to the surface and passes over the next four and so on. This is a 4/1 satin weave. It can also be done the other way, i.e. the weft yarns float over the warp yarns. This is a 1/4 satin weave. Across the width of the loom each warp yarn loops under a filling yarn one yarn below that of its neighbour.

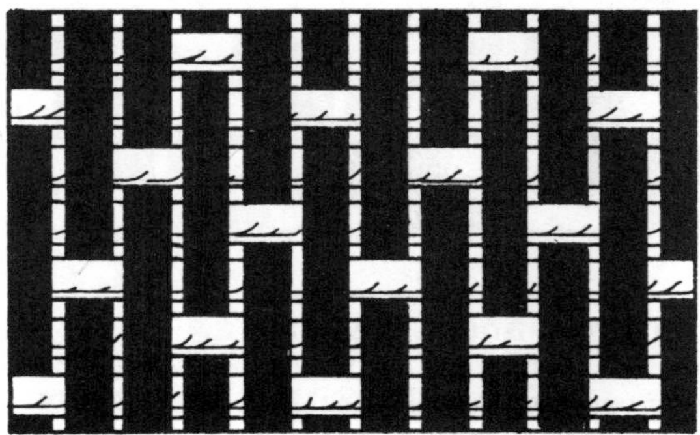

There are many variations on the satin weave. The floating yarns may interlace every fifth, eighth or twelfth yarn. They are referred to as five-shaft construction, eight-shaft construction and so on and may be warps floating over weft or weft floating over warp, and are known either as warp face satin or filling (weft) face satins.

The yarns that pass over the top are floating yarns and produce a sheen on the fabric. The amount of sheen varies according to the fibre used; for example, cotton satin has less lustre than nylon satin.

Satin weave fabrics fray readily and have a very easily defined right and wrong side.

4 Twill

A diagonal weave in which the yarns float over two or more before passing under the next yarn. As with satin, there is a progression of interlacing and this creates diagonal ribs on the face of the fabric. The angle of the diagonals varies in steepness and the prominence of the ribs is varied by the type of yarn used. Twill weaves may be either warp faced or filling faced, in a similar manner to satin.

The right side of twill fabric is easily determined, the fabrics fray readily but, in general, are very hard-wearing.

5 Herringbone and Chevron

Twill weaves in which the twill line rib zigzags across the cloth and does not continue in a diagonal line. This produces a distinctive striped effect with short diagonals across each stripe. Two or more colours are normally used in order to emphasize the weave.

The fabrics normally fray readily.

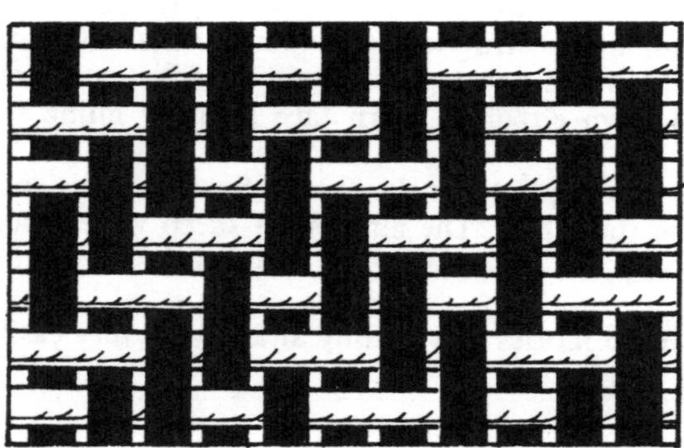

6 Rib

This is a variation on the plain weave. Fine and coarse yarns are alternated, often of different fibres to create a ribbed effect.

In handling these fabrics, entire ribs can easily pull away. In general, the fabrics do not wear well, especially if poor quality yarns have been used for either the warp or the weft. With some fabrics, such as poplins and taffeta, it is difficult to determine which is the right side.

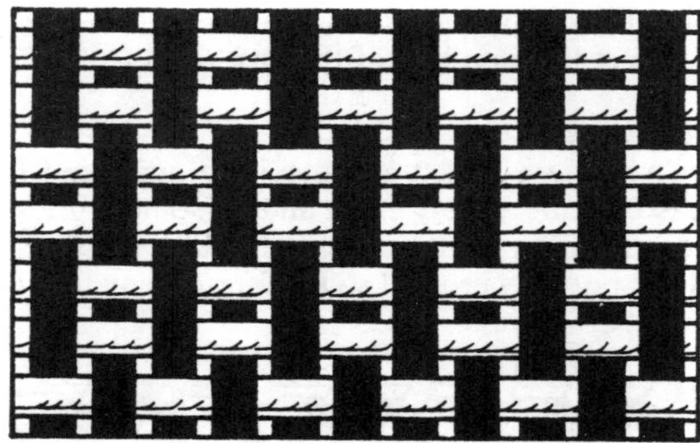

7 Jacquard

Characteristically complicated patterns are produced by a machine named after its inventor. The mechanism controls many more heddles than in the simpler weaves, enabling even single warp yarns to be lifted when necessary. Designs are not confined to variations of straight lines as they are with the basic weaves, but curves, flowers, scrolls and large patterns can be produced.

The design is made on a punch-card which is placed in the machine. Jacquard fabric has always been expensive as weaving is slow, but computer response mechanisms are being introduced which will make it a faster method of production.

Jacquard fabrics often fray readily. Designs are often one-way.

8 Dobby

A dobby weave produces small, simple, often geometric patterns. The dobby is an attachment fitted to a plain-weave loom and it raises or lowers harnesses in order to form patterns.

An example of a dobby pattern is bird's eye. The pattern does not usually affect the handling of the basic cloth.

9 Leno (Gauze)

The warp yarns are pulled alternately to right and left or up and down, so creating a wavy effect and, in some fabrics, an open mesh. There are many variations on the leno weave. The yarns are not twisted but only crossed so the fabrics may fray easily and may not be hard-wearing.

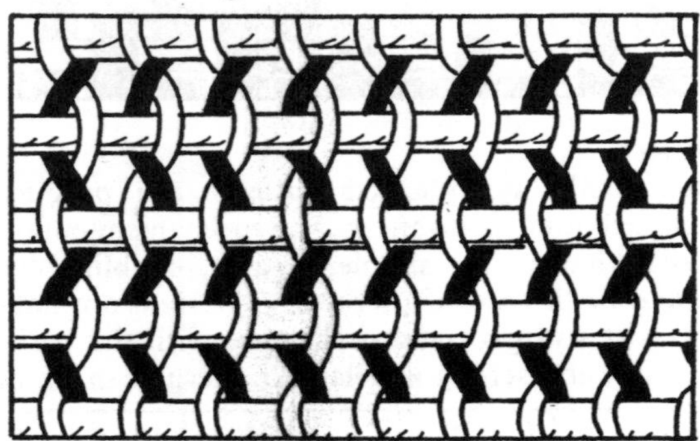

10 Lappet

Similar in effect to embroidery, additional designs are stitched on to the basic fabric as it is woven, using needles above the fabric and an additional yarn which is carried across the back while not in use. Excess floating yarns are cut away on the reverse side but they are fastened off, so there is no danger of spots coming off voile, for example.

11 Swivel

Also similar to embroidery in that figures and patterns are woven into the fabric during weaving, but it is done with additional shuttles, each carrying yarn and working with a swivel action in one area of the fabric. The excess yarn is carried on the back and cut away later. The designs often pull or wear away as the ends of yarn are not fastened off.

RIBBON AND BRAID

A *ribbon* is a fabric woven in the width in which it is to be sold and used. It has woven edges. Only very rarely are ribbons woven wider than 15cm. Like wide fabrics, ribbons are composed of warp and weft yarns — the edges are usually pronounced and often thicker than the main part of the ribbon, Millinery Petersham being the exception.

In contrast, a *braid* is plaited from three or more threads all belonging to one system of threads.

The traditional ribbon-weaving centres of Europe are Coventry, St Etienne, Basel and Wuppertal. Ribbons are primarily used for decoration and for many functional purposes in fastening. Ribbons are now predominantly woven from nylon, polyester, viscose and triacetate, but cotton is used as the weft in some cases (see Petersham). The warp threads run parallel to the edges; the weft from edge to edge at right angles.

Some terms are commonly used in the ribbon industry. It is interesting that many are also used with reference to wide width fabrics:

Barathea

A ribbon of medium weight and pebbled appearance, not often used now except as ties for masonic aprons. See also page 100.

Bayadère

A ribbon having thick warp threads, that are usually uncoloured, and bands of weft in different colours of uneven width, normally of at least three colours. A bayadère has pronounced ribs running parallel with the edge.

Bord Tiré

The description for a scalloped edge created by the weft not extending through to the full width of the ribbon.

Braid

This is not a ribbon, being plaited not woven.

Check

Usually of taffeta weave and having rectangular fields of colour formed by crossing a striped warp with weft in similar multicolours.

In a Gingham Check all fields of colour are true squares; most Ginghams are white with a colour. See also page 160.

Tartan, another type of check, is a ribbon woven in one of many very old and traditional plaid designs as used by Scottish

Highland families. Unlike broad tartans, which are usually in twill weave, ribbon tartans are of taffeta weave. See also page 238.

Ciré

The description of a ribbon with a very high lustre reminiscent of patent leather. It is created by friction calendering a satin ribbon, sometimes by adding a wax finish as well. See also page 128.

Facing Ribbon

A term synonymous with Faille. See below.

Faille

A medium-weight ribbon of plain weave, having a fairly pronounced rib but not as pronounced as in a Petersham. Its most common use is for backing the edges of knitting, to strengthen both the buttonholes and button stitchings. See also page 151.

Galloon

A term not used a great deal now except in the shoe trade, where it is applied to a ribbon which binds the edge of ladies' court shoes. See also page 159.

Gaufré

The French term for embossed. The design in relief on a metal roller is impressed on to a softer roller below creating a 'negative' image in depressions. The ribbon is passed between these heated rollers under pressure and thus the design is imprinted on to the ribbon.

Grosgrain

The French term for Petersham — sometimes used in the English language. See also page 165.

Jacquard

A term derived from its inventor Joseph-Marie Jacquard, denoting firstly a part of a loom, but also a fabric or ribbon woven by using this device. A Jacquard permits every single warp thread to be lifted — or lowered — individually, thus allowing the designer unrestricted scope for complicated patterns. See also page 51.

Messaline

Woven in plain weave with a very thin weft and then heavily calendered to give a mock satin effect. Sometimes used for tricolours. See also page 195.

Narrow Fabric

A term which embraces all fabrics under 45cm in width, whether ribbons, tapes, webbings, elastics or braids.

Organdie

As in broad fabrics, a thin, lightweight fabric, stiffly finished, of plain weave with distinct 'see-through' characteristics. See also page 203.

Petersham

This term has to be divided into two:
Millinery Petersham, traditionally used to trim hats but now widely used on many other garments. The weft, usually cotton, is distinctly heavy relative to the warp, thus forming pronounced ribs across the ribbon. The return of the weft creates a gimp-like effect.
Skirt Petersham, used almost solely for strengthening and giving shape to the waistbands of skirts. In recent times shaped Petershams have reappeared on the market, the best qualities having a curve which is quite permanent and shrink resistant.

Picot

A description for a decorative edge having loops at regular intervals. Corded and pronounced loops are the characteristics of a warp picot, flimsy loops are more usually created in weft. This type of picot can also be seen on some elastics, e.g. lingerie elastics.

Satin

Single: A ribbon with a smooth and shiny surface on one side only, created by allowing the warp to 'float' over several bars of weft, thus increasing the light reflection. Calendering increases the lustre.
Double: As above, but with both surfaces smooth and shiny.
Satin Faille: A single satin, having a faille-like reverse side, and of firmer construction. See also pages 48, 151 and 223.

Seersucker

A plain-weave ribbon with an uneven or waffled surface created by employing two different types of yarn — shrinking and non-shrinking in alternating stripes. See also page 225.

Taffeta

A term derived from the Persian *Taftah*. A plain-weave ribbon, nowadays nearly always in nylon, used very widely in Britain, and perhaps best known in its traditional role as a hair ribbon. See also page 236.

Velvet

The aristocrat of ribbons, ideally woven from nylon so as to be crush resistant. The distinguishing feature of velvet is a surface of short cut tufts of fibres standing so close together as to present a uniform surface. Velvet ribbons are woven in double layers, the pile 'running' between the two and then cut halfway between the two layers to provide two ribbons. See also page 244.

Knits and Jerseys

Knitted fabric is made from one continuous yarn or from a number of continuous yarns. Any fibre may be used and a variety of thick and thin yarns and textured and fancy yarns can be put together. Spun and filament yarns are both used. The advantages of knit fabrics are that they are, on the whole, easier to sew than wovens; they are comfortable to wear because they 'give' with the body; less precise fitting is needed because of this elasticity, and most knits are easier to care for than wovens.

Knitting machines produce fabric much more quickly than weaving looms so knits are usually profitable to the manufacturer.

There are two main methods of knitting.

1: WARP KNITTING

Many yarns are set up, one to each knitting latch, and each yarn proceeds to form stitches in a warp direction, i.e. lengthwise along the fabric, but, as it does so, the yarn also loops through the stitch on each side.

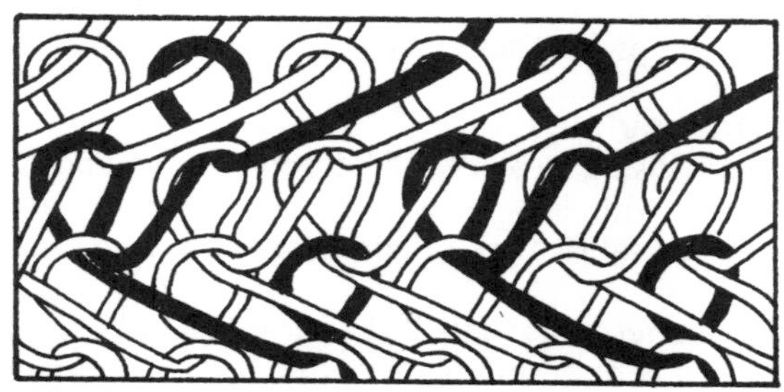

The machine may be flat with a row of needles at the base, producing a flat fabric with selvedges, or it may be circular thereby producing a tube of knitting. In both cases the fabrics are very wide.

Warp knits can be identified by a characteristic wavy effect on the wrong side. The fabrics do not ladder when cut and are firm to sew. There is a limited amount of 'give' in warp knit.

2: WEFT KNITS OR FILLING KNITS

One yarn traverses horizontally on either a flat or circular knitting machine. This produces a flat or tubular fabric that can be identified by lengthwise rows or wales of knitting on the right side, looking exactly like hand knitting. The wrong side looks like the purl side of hand knitting. The stitch can be varied by the introduction of ribs, purl stitches, tucks for lacy effects, etc.

Weft knits 'give' considerably in both directions and they may ladder when cut, but they tend to be better quality fabrics than warp knits. Cut edges tend to curl up in handling. Both warp and weft knit fabrics may be plain or printed.

Jersey

This is the name given to tubular weft or filling knit fabric that is made with the plain stitch only.

Double Jersey

This is made using two sets of latched needles and producing a firmer fabric with less 'give'. The cut edges do not curl in handling and the fabrics keep their shape in wear.

When paper patterns are labelled 'for knits only', it indicates that the pattern is only suitable for stretchy fabrics, because ease and shaping are reduced and the style relies on the qualities of the fabric for effect. These knits are unlikely to be warp knits and will be found amongst the weft knits, including jersey but not double jersey.

To check that a fabric is a knit of this type, measure a piece 10cm long across the width of the fabric, take hold of this length and stretch it along a tape measure or ruler until it reaches 15cm. If it stretches easily and goes beyond, and also returns when released to its original size, then the fabric is suitable for a 'knits only' pattern.

Non-Woven Fabrics

It is not easy to describe what is meant by a non-woven fabric, so I will quote from a description I have read. This says that a non-woven fabric is a sheet structure made from fibres held together by mechanical, chemical, thermal or solvent means; or by a combination of these. The term does not include paper, or fabrics which are woven, knitted, tufted, stitch-bonded or made by wool felting.

In comparatively simple terms, a non-woven may be described as a fabric having textile-like properties, which is prepared by bonding fibres together, rather than by the traditional method of spinning into yarns, followed by weaving or knitting.

PRODUCTION

Precise manufacturing details, such as the percentages of various fibres used, type and method of bonding the web, will depend on the use to which the result will be put. As our concern is with non-wovens for use as interfacings, I will deal only with the basic manufacture of these, namely Vilenes.

Fibres The fibres principally used are polyester, nylon and viscose with, occasionally, small amounts of acrylic. These fibres are blended in varying amounts, depending on the type of interfacing being made.

The staple fibres normally employed are usually in lengths of between 3 and 7cm, arriving in tightly packed bales direct from the main fibre manufacturers.

Recipe Each grade of Vilene has its own precise fibre and binder recipe, which has been selected to provide an interfacing with the required performance in the particular garment application. Recipes are constantly under evaluation, so that new interfacings can be introduced to keep in line with changes in fabric manufacture and fashion.

Fibre Blending The correct quantity of each fibre is weighed, according to the recipe, and fed by hand into the blending machine. At this point, the various fibres are in the form of highly compact pieces and require to be opened and blended. This is achieved by passing the fibre mix through a willowing machine, which teases the fibre into a lofty open form in preparation for the carding process.

Carding and Web Forming The opened fibre is fed into the carding engine, which consists of a series of revolving rollers, covered with closely-spaced pins or wire teeth, which separate the small fibre bundles into individual fibres, and these are removed from the final roller by a high-speed comb and passed on to a moving conveyor in the form of a lightweight, uniform web. The weight of fibre passing through the carding engine is adjusted to produce the various grades of interfacing required. This fine web of fibres is next folded down on to a conveyor, moving at right angles to the carding engine, forming a multiple-layer fibre web in which

the fibres are arranged to give balanced strength to the length and width directions in the finished interfacing.
Calendering This thick web of fibres is compressed through a pair of heated rollers to increase the density and strength of the web in preparation for the bonding process.
Bonding The compressed web is impregnated with a foamed bonding agent, usually based on an acrylate latex, applied as the web passes between a pair of spaced metal rollers. The amount of bonding agent applied is carefully controlled to give the desired ratio of fibre to binder in the final interfacing.
Drying and Curing The impregnated web is dried and cured by passing over steam-heated cylinders. The curing process ensures that the non-woven textile interfacing is fully resistant to all normal washing and dry-cleaning processes.

The material produced is then wound up on large batch stands. A single batch of lightweight interfacing may carry as much as 14,000 metres when cut to the normal sales width. A sample is taken from each batch produced, for extensive laboratory quality control tests, to ensure that the product always reaches the required standard of performance.

SEW-IN QUALITIES

Trimming The batch of material is now cut down the middle, and the edges are trimmed to produce two rolls of interfacing at the required width.
Inspection These large rolls of cut material are finally carefully examined by passing over brightly-lit inspection tables to ensure that the appearance and handle of the material is satisfactory and, at the same time, the interfacing is rolled in twenty-four metre lengths before dispatch to the retail stores.

IRON-ON NON-WOVENS

A base material is produced in the same way as that employed for the manufacture of a sew-in interfacing, but before the final cutting process, a fusible adhesive is applied to one side of the fabric.

Applying the Adhesive

Adhesives are applied in various forms.

1 Printed Adhesives

The adhesive employed is initially in the form of a thick paste, which is applied to the interfacing through fine holes in a printing roller to provide fine adhesive dots in a uniform pattern on the fabric surface.

These are dried under infra-red heaters and slightly fused. The adhesive dots are re-activated in the ironing process when the interfacing is applied to the outer fabric in garment making.

2 Powder Adhesives

Adhesives in powder form are applied by scattering the powder on to the surface of the base fabric, the particles of powder being then attached by slightly fusing them under an infra-red heater. The adhesive powder particles are re-activated in the iron-on process, when the interfacing is applied to the outer fabric in garment making.

As with sew-in interfacings, the final process is cutting and inspection, followed by rolling into twenty-five-metre lengths for sale through retail stores.

IRON-ON WUNDAWEB ADHESIVE NON-WOVEN

In addition to the range of iron-on interfacings, a 100 per cent adhesive non-woven is available for use in hemming clothing, curtains, etc., without sewing. The adhesive is initially in the form of granules and these are melted and converted into a large number of adhesive fibres, which are sprayed on to a moving conveyor to form the iron-on non-woven web.

After rolling on to a batch, the material is inspected and is then cut into 3-cm wide bands and packaged in transparent plastic containers mounted on display cards for sale through retail stores.

Testing

Routine laboratory and studio tests are carried out on Vilene qualities to check that weight, thickness, strength, extension, bursting point, crease recovery, washing and dry-cleaning performance all meet stringent quality control standards.

Iron-on Vilene qualities are also tested after application to typical outer fabrics, to ensure that the adhesive bond strength is satisfactory after washing and dry cleaning processes.

Lace

Machine-made piece lace is really the concern of a book dealing with fabrics, but hand-made laces came first and machine-made laces were largely based on them.

Lace-making goes back as far as the Bronze Age. It is interesting that early pieces of decoration made from horsehair and hair have survived for us to see, but those made from flax and cotton have perished. The first lace that we would recognize made with needle and needlepoint thread was produced in the fifteenth century in Italy. Lace-making then spread throughout Europe with new techniques added, such as working on a pillow using bobbins for holding the threads. Each country, and often each area, developed its own characteristics and various types of lace are still distinguished by their old names, such as Brussels and Valenciennes.

The art of lace-making has been very much revived now and, like all crafts, although it is time-consuming, it is satisfying to do and gives a great deal of pleasure to the craftsman. Pieces of old hand-made lace in a good state of preservation should be carefully restored and used or stored.

Machine-made Lace

Demand for lace has always exceeded supply even from early times, so it was inevitable that a machine-made imitation lace would be produced. The first machine was made in Nottingham and it produced a net base on which patterns could be embroidered by hand. Later, in 1813, a further development occurred and a machine was invented that could make the base and also do the embroidery. This invention also took place in Nottingham, and from then on Nottingham lace became famous throughout the world.

Leavers Lace

Another name that became familiar to anyone interested in textiles was that of Leaver, the man who invented the machines. Leavers Laces are still made in the Nottingham area and the name still represents a particular type of product of high quality.

Most textile looms use only two sets of threads but a lace machine uses warp, weft or beam and also bobbin threads. The result is a fabric that is neither knitted nor woven. The production of any kind of lace or net requires skill and precision in setting up the loom.

Additional beam threads are used for outlining the pattern. The warp threads are suspended so that there is just enough space for a fine disc, carrying the bobbin threads, to slip between. The bobbins swing pendulum fashion, while the warp threads move from side to side according to the pattern being made. The movement of one set of threads across the others produces the twists that are characteristic of Leavers Lace.

After weaving, the lace is scoured to remove dirt and lubricant. It is then dyed and pinned out to the correct even width and hot-air dried. Finally it is inspected and repaired.

Net

To produce net, two sets of bobbins are used, one on the front and one on the back of the machine. These cross to right and left alternately, so forming a diagonal line of twists in front of and behind the warp. This produces a firm twist net. The size of the mesh can be varied according to the use for which the net is intended.

Schiffli Embroidery

The Schiffli machine embroiders various patterns on plain net to produce imitations of hand-embroidered lace. If the background fabric is then dissolved or burnt out, Guipure Lace is the result. If the embroidery is applied to fine plain-weave cotton, then Broderie Anglaise or Eyeletting is the result.

To produce the embroidery, the machine has a set of automatically controlled needles moving backwards and forwards over the net in a similar action to that of a sewing machine needle. This lace is sometimes called 'Needlerun' and can be identified by the fact that the design is light rather than solid, and the decoration is formed with stitches similar in appearance to machining.

Lace Yarns

Because of the delicacy of even heavy lace, all yarns have to be of good quality. Some yarns have to be twisted more than for ordinary weaving to make them more durable.

Fibres

Most fibres can be used for making lace and net, but the most common are probably cotton, nylon and viscose.

Grain

Lace and net have no defined grain direction. In theory, pattern pieces may be placed in any direction and the hang and wear will not be affected, and in the case of plain net this may be done. However, with patterned lace the placing of the pattern will be governed by the design of the lace, position of flounced edge, main motif, etc.

Matching

With an all-over lace design pieces can be joined almost invisibly by overlapping one piece on the other and matching up the motifs as nearly as possible. Work satin stitch by hand or machine to join, outlining the motif. Surplus on both pieces of lace can be trimmed away close to the stitching.

Dyeing and Printing

The colour of fabric is probably more important than anything else — including pattern, structure, weight and fibre content — because, if it is well displayed, a customer will buy a piece of fabric because she likes the colour, learning later about its other properties. Often she will change her plans about what garment to make to fit in with the fabric she likes: even more often, she will buy it and simply put it away until she decides what to use it for.

METHODS OF DYEING

Fabrics are either yarn-dyed (also known as loom-state) or piece-dyed. If a fabric is yarn-dyed, the yarn is left in hanks or wound on cheeses and is dyed in that state before weaving. Piece-dyed fabrics are first woven into what is known as 'grey' goods and afterwards dyed or printed. The advantage of this method is that the lengthy process of producing the fabric is over, it can be stored and then coloured to order to keep in step with demand, fashion changes and individual orders. Yarns dyed in hank state are used for colour-woven fabrics, i.e. woven checks, stripes, etc.

Dyeing is complicated and liable to error. Some fibres have a better affinity for dyes than others, some will only accept a limited range of colours. Some dyes are not fast or fixed, some are even resistant to fixing, and the colour bleeds on washing. Many colours will fade if exposed to sunlight, due to the types of dye used. The quality of dyes and dyeing techniques are constantly improving. This may be due in part to the use of progressively more sophisticated fabric finishes that demand more permanently dyed fabric as the base.

Natural dyes, mainly vegetable, have always been used, and, while they seem very suitable for such yarn as hand-spun wool, the colours, though natural, are very limited in range. Synthetic dyes had to be found that would penetrate all fibres in a wide range of colours.

Dye must be thoroughly dissolved in water or other liquid before the yarn or fabric is immersed. Undissolved particles will remain on the surface and will later bleed.

Direct dyes are easiest to apply as the dyeing takes place in one immersion without any setting or fixing process. The possible colour range is wide but the dyes are not fast to sunlight.

Disperse dyes have been developed to overcome the problems of dyeing the non-absorbent fibres such as polyester. In this method of dyeing the fibre is subjected to heat, causing swelling, at which point the dye is introduced under pressure.

Pigment dyes are quick and easy to apply and can be used satisfactorily on all fibres. The dye particles are applied to the fibre with the aid of a binding agent.

Sulphur dyes are inexpensive and easy to use but the colour range is limited.

Acid dyes are bright in colour, expensive and fast to light.

Basic dyes have been used for a long time but are now mainly used on acrylic fibre because on this they give good results, producing bright fast colours.

Napthol dyes, also known as azoic dyes, involve immersing the fibre in napthol before the dye bath. Used mainly to produce bright colours and black.

Chrome dyes are used mainly on wool. They involve additional chemicals in order to achieve penetration of the fibre.

Vat dyes are fast and resistant to bleach and light. Expensive to use.

Mordant: the mordant is a chemical additive used when necessary to bind the dye to a fibre that would not otherwise accept it.

Dyeing is a highly technical skill requiring years of experience after training. A dyer has to know for certain which type of dye to use on which fibres to produce specific results and a great deal of time and money is spent in experimenting in laboratories.

Unfortunately, when buying fabric, there is no way of knowing what sort of dye has been used, nor whether it is fast.

METHODS OF PRINTING

The main methods of printing used in producing large quantities of fabric are:

Roller Printing

The design is engraved on a copper cylinder. A separate cylinder is engraved for each colour, each representing a different part of the design. Dye is mechanically applied to the rollers, carefully removing excess dye so that only the engraving contains dye. The fabric to be printed, backed by a soft absorbent cloth, is passed over the copper cylinders and kept in place at an even pressure by a large iron roller. As the printed fabric emerges it is dried and finished. Roller printing is inexpensive once the copper rollers have been engraved. The method is used where large quantities of fabric are required, for the expense of the copper rollers could not be recovered if only short lengths were produced. The disadvantage is that the number of colours that can be used is limited.

Warp printing is a process in which the design is applied with rollers to the warp yarns only; the weft or filling yarns are white. It is an expensive process, producing an identifiable blurred pattern. Used mainly in furnishing fabrics.

Discharge Printing

The fabric is first piece-dyed to give it a solid background, then a chemical is applied, in the design required, to remove the background colour. These areas are then reprinted with other colours, often leaving parts of the design uncoloured. It is an excellent method of printing, expecially where small, scattered prints are required.

Discharge printing is especialiy effective on spun viscose and acrylic.

Paper Printing

A comparatively recent development in which rolls of paper the width of the fabric are printed with the required design, using thermoplastic ink. The base fabric and the paper pass together through large heated cylinders and the heat transfers the ink to the fabric. The fabric is dried, but no other finishing is necessary.

This is an inexpensive method of printing and is the one mainly used for printing knit fabrics. It is the most successful method of printing synthetic jersey. The printing is very quick and large quantities of fabric can be produced in a short time.

The disadvantage of paper printing is that the rolls of paper are expensive to purchase and they can be used only once. This also means that a design can only be repeated if the printed paper is available. However, a manufacturer can print a small amount, keeping reserves of paper, and repeat it quickly if it proves a popular design.

Screen Printing

Once referred to as silk-screen printing because the fine screens were always made from silk. They are now also made from polyester and nylon fibre.

The design is applied photographically to a series of fine mesh screens set in frames, one frame for each colour to be used. As the fabric passes along a conveyor belt the screens are lowered in sequence, each one transferring a pattern of dye. The fabric is then dried.

Screen printing is a very quick method of printing which probably compensates for the high cost of the machinery involved. The main advantage of the method is that many colours can be used.

Short lengths of expensive fabric are screen printed by hand. The method is largely the same, although the design is usually painted on the screen by hand and then, after applying dye, each screen is lowered on to the fabric to transfer the design. It is a very slow process.

Resist Printing

A resin paste is applied to the fabric in a pattern, after which the cloth is dyed. The dye cannot penetrate the paste. After dyeing, the paste is removed, producing a fabric of solid colour with small white patterns.

The disadvantage of the method is that a variety of colours cannot be used.

* * *

Printed patterns vary in size and complexity of colour according to the method of printing being used. It is possible to guess what form of printing has been used by examining the pattern for accuracy and by counting the colours used. Also, with the cheaper methods of printing, the reverse side of the fabric remains white. The price of the fabric is also a guide. With good quality prints the retailer will often be acquainted with the method of printing, if only so that he can justify the high price.

The disadvantage of prints is that they are nearly always off the straight grain of the fabric. It is perfectly possible to begin printing with the end of the fabric accurately placed with the weft threads exactly at right angles to the warp, or the wales of knitting straight, and it is possible to control and regulate the fabric so that the print remains on grain, but few manufacturers take the trouble to ensure this is so.

Examine the fabric carefully before purchase to ensure that the print is not so badly off-grain that it will be impossible to make a satisfactory garment. Avoid printed checks, stripes, spots, geometric designs if they are off-grain. Large patterns will also have to be evenly placed on curtains and bedspreads as well as on clothes. Small all-over prints are safest, as the fabric can be used correctly on the grain.

Most prints are also one-way. Examine carefully before purchase and buy extra fabric if necessary to accommodate cutting all pieces in one direction.

Finishes

Finishes are processes applied to fabrics after weaving or knitting, although sometimes best results are obtained by applying certain finishes before the fabric is constructed.

Some fabric finishes are basic, some improve the performance of the fabric, and some are purely decorative. The basic finishes are permanent, but the others may not be. Some fabrics are labelled with the finish that has been applied in order that it shall not be destroyed by subsequent laundering or dry-cleaning.

All finishes are applied only to specific fibres where such a finish is an advantage, and is also successful. Occasionally a finish is deliberately applied to conceal faults in the fabric or inferior yarn. Most basic finishes are invisible and are now taken for granted. Decorative ones are clearly visible, but some finishes applied to improve performance are not visible.

All techniques add to the cost of the fabric, but few fabrics are sold unfinished because the consumer now demands a high standard of performance.

The following finishes are applied to the yarn or the fabric; the decorative finishes included are those not involving the addition of other fibres.

BASIC FINISHES

Grey goods, or loom-state cloth, are 'finished' by converters by bleaching and cleaning before further finishes can be applied.

Bleaching

Most fabric is bleached. It is often necessary to bleach the yarn rather than wait until it has been woven or knitted. The chemicals vary according to fibre content, but the process tends to reduce slightly the strength of the basic fibre.

Desizing

Size in warp yarns has to be removed. This is done by applying an enzyme which acts on the starch; the resulting substance is removed by washing. Desizing of silk, the removal of the gum, is carried out with caustic soda.

Washing

All fabric is washed to remove dirt and impurities, grease and any marks inadvertently applied during production. Some fabrics are boiled for quite long periods, some immersed in hot alkaline solution.

Scouring

A cleaning process applied to wool after weaving.

Singeing

Projecting fibre ends are burned off the surface of some fabrics. In some cases, this is done after dyeing. The advantages of singeing are that it removes roughness and also reduces the possibility of pilling. Fabric to be napped or brushed is not singed.

The above basic finishes are often combined; for example, bleaching may be done at the same time as fabric is cooled in water following singeing.

Decating

A process applied to woollen fabrics which develops the lustre of the fibre, or to man-made fibre fabrics to improve the feel and colour. The fabric is wound around perforated rollers and immersed in hot water, or subjected to steam.

Beetling

A process applied to linen and cotton, in which the yarns are flattened to produce a firmer, closer weave.

Tentering

A process applied to woven fabrics. Clips are inserted in the selvedges, and the weft yarns are pulled to straighten and tighten them to ensure that they run at right angles to the warp yarns. This finish is normally applied when the fabric is still wet from undergoing some other basic treatment.

Knitted fabrics are sometimes tentered with little blobs of adhesive along the edges, to avoid damage by hooks.

PERFORMANCE FINISHES

Crabbing

The cloth is stretched over rollers and passed into hot water or steam, after which it is put into cold water and then pressed.

The warp and weft yarns are set in position and ensure stability during further processing.

Laminating

Foam is applied to the wrong side of some curtain and dress fabrics to increase warmth and to make a stable, crease-resistant fabric.

Fulling

A woollen finishing process which improves body by the application of pressure with heat, making the fabrics more compact.

Carbonizing

This process destroys vegetable matter in woollen yarn, resulting in a fabric that dyes more evenly and has a softer texture.

FINISHES AFFECTING WEAR AND HANDLING

Mercerization

Used largely on cotton yarn but also on linen. Caustic soda causes the fibre to swell, it becomes soft and lustrous and its strength is increased. As well as making the fibre more attractive, the process makes the yarn more receptive to dyes. Mercerized yarns are used for dress and furnishing fabrics and for sewing threads.

Napping and Brushing

This finish increases warmth and softness, but fabrics brushed excessively are weakened. Napping and brushing are usually done with wire rollers on one side of the fabric only or, in the case of lightweight fabrics such as viscose and cotton, on both sides. The finish is sometimes applied to inexpensive fabrics to cover imperfections.

Most fibres can be brushed. The yarn is subjected to only a slack twist, so that after weaving or knitting the fibre is easily teased. An application of steam will fix the nap in one direction, if this is required.

Sueding produces a similar effect to brushing. It is usually applied to one side only.

Shearing

Pile fabrics and those that have been napped are sheared to trim the pile evenly. Decorative effects can be achieved by the same, lawn-mower-type processing.

Grey goods may also be sheared to remove fibre ends, etc.

Shrinkage

Fibres are spun and woven under tension, so that the fabrics are stabilized and shrunk evenly. The method of shrinkage varies widely according to the fibre-content, type of yarn and type of fabric. Initial shrinkage does not always prevent further shrinkage in wear. For example, curtain fabrics will often be liable to shrinkage, even though initially processed, due to the fact that some fibres will absorb moisture from the atmosphere if the level of humidity is high. In addition, some fibres are less stable than others.

Shrinkage processes are carefully controlled and highly sophisticated. The majority of dress fabrics made from man-made fibres, cotton or silk have been permanently shrunk if they are offered for sale at a good price. Top quality wool will not shrink either. If in doubt, however, the fabric should first be washed or damp-pressed, and curtains should be cut with at least 10cms extra length.

Shape Retention

Crease-resistant finishes can be applied to cotton and viscose fabrics to assist in shape-retention. These finishes include drip-dry and minimum iron.

Permanent press finishes are applied to finished garments, such as trousers and pleated skirts, and also to fabric which will produce pleated goods. Fabrics will be labelled with the name of the process which shows that it is permanent.

Glazing

A polished or glazed surface can be obtained by the application of starch, glue or shellac, and the surface of the fabric is ironed, under pressure, with rollers. The process is often applied to cotton, and the resulting fabric is stiff and shiny on one or both sides. Fabrics finished by glazing are highly resistant to dirt penetration, so glazing is often applied to curtain fabrics as well as to some dress cottons.

Schreinering

A method of adding shine to the right side of low-priced cotton fabric. The fabric is slightly engraved with shallow ridges which reflect light and therefore add shine to the fabric.

Slippage Resistance

In fabrics with a low thread count, slippage of yarns may occur in wear, particularly with slippery yarns such as acetate. Additional firmness to prevent movement can be added by immersing the fabric in synthetic resin.

Stain Repellance

Stain-repellant finishes, including alcohol-resistants, can be applied to some fabrics, such as velvet, that are likely to be adversely affected by staining. Fabrics will be labelled if they are so finished; recommendations for washing and dry cleaning should be carefully followed.

Waterproofing

In this process, fabrics are completely sealed with vinyl resin, rendering them waterproof. In addition, they are then proof to wind, sunlight, stains, moths, etc.

Water Repellance

Some fabrics are water repellant to a certain degree owing to their fibre properties and also the type of weave. A water-repellant finish can be applied to some fabrics, such as polyester/cotton, which are then used for raincoats and anoraks. Other fabrics, such as quilted material with nylon top fabric, can also be made water repellant.

Permanent Stiffening

By a chemical process, a change in the structure of the cotton fibre can be brought about which gives the fabric more stiffness, and makes it smoother and more resistant to dirt.

Some permanent processing, applied to the collars and cuffs of ready-made shirts, involves inserting a specially treated fabric between two layers of cotton and baking the sandwich at controlled temperatures.

DESIRABLE FINISHES

Anti-static

Man-made fibres, particularly nylon and polyester, tend to build up static. A few fabrics, mainly lightweight and intended for lingerie or linings, can be treated to reduce this tendency. It is not always effective nor permanent. Washing the garment in fabric softener will lessen the static, if it builds up as the garment ages.

Anti-bacterial

An antiseptic finish can be applied giving the fabric a self-sterilizing quality and rendering it unaffected by perspiration and other body odours. Garments may be washed or dry cleaned.

Absorbency

The absorbency of some fibres can be increased, making the fabric more comfortable to wear. Natural and man-made fibres may be treated in this way, particularly for nightwear, sports clothes, towels, etc.

Flame-proofing

A flame-resistant process can be applied to some fabrics that are used for nightwear, and which also burn readily, for example, brushed cotton and winceyette. However, the process only ensures that the flame is retarded and that the fabric smoulders slowly rather than burns.

It is very difficult to buy specially treated flame-retardant fabric by the metre, as both manufacturers and shops say that there is only a small demand. They point out that flame-retardant adds considerably to the cost, without giving the customer anything that is instantly visible. Furthermore, some finishes destroy the attractiveness of the fabric, making it hard to the touch and stiff, spoiling the quality of the dyes, and the finish can be removed by bleaching or washing in soapless detergent. Unfortunately, it is not advisable to add a flame-retardant finish at home, as the chemicals likely to be used are toxic.

When choosing fabrics for children's clothes and nightwear, it is best to look for dense, thick and tightly woven or knitted fabrics, for they are the most likely to have some flame-retardant qualities. Wool and modacyclics, such as Teklan, are naturally non-flammable fibres. Nylon melts and does not flare, but melted beads of the fibre can give severe burns. Viscose fibres such as Viloft and Vincel have good flame-retardant properties. Polyester cotton and acrylics are generally flammable unless specially treated. Note also that quilted fabrics may have a filling that is flammable (e.g. polyester).

Mildew-proofing

Mildew and mould are problems in some countries where the level of humidity is high. Cellulosic fibres are particularly susceptible and so is silk and wool. Fabric can be rendered proof, and the finish does not wash out.

Moth-proofing

Once an enormous household problem, damage to woollen carpets and clothes by moths has largely been eliminated by the application of chemicals added to the dye.

DECORATIVE FINISHES

Crinkle Finish

This is achieved in three different ways: with engraved rollers, giving a finish that washes out eventually; by applying caustic soda in patterns; by the application of heat to thermoplastic fibres.

Embossing

Similar to crinkling, but aided by the use of heat, producing permanent effects on thermoplastic fibres. Other fibres are chemically finished to ensure the embossing is permanent, but wool cannot be embossed. Pleating is a variation of embossing.

Puckering

Damask effects are produced in nylon and polyester fabrics by applying a chemical which will partly dissolve the fibres. As the fabric dries, those parts shrink, thus causing a permanent puckered effect.

Burnt-out Finish

Fabrics made from two fibres, e.g. polyester and cotton, may have chemicals applied in a pattern to burn away one of the fibres, leaving opaque and sheer areas in the solid colour fabric.

Transparent Finish

Cotton is immersed in acid in a carefully controlled process, the acid thins and weakens the cotton which is removed when transparent. The fabric is mercerized and then dyed. Patterns can be produced by applying an acid-resistant substance to certain areas before immersing the whole fabric in acid. Sheer cotton fabrics such as organdie are produced in this way.

Moiré Finish

Moiré, or water-marking, can be obtained by impressing ridged rollers on to fabric in a heat-controlled process. Ribbed fabrics respond best, as the filling yarns move slightly when in contact with the ridges of the rollers. Light reflects on the wavy surface of the fabric, giving the characteristic 'watered' effect.

Water-marking may or may not be permanent, depending on the fibre content. Washing and dry cleaning instructions must be followed to preserve the finish.

Care of Textiles and Fabrics

As the production of textile fibres, particularly man made, has increased, and as the export of these fibres and garments has increased, it has been found necessary to introduce a code of labelling and textile care which is common to all countries.

TEXTILE CARE

This consists of simple symbols which, once interpreted, can then be recognized no matter what is the country of origin. The first column contains the diagrammatic symbols, and in the second there is a brief explanation, usually in English and in the language of the country of origin.

Some printed furnishing fabrics have the code printed on the selvedge, a great help in caring for curtains, etc.

THE INTERNATIONAL CARE LABELLING CODE

Symbol	Machine	Handwash
4 50	Hand-hot	Hand-hot
	Medium wash	
	Cold rinse. Short spin or drip-dry	
	Do not use Chlorine Bleach	
	Warm Iron	
P	**Dry Cleanable**	

The code basically consists of these four symbols.

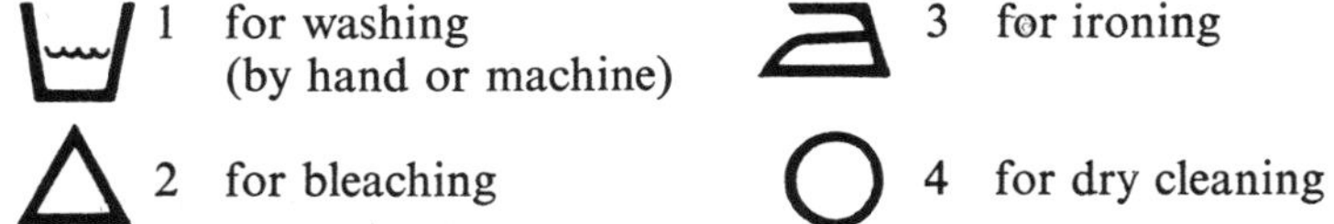

1 for washing (by hand or machine)

3 for ironing

2 for bleaching

4 for dry cleaning

The symbols are always presented in the same sequence. In the UK they are mainly found arranged vertically; in other European countries they are more usually arranged horizontally.

N.B. Care labels may also include symbols recommending a particular drying method — see Drying, page 82.

WASHING

The number and the temperature shown in the tub symbol indicate a particular washing process.

Each washing process describes the best method of washing and rinsing a particular group of fabrics and recommends:

- maximum wash temperature
- the amount of agitation during the wash
- the method of water extraction.

Symbol	Washing Temperature Machine	Hand	Agitation	Rinse	Spinning/ Wringing
1 (95)	very hot 95°C or boil	hand hot 50°C or boil	maximum	normal	normal
2 (60)	hot 60°C	hand hot 50°C	maximum	normal	normal
3 (60)	hot 60°C	hand hot 50°C	medium	cold	short spin or drip dry
4 (50)	hand hot 50°C	hand hot 50°C	medium	cold	short spin or drip dry
5 (40)	warm 40°C	warm 40°C	medium	normal	normal
6 (40)	warm 40°C	warm 40°C	minimum	cold	short spin
7 (40)	warm 40°C	warm 40°C	minimum do not rub	normal	normal spin do not hand wring
8 (30)	cool 30°C	cool 30°C	minimum	cold	short spin do not hand wring
9 (95)	very hot 95°C to boil	hand hot 50°C or boil	maximum	cold	drip dry
	(hand in tub)	**Do not machine wash**			
	(crossed tub)	**Do not wash**			

WASHING TEMPERATURES

100°C	Boil	Self-explanatory
95°C	Very hot	Water heated to near boiling temperature
60°C	Hot	Hotter than the hand can bear. The temperature of water coming from many domestic hot taps

WASHING SYMBOLS

Fabric	Benefits
White cotton and linen articles without special finishes	Ensures whiteness and stain removal
Cotton, linen or rayon articles without special finishes where colours are fast at 60°C	Maintains colour
White nylon; white polyester/cotton mixtures	Prolongs whiteness — minimizes creasing
Coloured nylon; polyester; cotton and rayon articles with special finishes; acrylic/cotton mixtures; coloured polyester/cotton mixtures	Safeguards colour and finish — minimizes creasing
Cotton, linen or rayon articles where colours are fast at 40°C, but not at 60°C	Safeguards the colour fastness
Acrylics; acetate and triacetate, including mixtures with wool; polyester/wool blends	Preserves colour and shape — minimizes creasing
Wool, including blankets, and wool mixtures with cotton or rayon; silk	Keeps colour, size and handle
Silk and printed acetate fabrics with colours not fast at 40°C	Prevents colour loss
Cotton articles with special finishes capable of being boiled but requiring drip drying	Prolongs whiteness, retains special crease-resistant finish

50°C	Hand hot	As hot as the hand can bear
40°C	Warm	Pleasantly warm to the hand
30°C	Cool	Feels cool to the touch

CARE OF TEXTILES AND FABRICS

Sorting and washing, using the numbered processes of the International Code, will give you the best results. Where a washing machine shows the wash tub symbols on the control panel, the complete process will have been provided for you, and all that is necessary is to match the number on the label to the machining programme. On other machines or when washing by hand, apply the label instructions to particular circumstances. To help, details of the processes are printed on all washing powder packs.

When washing in launderettes, because of the simpler range of settings, it may be practical to combine loads and select the safest wash for all the articles in that load.

Warning: Any attempt to mix loads without selecting the mildest conditions may result in serious colour problems, loss of shape or shrinkage, and even permanent damage to the fabric.

WASHING PROCESSES

1 This process is used for white cotton and linen articles without special finishes and provides the most vigorous washing condition. Wash temperature can be up to boiling (100°C) and agitation and spinning times are maximum. This ensures good whiteness and stain removal.

2 Process 2 is for cotton, linen or rayon articles without special finishes, where colours are fast at 60°C. It provides vigorous wash conditions but at a temperature which maintains fast colours.

3 Used for white nylon or white polyester/cotton mixtures, this process is less vigorous than either 1 or 2. The wash temperature (60°C) is high enough to prolong whiteness, and cold rinsing followed by short spinning minimizes creases.

4 This process is for coloured nylon; polyester; cotton and rayon articles with special finishes; acrylic/cotton mixtures; coloured polyester/cotton mixtures. In all respects except for washing temperature it is the same as Process 3. The lower temperature, hand hot (50°C), safeguards the colour and finish.

5 Suitable for cotton, linen or rayon articles where colours are fast at 40°C, but not at 60°C, this process has warm wash (40°C), medium agitation, normal spinning or wringing. The low wash temperature is essential to safeguard colour fastness.

6 This is for those articles which require low temperature washing (40°C), minimum agitation, a cold rinse and a short spin, e.g. acrylics; acetate and triacetate, including mixtures with wool; polyester/wool blends.

These conditions preserve colours and shape, and minimize creasing.

7 Similar to Process 6, this process is for wool, including blankets, and wool mixtures with cotton or rayon; silk which needs low temperature washing (40°C) and minimum agitation but requires normal spinning. Washing in this way preserves colour, size and handle. These fabrics should not be subjected to hand wringing or rubbing.

8 Unlikely to appear on UK-produced goods, this is for silk and printed acetate fabrics, with colours which are not fast at 40°C, requiring to be washed at a very low temperature (30°C), with minimum agitation and spinning.

9 Again rarely to be found on UK-produced goods, this process is for cotton articles with special finishes which benefit from a high temperature (95°C) wash but require drip drying.

This symbol indicates those articles which must NOT be machine washed.

Articles which must not be washed at all will bear this sign.

Bleaching

This symbol indicates that household (chlorine) bleach could be used. Care must be taken to follow the manufacturer's instructions.

When this symbol appears on a label, household bleach must **not** be used.

Ironing

The number of dots in the ironing symbol indicates the correct temperature setting — the fewer the dots, the cooler the iron setting.

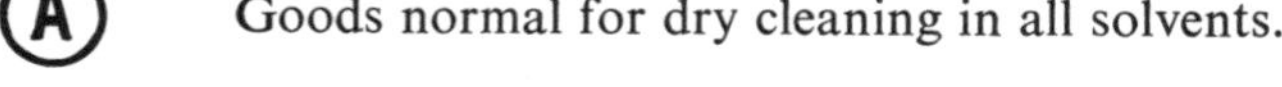

Cool **Warm** **Hot** **Do not iron**

Dry Cleaning

The letter in the circle refers to the solvent which may be used in the dry-cleaning process, and those using coin operated dry cleaning should check that the cleaning symbol shown on the label is the same as that in the instructions given on the front of the machine.

Ⓐ Goods normal for dry cleaning in all solvents.

Ⓟ Goods normal for dry cleaning in perchloroethylene, white spirit, Solvent 113 and Solvent 11.

Ⓟ May be dry cleaned professionally. Do not 'coin-op' clean.

Ⓕ Goods normal for dry cleaning in white spirit or Solvent 113.

Do not dry clean.

Drying

Care labels may also include one or other of the following symbols recommending a particular drying method.

Tumble drying beneficial but not essential.

Line dry.

Drip dry: for best results hang while wet.

 Dry flat: do not hang to dry.

Extract from H.L.C.C. Booklet, 'The International Textile Care Labelling Code'.

FABRIC CARE

Even choosing a suitable fabric and making it up well can be wasted effort if the garment is not cared for. The following is an extract from information published by the Association of British Launderers and Cleaners.

Drip-dry Garments

Drip-dry garments — often shirts — and fabrics are made from specially treated cotton or man-made fibres, or a mixture. The fabrics are less absorbent and therefore dry more easily. However, if they are washed at too high a temperature, the 'finish' may be destroyed. It is unwise to use bleach on resin-finished cotton, as this may combine with the finishing agent so that it cannot be rinsed out. The damage may not be immediately apparent, but before long the fabric could rot. The same advice applies to crease-resistant garments like cricket flannels.

The main rule to remember is not to allow such articles to become too soiled, as marks cannot be removed by high temperature washing.

Ironing and Pressing

Most fabrics are improved by ironing. Even non-iron fabrics look better with a gentle pressing. Always make sure that you know how the fabric should be ironed before you begin. The safest precaution is to use an iron with a pre-set temperature control. The control is then set to the temperature suitable for the fabric. The British Standards Institution advises the use of irons with dot symbols. One dot indicates a cool iron, two for warm and three for hot. These dots correspond with the instructions on Care Labels.

Some man-made fabrics (e.g. acetate, acrylics, etc.) are liable to damage unless ironed with a cool iron. Remember that it takes time for the temperature to alter when you change from one setting to another, so allow for this, particularly when changing to a lower setting. For this reason it is better to iron the fabrics needing a cool iron first and gradually increase the temperature for other fabrics. Never use a steam iron on acrylics.

STAIN REMOVAL

Always deal with stains promptly. Unknown large or difficult stains, or stains not listed below, should be sent to your launderer or dry cleaner for professional treatment. Always mention the nature of the stain if you know it.

When treating stains at home, identify the fabric before you start and find out if it is washable or dry cleanable.

Washable Fabrics

Always treat stains as soon as possible to prevent setting. Many stains can be removed by immediate soaking in clear water or water and detergent, followed by a normal wash. Detergents containing enzymes are useful for protein based stains, e.g. egg, blood, etc.

Where this is unsuccessful or impracticable, special treatment of the stain may be necessary. In this case consult your launderer or dry cleaner.

Dry Cleaning Fabrics

In most cases, send article as soon as possible to an expert cleaner, explaining what caused the stain. Inexpert treatment can produce a different stain or mark that is permanent. Dress materials (with surface effects), such as satin, taffeta and velvet, should always be left to the professional. Attempts to remove a stain on such material often results in the removal of the surface effect.

When removing stains from other fabrics always keep the stained side down. Start by dabbing with a dampened clean white cloth, in a circle outside the stained area, working gradually inwards. Keep a pad of clean material underneath the stained area. Do not apply solvent directly on to the centre of the stain. Do not rub, use a light dabbing movement.

If the stain is on leather, suede or other animal skins, a solvent, e.g. Swadegroom, may be used on small areas — so long as the product is made for use on natural skins. Always keep the garment on a well-shaped hanger when not in use, and allow it to dry away from direct heat if it is wet. For best results, have leather or suede cleaned before it becomes badly soiled. A list of cleaners specializing in suede and leather garments is available from the Services Adviser, Association of British Launderers and Cleaners.

Some Specific Stains

Blood

Blood stains are very difficult to remove unless treated quickly. If the stain is obstinate, send the garment to your launderer or dry cleaner.

Washable fabrics. Soak articles in cold water as soon as possible. Never use hot water as this will set the stain. Enzyme detergents are useful here. If the stain is an old one, treat it with cold water containing a few drops of ammonia. Allow the ammonia to soak into the stain for two or three minutes and then sponge with cold water until the smell of ammonia disappears.

Dry cleanable fabrics. Sponge as soon as possible with cold water containing a few drops of liquid detergent. Do not rub.

Felt Tipped Pen Ink

This ink has a different base to that of fountain pen ink and even professional treatment may not remove the stain completely. No home remedy should be attempted.

Ballpoint Ink

Washable fabrics. Use undiluted liquid detergent. Sponge with cold water to remove all traces of detergent.

Dry cleanable fabrics. Methylated spirit should remove the worst of the ink — but this should be used very carefully. Ballpoint ink stains on dry cleanable articles usually respond to professional treatment, so after home stain removal, they should not be left long before a thorough dry clean, otherwise the remaining stain may set.

Fruit Juice

Washable fabrics. Stretch the stained part over a bowl and pour warm water (40°C) through the stained material. Some fruit stains change considerably with time and on drying may be difficult to remove. If this has happened, professional treatment is advised.

Dry cleanable fabrics. Most articles may be dabbed with a clean pad that has been soaked in water and partly wrung out. If in doubt, test a part of the garment that does not show.

Grease

Washable fabrics. Dab the stain with liquid detergent as soon as possible. If badly stained, soaking may be necessary.

Dry cleanable fabrics. Requires professional treatment.

Lipstick

Some lipstick stains may be removed by oil of eucalyptus, but if this is not successful, send the garment for dry cleaning.

Mildew

The removal of mildew is always difficult, and often impossible, so never leave damp articles lying about for any length of time. If articles are badly mildewed send them to your launderer as soon as possible.

Milk or Coffee

Washable fabrics. Small stains should be dabbed with warm water containing liquid detergent. Larger stains should be treated by pouring warm water, with liquid detergent, repeatedly through the fabric. Wash the article thoroughly afterwards.

Dry cleanable fabrics. Dab with a clean pad soaked in water. Should this be unsuccessful, have the garment professionally cleaned. If the drink has sugar in it, advise your dry cleaner.

Oil

Washable fabrics. Apply liquid detergent to the dry material. Rinse out thoroughly.

Dry cleanable fabrics. Dab the stain, when fresh, with a home brand of stain removal fluid, starting in a large circle outside the stain and working inwards. Always keep a pad of clean cloth underneath.

Rust

Washable fabrics. Moisten the stain with lemon juice. Do not let the juice dry on the fabric. Rinse quickly in water containing a little ammonia. Rinse out ammonia. Never use liquid bleach as this will not remove the stain and is certain to rot the fabric eventually.

Dry cleanable fabrics. Should be treated professionally as a high degree of skill is required.

Scorch

Removal of scorch marks depends on the degree of burning. Slight scorching on natural fabrics may be removed by brushing with a stiff clothes brush. This removes the burnt fibre ends. Man-made fibres will harden and damage is usually irrevocable.

Tea

The important thing is to dilute the stain with hot water, before it dries. Where soaking is not possible, dab frequently with a wet pad. If the stain persists, send article to your launderer or dry cleaner.

Wine

Washable fabrics. Should be easily removed by normal washing. Do not allow stain to dry in.

Dry cleanable fabrics. Dab the stain with a clean pad, taking great care not to rub the material. Early professional treatment is required for delicate materials and it is better not to do anything to them yourself, particularly if the fabric has a sheen or special finish to it.

Part Two

A to Z of Fabrics

Many fabric names are in this list, including some that are now rare, and some descriptive terms that have fallen into disuse with the development of modern fabrics.

HOW TO USE YOUR A TO Z

In cases where a type of fabric is produced in different versions, and each one is known by a different name, you will find each name listed separately. For example, general information on handling lace will be found under L, but a short description of Brussels Lace will be found under B.

The most common fibre names are listed; others, including foreign equivalents, will be found in the list of fibre trade names at the end of the section.

Where there are two possible positions in the alphabet I have directed you to both. For example crêpe, polyester crêpe. In cases like this both names are listed, though the advice on handling may be the same for both.

Sizes of machine needle given are Continental, followed by the British equivalent.

In many of the entries there is a symbol or a series of symbols. These will give you, at a glance, the principal properties of that fabric.

KEY

 Suitable for furnishings

 Suitable for underwear

 Drapes or gathers well

 Suitable for children's wear

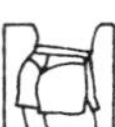 Suitable for sports wear

 Rainproof or showerproof

 Suitable for tailored styles

 Suitable for men's suits

 Suitable for trousers

 Pleats well

 Dry pressing

 Steam pressing

Dry clean

 Washable

 Use zigzag machine stitch

With this A to Z at hand you should have no qualms when buying and choosing fabrics.

A

ABBOT CLOTH
(or Monk's Cloth)

Heavy coarse cotton or linen fabric loosely constructed, usually in basket weave. It is rough surfaced and hard-wearing, but has a tendency to lose shape under pressure due to the looseness of the weave, so its use is confined to curtains, loose covers, etc.

Width
114cm (45in).

Handling
The thick yarns of the cloth will tend to make it fray easily, so do not cut until ready to sew. Allow plenty of seam and hem allowance. Neaten all raw edges. Hems should be turned twice and machined.

Thread
Synthetic or cotton.

Needle
Machine: 100 16. Large stitch.
Hand: 5 or 6. Keep hand-sewing to a minimum as it is difficult to control the loose yarns.

Pressing
Hot iron plus moisture.

Care
Wash if facilities are available to take the bulk, or dry clean.

ABBOTSFORD
The name given to a variety of dress weight fabrics that are in a muted check design. The fabric is always slightly napped on one side, and may be made from cotton, wool, viscose, modal or acrylic.

ABERCROMBIE

A Scottish tartan woven with a blue and black ground and green and white overcheck. Traditionally all-wool but it may now contain a proportion of polyester or acrylic fibre.

Used for kilts, pleated skirts, bias cut skirts, pinafore dresses, children's clothes. It is a medium-weight fabric, not usually heavy enough for outer wear.

Width
140cm (54in).

Handling
One-way design, so cut out accordingly. Lay out fabric so that checks are level and cut out so that checks match at seams.

Thread
Synthetic or mercerized.

Needle
Machine: 90 14. Insert pins across seams at intervals and stitch slowly over them to prevent checks from slipping.
Hand: 7.

Pressing
Hot iron, damp cloth. Pressing block for pleats.

Care
Dry clean. Wash only if labelled washable.

ACETATE

This is cellulose ester fibre, which is not affected by moths or mildew, and has very good draping qualities. In staple form it can be blended with other fibres to produce a wide variety of fabrics of different weights and types.

It is inflammable, but flame-resistant types have now been developed, especially for furnishing fabrics.

Special dyes, known as disperse dyes, were first produced for use with acetate, in Switzerland, and as it is selective about which dyes it accepts, interesting colourings can be obtained when it is mixed with other fibres.

Acetate is not exactly crease-resistant, but it tends to spring back to shape rather than remain crushed. It is not hard-wearing. Acetate fabrics are washable and as the fibre does not readily absorb moisture, they dry quickly, especially if rolled in a towel first to remove excess moisture. Press with a warm iron while slightly damp, or with a steam iron.

Acetate is thermoplastic, so it can be permanently pleated. But it is also possible to make a permanent crease by mistake if pressing with too hot an iron!

See also page 34.

ACETATE JERSEY

Knitted fabric, plain or printed, made from acetate or triacetate fibre.

Handle as for Nylon Jersey (see page 202), but wash by hand as creases may become permanent if set in with hot water. Drip dry, do not wring or spin. Iron slightly damp with a warm iron.

ACRILAN

Trade name for acrylic fibre produced by Chemistrand Co.

See Acrylic (below).

ACRYLIC

Generic term for light but bulky man-made fibre with soft, woolly handle, which is often used with natural and other man-made fibres to make wool-like fabrics and knitted goods. Of all man-made fibres it is the closest to wool.

Acrylic fibre is produced mainly from acrylonitrile. The fibre is absorbent and warm, resistant to mildew and moths, washable and dry cleanable, but fabrics have a tendency to 'pill' after some wear and knitted acrylics easily lose their shape. Skirts may 'seat', trousers may bag at the knees.

Press lightly with a medium hot iron and slightly damp muslin cloth, but leave fabric undisturbed until cool or it will lose its shape.

See also page 35.

ACRYLIC SHEER

A heavy, rather stringy open-weave vision net for curtains, often in two-colour plain weave.

All acrylic fibre is very soft and difficult to press, but a firmer net of this kind contains about 20 per cent flax which improves its texture and handle.

Width
120cm (48in).

Handling
Easy to cut on the grain but difficult to tack as the weave is so open. Do not use adhesive web because adhesive passes through fabric to the iron.

Thread
Synthetic.

Needle
Machine: 100 16. Large straight or zigzag stitch.
Hand: 6.

Pressing
Warm iron.

Care
Medium hot wash. Do not spin.

AERTEX

  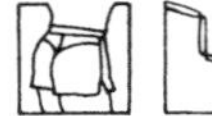 

Trade name for a British cotton cellular cloth. The fact that it is cotton and of open texture makes it cool and absorbent and comfortable to wear.

Used for underwear, sports clothes, shirts for children and adults. It is not generally available as piece goods, but ready-made clothes may need repairing.

Width
Various.

Handling
A soft fabric presenting no problems. If seams are split they should be reinforced with cotton tape before stitching up, or the cellular structure will not withstand the stitching.

Thread
Synthetic or mercerized.

Needle
Machine: 90 14. Slight zigzag stitch.
Hand: 6.

Pressing
Hot iron or steam iron.

Care
Hot wash by hand or machine. Boil. Iron slightly damp with a hot iron.

AGARIC
Cotton fabric with a loop construction, like towelling.

Handling
As Towelling, page 239.

AJOUR

Lacy, openwork embroidery, normally cotton with viscose fibre. A decoration used on blouses and underwear.

Thread
Machine embroidery or synthetic.

Needle
Machine: 70 9.
Hand: 9 or 10.

Pressing
Place right side down on to folded towel and press lightly with warm iron or steam iron.

Care
Wash by hand in warm water with soap flakes or liquid soapless detergent.

ALBERT CLOTH
Double-faced, reversible coat fabric, often with a different face and back. Made from wool, it is a good quality cloth used to make expensive overcoats for men, sometimes with velvet collars.

Handle as Reversible Cloth, page 220.

ALENÇON LACE
Usually made in a floral design with a heavy corded thread outlining it. The background is fine mesh or net.

ALEXANDRIA

Fine, lightweight dress fabric made of cotton and wool with a small woven design. Possibly its name derives from the very early silks and wool fabrics, made in the ancient city of Alexandria, which featured small designs such as flowers and scrolls.

Used for blouses, dresses and children's clothes.

Width
90cm (36in).

Handling
It gathers well. Use fine nylon zip and light interfacing.

Thread
Synthetic or mercerized.

Needle
Machine: 80 11. Medium stitch.
Hand: 7.

Pressing
Hot iron and moisture.

Care
Wash.

ALLIGATOR
The skin of the reptile, easily recognizable by square boxy markings. Used mainly for shoes and handbags. Not normally available for sewing.

ALL-OVER LACE
Any piece-lace with a pattern repeated regularly all over, no edgings, borders, etc.

ALOE LACE
A very fragile type of lace, usually made in Italy, but some comes from the Philippines. Very expensive. Made from the fibre of the plant, aloe.

ALPACA

Alpaca fibres (from the silky wool of a llama-like animal) are sometimes blended with cotton, wool, or rayon, mainly to reduce the cost, though alpaca is not as expensive as camel cashmere. Imitation alpaca is made from viscose and acetate yarns.

Alpaca was once widely used for dress fabrics, but is now mainly confined to men's light suits in black or grey. Sometimes still used for nurses' uniforms.

Width
Usually 140cm (54in), but may be less.

Handling
Use for crisp tailored clothes.

Thread
Synthetic or mercerized.

Needle
Machine: 100 16. Large stitch.

Pressing
Hot iron and damp muslin.

Care
Dry clean.

See also page 43.

ALPACA CRÊPE
A soft acetate or polyester crêpe with dull surface, fairly soft to handle. Used for dresses.

See Crêpe, page 135.

ALTAR CLOTH
A very fine sheer, crisp fabric used, as the name suggests, for church cloths.

Handle as Lawn, see page 183.

AMAZON

Fine dress fabric with a worsted warp and woollen weft, usually in satin weave in plain colours. It is lightly milled and raised to give a fibrous effect but this does not conceal the twill effect of the satin weave.

Width
140cm (54in).

Handling
Expensive so used only occasionally, mainly for women's clothes.

Thread
Synthetic or mercerized.

Needle
Machine: 90 14. Medium stitch.
Hand: 6 or 7.

Pressing
Hot iron and damp cloth.

Care
Dry clean.

ANGORA
From the Angora rabbit, the hair is always mixed with other fibres, often wool or acrylic, to reduce the cost. Fabrics must be labelled as containing rabbit hair to avoid confusion with mohair, the hair of the Angora goat.

Any fabric containing Angora rabbit hair is characterized by the appearance of short white hairs.

Handling
Handle as for the main fibre in the fabric.

See also page 43.

ANTIQUE LACE
A term used to describe handmade bobbin lace where heavy threads have been used. Designs are often irregular.

ANTIQUE TAFFETA

A very heavy, stiff fabric, not found much now, but it is the best type for curtains, etc.

See Taffeta, page 236.

ANTWERP POT LACE
A bobbin lace which always had motifs of baskets or vases of flowers as decoration.

APPLIQUÉ LACE
Any fabric where separate lace motifs are applied to a background.

ARABIAN LACE

An écru-coloured piece-lace corded in a darker shade.

Used for curtains.

ARGYLL
Diamond-shaped design for knitted fabrics using two or, more usually, three colours of yarn. Often used for jerseys and hosiery, but also incorporated into knit fabrics.

Handling
Handle as for knit fabric. Pattern must be matched.

ARMENIAN EDGING
Narrow lace trimming with formal, often geometric designs.

ARMURÉ
French term for a variety of fabrics which have an embossed or pebbled surface, imitating bird's eye effect, piqué, stripes, crêpe and ribs. Sometimes they also have a woven design.

Made from any fibre or blends of various fibres, this is mainly a dress weight fabric.

Handling
Handle according to the fibre content, taking care not to impair the embossing when pressing.

See also page 75.

ARRAS
(a) French lace.
(b) Worsted cloth that was produced in or around Arras.
(c) Tapestry work made famous centuries ago in the city of Arras.

ARTIFICIAL SILK
Sometimes known as Art. Silk, the name given to the early viscose fibre (rayon) fabrics because they were made to imitate the more expensive pure silk cloth. The term should no longer be used, but is still in existence on the temperature setting dials of older domestic irons.

ART LINEN

Linen fabric made with a cylindrical thread. It is soft but firm enough to use as a base for embroidery, and is used for drawn-thread work. Colours: écru, white or unbleached.

Width
Various.

Handling
Fabric will fray; allow for this. Handling while working embroidery increases risk of fraying.

Thread
Mercerized.

Needle
Choose size and type according to weight of fabric, type of embroidery, etc.

Pressing
Hot iron and moisture on wrong side. Press lightly if embroidered.

Care
Hot wash by hand.

ARTILLERY TWILL
See Whipcord, page 250.

ASBESTOS
A fibre produced from asbestos, spun alone or with cotton. The fabric is produced mainly in plain or twill weave and is used largely for industrial purposes, including protective clothing, but also for theatre curtains, ironing board covers, fire blankets. It is made in a variety of weights, but it is rarely found on sale as a piece-goods fabric. If it has to be handled in the home, use synthetic thread and a large stitch.

ASTRAKHAN
The fur of the caracul lamb, recognizable by its glossy curls. Brown, beige or black.

ASTRAKHAN CLOTH

Heavy woven or knitted, synthetic or wool, curly-piled fabric made in imitation of astrakhan fur. Used for coats, jackets, collars, bags, etc. Good quality cloth contains some mohair to add lustre and curl.

Width
Probably 140cm (54in). Possibly 150cm (60in).

Handling
Handle as Fur Fabric, page 156.

ASTRAKHAN FUR
Luxurious and expensive fur taken from young lambs in the Astrakhan area of Russia. Used for coats, hats and trimmings for men and women.

See also Fur Handling, page 157.

ATLAS

Satin-weave rich fabric made from silk or man-made fibres.

Used for dress fabrics, mainly evening wear.

A less expensive Atlas is made with a cotton weft and is used as a lining fabric.

Width
90, 114 or 140cm (36, 45 or 54in).

Handling
Fabrics fray, so allow for this when cutting out. Cut linings slightly larger to avoid strain in wear.

Thread
Synthetic or mercerized.

Needle
Machine: 80 11. Medium stitch.
Hand: 8.

Pressing
Warm iron on wrong side only. If pressing on right side, protect with dry cloth to avoid marks.

Care
May be washable, but check the label on the fabric and dry clean if in doubt.

AZLON

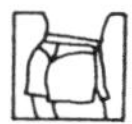

Generic term for regenerated protein fibres from peanuts, soya beans, corn, milk, etc. They are soft and smooth and blend well with other fibres.

Used for knitted garments, sportswear and coats.

B

BABY LACE
The very narrow lace edging of the Valenciennes type.

See page 244.

BAG CLOTH
A woven cloth of inferior quality yarns, heavily sized to prevent penetration. Used, as the name implies, for bags and sacks to hold dry goods such as flour, beans, lentils, etc. The sizing washes out leaving a soft fabric useful for dusters and cleaning cloths.

BAGHEERA VELVET
A piece-dyed velvet with a rough surface. Used for outer wear as the rough surface makes it largely uncrushable.

See Velvet, page 244.

BAININ

Hand-woven woollen homespun fabric from Ireland.

Used for coats, skirts, stoles.

Width
140cm (54in), 90cm (36in), or less.

Handling
Hand-wovens are loosely constructed, so allow for fraying.

Thread
Synthetic or mercerized.

Needle
Machine: 90 14. Medium to large stitch.
Hand: 6-7.

Pressing
Hot iron and damp cloth.

Care
Dry clean.

BAIZE (1)
Originally made in Spain and used as a wall covering, this is a loosely woven, short napped fabric, made to imitate felt. Usually dark green, plain weave. Rarely found on sale as piece goods.

See also Blazer Cloth, page 104.

BAIZE (2)
A coarse woollen cloth of plain-weave construction made in Great Britain for centuries. It is now a thick cloth with a napped surface. Rarely found on sale as piece goods.

BALBRIGGAN

A light knit fabric made on a circular knitting machine. It was originally made at Balbriggan in Ireland and used for hosiery.

Now used for sportswear, underwear, and pyjamas.

Usually made from cotton, it may have a slight fleece on the wrong side.

Handling

Handle as for Cotton Jersey, page 132.

BALLOON CLOTH

A plain-weave cotton made from high quality fine yarn and very closely woven.

Used occasionally for ready-made shirts, for typewriter ribbons and, of course, for balloons.

BAN-LON

Registered trademark of Bancroft and Sons. Fabrics made of yarns specially treated by their Textralized process which adds bulk, moderate stretch and texture to synthetic thermoplastic yarns. Fabrics made from these yarns are soft, strong, easy to wash, quick-drying and crease- and shrink-resistant.

BANNOCKBURN

The name of a Scottish town that has long been the centre of an area producing a top quality tweed for suits and coats. Its characteristic is that a single colour yarn is alternated with a yarn made of two colours; the yarns are twisted together before weaving.

BARATHEA

Expensive fine English cloth, closely woven with slight diagonal weave appearance and broken rib effect. Feels smooth but has a granular appearance. Originally in worsted and silk, but now made with synthetic fibres such as viscose and acetate and polyester.

Used for men's evening clothes in black, and in many colours for coats and skirts for women.

Width

140cm (54in).

Handling

A springy suiting, so keep to plain tailored styles. Pleats well. Cut pieces one way as slight shading may occur. Right side of fabric not always easily distinguishable from wrong. Use firm interfacing.

Thread

Synthetic or mercerized.

Needle

Machine: 90–100 14–16. Large stitch.
Hand: 6–7.

Pressing

Hot iron and damp muslin. Sharp pressure to avoid iron marks.

Care

Dry clean unless labelled washable.

BARK CRÊPE
Heavy crêpe with rough texture, like tree bark, usually viscose or polyester. A stiff fabric for evening wear.

BARMAN LACE
The name given to machine-made reproductions of French and Belgian hand-made laces.

BARRÈGE (or Barège)
Very sheer fabric of wool and silk or cotton used for veilings. Originates from Barège in the Pyrenees.

Unsuitable for clothing. Drapes well but will not withstand strain in wear. Rarely found on sale as piece goods.

BATISTE

Plain-weave, fine, smooth finish cotton fabric, but may now be polyester. Slightly heavier than voile, in white or plain colours. It creases easily but is strong, wears well, and washes and boils.

Used for handkerchiefs, underwear, shirts, blouses, nightwear, children's clothes.

Width
90cm (36in) or 114cm (45in).

Handling
Easy to sew, minimal fraying. Use lightweight zip. Use French seams or machine fell on nightwear and baby clothes.

Thread
Synthetic or mercerized.

Needle
Machine: 80 11. Small to medium stitch.
Hand: 8.

Pressing
Hot iron and damp cloth or steam iron.

Care
Hot wash. Iron damp.

BATTENBERG LACE

A coarse type lace often made from linen thread and used mainly in small areas, such as collars and cuffs, although it is a popular heavy curtain lace.

BEADING LACE
This describes very narrow insertion laces. These are often openwork hemstitching or faggot-stitch, or they may have slits for inserting ribbons.

BEAVER CLOTH

Expensive coating material which has been heavily napped and raised and made to look like beaver fur. Woven in a variety of weights in single or double satin weaves from high quality woollen yarns.

Used for overcoats and winter jackets for men and women.

Width
140cm (54in).

Handling
Frays little. Cut one-way with pile running from top to bottom. Piped buttonholes or perfectly tailored hand-worked ones. Firm interfacing.

Thread
Synthetic or mercerized.

Needle
Machine: 100 16. Large stitch.
Hand: 5 and 6.

Pressing
Hot iron and damp cloth on wrong side. Sharp pressure to avoid iron marks. Brush surface on right side after pressing.

Care
Dry clean.

BEDFORD CORD

Originated in Bedford, Great Britain, but apparently Bedford, Massachusetts also claims the honour. Firm heavy fabric used for trousers, riding breeches, uniforms, upholstery. Typified by narrow warp cords. Made with carded cotton yarns, woollen or worsted yarns, viscose acetate polyester or combinations of yarns. The wales are wide and stiffer yarns are usually present. Light Bedford Cord used for dresses, children's clothes.

Width
140cm (54in) if wool. 90cm, or 114cm (36in or 45in) if other yarns.

Handling
Cut with cords or wales running the length of the cloth. Use heavy metal zip and firm interfacing.

Thread
Synthetic or mercerized.

Needle
Machine: 100 16. Large stitch.
Hand: 5 and 6.

Pressing
Hot iron and damp cloth. Sharp pressure to avoid iron imprints.

Care
Dry clean unless labelled washable.

BEMBERG
Trade mark of early cuprammonium rayon produced by the American Bemberg Company. Fabric is still often labelled 'Bemberg' but must include fibre content description as well.

See Cupro, pages 36 and 138.

BENGALINE

The original cloth came from Bengal but an imitation is the familiar crosswise rib fabric made of viscose, silk, wool or cotton. Similar to Poplin or Faille in appearance but heavier.

Used for coats, suits, dresses, and ribbons; can also be made as a curtain fabric.

Width
Various according to fibre content.

Handling
A stiff fabric requiring plain ungathered styles. Use firm interfacing. Cut with ribs running across the garment. Neaten all raw edges.

Thread
Synthetic or mercerized.

Needle
Machine: 80–90 11–14. Medium stitch.
Hand: 7–8.

Pressing
Temperature of iron must be set according to fibre content. A steam iron would be suitable for all types of fabric. Press lightly if viscose or silk to avoid leaving iron marks.

Care
Dry clean. Wash if labelled washable.

BILLIARD CLOTH
Woollen cloth made from fine Merino wool. Heavily milled with a fibrous finish. Dyed green or red for billiard or card table tops. Plain or twill weave, the cloth is of the highest quality and must obviously be smooth and even, but have body.

BINCA OR BOLDWORK CLOTH
A very distinctive embroidery fabric made in a range of colours. It is characterized by the fairly large square holes between the blocks of threads. Often used as a beginner's embroidery fabric for children.

BINCHE LACE
A six-point star-shaped ground net of snowflake effect with a scroll pattern on it. A Flemish lace.

BIRD'S EYE
A weave which suggests the eye of a bird, the cloth is usually fine clear-finish worsted and the design gives the appearance of small indentations. It may be simulated in cotton or viscose, in which case it has a small diamond pattern with the bird's eye indentation in the centre. Cotton fabrics are often used as towelling.

Width
Worsted: 140cm (54in).
Others: 90cm or 114cm (36in or 45in).

Handling
Handle according to fibre content.
See Worsted, page 251.

BISSO LINEN
See Altar Cloth, page 96.

BLANKET CLOTH

May have been named after Thomas Blanquette, a Flemish weaver living in England in the fourteenth century, but now means any thick cloth with a heavy nap, suitable for rugs, dressing-gowns, blankets, casual coats, shawls, stoles.

Warmest made in wool or worsted, but now also made from other fibres or mixtures. Not hardwearing if made into clothing.

Width
140cm (54in) or wider.

Handling
It does not fray so edges may be finished with loopstitch or other decorative stitch. Avoid too many thicknesses at one point. Coat edges could be bound with braid to reduce bulk. Lining unnecessary.

Thread
Synthetic or mercerized.

Needle
Machine: 90–100 14–16. Large stitch.
Hand: 6–7.

Pressing
Hot iron and damp cloth, very light pressure to avoid flattening the fabric surface.

Care
Dry clean. Wash if labelled washable. Blankets are washable.

BLAZER CLOTH

A type of Flannel or Melton used for blazers. Usually wool but can be mixtures. It was traditionally striped, but is now also in plain colours. The right side is usually slightly napped.

Width
140cm (54in).

Handling
Used for blazers because it is not necessary to line it. Neaten all raw edges. Use firm interfacing. Make piped buttonholes or very good tailored, worked button holes. Shrink before use.

Thread
Synthetic or mercerized.

Needle
Machine: 90 14.
Hand: 6–7.

Pressing
Hot iron and damp cloth. Allow to cool before moving.

Care
Dry clean.

BLONDE LACE
A silk lace with floral designs but with boldly defined holes in the flower heads. Very expensive.

BOBBIN LACE
Also called Pillow Lace, it is hand-made using fancy bobbins of bone, ivory and now wood, on a hard stuffed pillow, and using long pins with coloured glass or plastic heads to anchor the lace to the pillow. Punched paper patterns are first fixed to the pillow. A very old craft.

BOBBIN NET
A machine-made copy of the original Bobbin Lace. A machine to do this was first invented in the early nineteenth century and produced a hole-mesh fabric.

BOLIVIA

An expensive, soft, plushy fabric usually of wool, and often containing a small amount of special fibre, such as Alpaca or Mohair.

It is closely woven and of fine texture with a cut pile surface. The pile is cut in ribs running in the warp direction. A thick firm fabric used for coats, cloaks, etc.

Width
140cm (54in).

Handling
A top quality expensive cloth to be tailored only by those with a great deal of expertise. Cut all pieces in one direction. Use heavy interfacing and make perfectly tailored hand-worked button-holes. Needs lining.

Thread
Silk or mercerized.

Needle
Machine: 90–100 14–16. Large stitch.
Hand: 8.

Pressing
Cover the pressing surface with a piece of soft cloth or a spare piece of Bolivia and press on the wrong side of the garment with a hot iron and damp cloth. Use firm pressure to achieve good results, but take care not to flatten the plush pile. Brush up the right side if necessary.

Care
Dry clean.

BOMBAZINE

One of the oldest fabrics known, this was a fine silk or wool fabric of plain or twill weave for formal clothes. In black it was the traditional mourning cloth. It is now made from silk warp and worsted filling with imitations made from viscose or cotton.

Width
Varies according to fibre.

Handling
May be fairly crisp so choose suitable interfacing. Used mainly for evening and wedding-gowns, if silk or viscose and has lustre.

Thread
Synthetic.

Needle
Machine: 90 14. Medium stitch.
Hand: 7.

Pressing
Medium hot iron on wrong side, or steam iron.

Care
Dry clean.

BONDED FABRICS
See Laminates, page 181.

BONDED FIBRE FABRIC
Known as non-wovens, these are made from a variety of fibres used on the same principle as in felt, but bonded together chemically as, unlike wool, they do not have inherent felting properties.

Bonded fibre fabrics or non-wovens have developed in many directions, which include household cloths and cleaning pads, industrial and military protective clothing, and as interfacing and other haberdashery items. As non-wovens do not fray and have no grain they can be used economically.

See also page 58.

BOOK MUSLIN

Inexpensive white muslin-type fabric heavily sized.

Used for stiffening bags, hats, wide belts, etc.

Width
90cm (36in).

Handling
Very springy, so only use for flat areas. Does not fray. Will blunt needles quickly. Difficult to hand sew. Use adhesive where possible.

Thread
Synthetic.

Needle
Machine: 100 16. Large stitch, straight or zigzag.
Hand: 6.

Pressing
Hot iron.

Care
Dry clean for safety as some types can lose their stiffness.

BOTANY TWILL

Cloth woven from botany quality worsted yarns in various weights. The weaves are 2 and 2 or 4 and 4 twills producing smooth fabric used for men's and women's suitings. An expensive cloth as botany is the top quality worsted yarn.

Width
140cm (54in).

Handling
This top quality suiting should be confined to suits, skirts etc.; it pleats well. Use metal zips and firm interfacing. The cloth will fray, so line jackets and neaten raw edges of other garments.

Thread
Mercerized or synthetic.

Needle
Machine: 90–100 14–16 Large stitch.
Hand: 7–8.

Pressing
Hot iron and damp cloth. Pressing block where necessary.

Care
Dry clean.

BOUCLÉ

Yarn with a curl or loop effect, made from two or more threads twisted together.

The fabric may be either woven or knitted. With the latter, the loops appear only on the right side. Fibres used for bouclé yarns may be wool, worsted, polyester, nylon, viscose, acrylic or blends. The resulting fabric has 'give' in it, due to the elasticity of the yarn. Knitted Bouclé tends to have quite a lot of 'give'.

Fabrics range from soft and lightweight to firm and coat-weight.

Width
Varies according to fibre.

Handling
Knits will not fray but edges will curl, so neaten all raw edges. Woven bouclé will fray readily so requires neatening. Use nylon zip and soft interfacings.

Thread
Synthetic or mercerized.

Needle
Machine: depends on thickness of fabric.
Hand: depends on thickness of fabric.

Pressing
Medium hot iron and slightly damp muslin with sharp pressure to avoid impairing the surface interest.

Care
Follow instructions according to fibre content.

BOUCLÉ KNIT

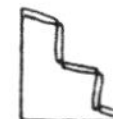   

Knit fabric with a bouclé effect on the right side. This is achieved by the introduction of an inlaid yarn fed into the knitting machine and trapped as the knit stitch is made. The fabrics are medium weight and are usually produced from polyester, nylon and acrylic yarns.

Used for sweater dresses, sweater-type tops, jackets.

Width
150cm (60in) or more.

Handling
There is usually an excessive amount of stretch across the width of the fabric, so cut pieces with the grain all one way, even though the fabric has an all-over bouclé appearance. The edges may tend to curl up when the fabric is cut, but this can be controlled when sewing starts by neatening all raw edges. Use stretch interfacing and piped buttonholes. If lining is required, use Nylon Jersey.

Thread
Synthetic.

Needle
Machine: 90 14. Medium stitch. Slight zigzag.
Hand: 6.

Pressing
Medium iron and damp muslin, or steam iron. Very light pressure.

Care
Usually washable, but follow the instructions.

BOURRETTE

Yarn spun from carded short fibres of lower quality waste silk. The resulting silk fabric is hairy and interspersed with nubs of fibre.

Used for blouses, shirts, soft jackets and skirts.

Width
90 cm (36in).

Handling
Fabric will fray during making up so neaten seams. Use light interfacing and nylon zips. Make good hand-worked buttonholes or machine-made ones.

Thread
Silk or synthetic.

Needle
Machine: 80 11. Small stitch.
Hand: 9.

Pressing
Press lightly on the wrong side with a dry iron. When finishing on the right side, protect the fabric with a dry cloth.

Care
Warm wash by hand in soap flakes or liquid soapless detergent. Roll in a towel to absorb surplus water. Iron on wrong side when nearly dry.

BOX CLOTH

A thick heavily-milled woollen cloth in 2 and 2 twill, which is buff or tan-coloured cloth like Melton.

Used for overcoats and suits, riding habits.

See Melton, page 194.

BOX LEATHER
This has always been known as a good quality leather. It is 'boarded', i.e. the surface is broken up with parallel creases, a process only applied to top quality smooth leather. Very expensive.

Used for shoes and handbags, not usually available for sewing.

BRAIDED FABRICS
Yarns of any fibre are interlaced and diagonally plaited, but only narrow widths can be produced for cord, shoelaces, braids for coats and uniforms.

See also Ribbon, page 52.

BRETON LACE
A net ground with heavy embroidered designs. A feature of it is that the embroidery threads are very often coloured.

BRIGHTON HONEYCOMB
A fabric, usually cotton, with a typical honeycomb effect but on the right side only.

See Honeycomb, page 170.

BRI-NYLON

A British polyamide fibre used mainly in the manufacture of carpets, lingerie, nightwear and lightweight knitwear. Surface can be brushed to form a short pile. Hard-wearing. Washes easily and dries quickly as it is not absorbent.

See also page 39.

BROADCLOTH

A term largely used in the United States. A heavy 'lustrous' faced woollen fabric. Set wide on the loom to allow for the shrinkage and made with a high nap which is then pressed down so that the weave is not visible, this gives it the compact look that is typical. It is hard-wearing as the yarn is made from best Merino wool. Generally twill weave but may be plain.

The name originally referred to any cloth wider than the usual 29in, and the inference was that the wider cloth was inferior, but now woollen broadcloth is a top quality fabric excellent for coats and jackets and all tailored clothes.

Width
140cm (54in).

Handling
This is a one-way cloth, so cut with the nap lying in one direction downwards on all pieces. Use heavy interfacing. Piped button-holes or very good tailored worked ones. The cloth will not fray, but the garment will need lining if it is a fitted coat or jacket.

Thread
Synthetic, mercerized or silk.

Needle
Machine: 100 16. Large stitch.
Hand: 6–7.

Pressing
Hot iron and damp cloth on wrong side, sharp pressure to avoid imprints. Press on right side, protecting garment with a piece of the broadcloth face down under the damp cloth. Press lightly.

Care
Dry clean.
(For Cotton Broadcloth, see page 131.)

BROADTAIL
A flat, lustrous fur, slightly wavy. The pelt of the young unborn Persian lamb.

BROCADE

Multi-coloured or self-coloured floral raised design, sometimes with metal threads added. Made on Jacquard loom, usually in satin weave. Originally always silk, it can now be viscose, cotton, acetate, polyester and many blends. In true brocade, the design is produced by additional coloured threads on the weft. These pass across the back of the cloth unused and are brought to the surface when required. The wrong side is easily discerned by those threads or floats. In addition threads can be woven into the back of the fabric. Some brocades are heavy, some are crisp.

As brocade is made from all fibres into a wide variety of weights of fabric, it is used for many purposes, including clothing, furnishings and upholstery.

Widths
90cm, 115cm, 120cm, 150cm (36in, 45in, 48in, 60in).

Handling
All brocades fray readily as the floats soon become detached when cut. Allow for this when cutting. Hems on curtains and furnishings should be doubled and machined and seams bound. On clothing, use open seams and neaten raw edges. Use nylon zips and medium to firm interfacing depending on weight. Dress brocades made from slippery yarns fray very readily so add extra seam allowances, applying non-fray liquid if necessary. Raw edges can be bound

with net to prevent fraying while not adding bulk.

Thread
Synthetic.

Needle
Machine: 90–100 11–16. Medium to large stitch.
Hand: 7–8.

Pressing
Press dress brocades with a dry iron on the wrong side only, using light pressure. Start by using the toe of the iron only to open seams. Take care not to impair the raised surface.

Furnishing brocades are more substantial. Use a medium hot iron or steam iron and medium pressure.

Care
Follow the care instructions on the fabric: some are washable but most dress brocades should be dry cleaned only.

BROCADE VELVET
Velvet with the pile sheared at different heights to form a design, sometimes check, sometimes floral. Plainer designs in dark colours are used for men's jackets. Some superb quality velvets of this type come from France. Very expensive.

BROCATELLE

A furnishing and upholstery fabric similar to brocade. Woven on a Jacquard loom, the cloth has an additional weft thread of cotton or rayon or linen to pad out the pattern producing high relief. The patterns are often twill on a plain or satin background. Heavy yarns used are plain and mercerized cotton, viscose, linen.

Width
114cm, 120cm, 150cm (45in, 48in, 60in).

Handling
Designs are usually one-way and will have to be watched on curtains, etc. Fabric will fray, so all hems should be double and machined and seams bound.

Thread
Synthetic or cotton.

Needle
Machine: 90–100 14–16. Large stitch.
Hand: 5–6. Keep hand-sewing to a minimum.

Pressing
Use a medium hot or steam iron and light, sharp pressure on both sides.

Care
Most fabrics for curtains and furnishings are washable, but check the instructions when buying.

BRODERIE ANGLAISE
The best quality fabrics are made in Austria and are expensive. The fabric is plain-weave cotton, or polyester and cotton, in which shaped holes, e.g. leaves, and round holes are punched and then embroidered. Most fabrics are white or plain pale colours with self-colour embroidery, but a few are embroidered in a contrasting colour. Some fabrics have more

embroidery than others, some have a border design, some a scalloped edge. Creases easily.

BRUGES LACE

A bar lace, originating from Bruges. Very similar in appearance to Honiton Lace. Woven as a tape with a fine thread. Coarse types are used for curtains, bedcovers and tablecloths.

BRUSHED ACRYLIC

A fabric described like this is usually thick, light and woolly—most often, acrylic fibre on a jersey backing with the right side brushed into a furry surface. Used for dressing-gowns, sleeping bags, baby coats, zip-front casual jackets, toys, collars and cuffs. Good in white, but colours tend to be either dull or garish.

Width
114cm, 150cm (45in, 60in).

Handling
The fabric is extremely inflammable and should be used with caution for young children's dressing-gowns. Very bulky, so choose simple styles with few pieces. Often improved by adding knitted collar and cuffs. Pile is usually brushed evenly but if it lies in one direction cut all pieces one way. It will not fray, but reduce bulk in seams by trimming away surface of seam allowances after stitching. If facings are needed, use a thin plain matching fabric. Use big plastic zip or heavy nylon zip and insert so that zip is visible and therefore pile will not catch in the teeth.

Thread
Synthetic.

Needle
Machine: 90 14. Large stitch. Avoid topstitching.
Hand: 6.

Pressing
Medium iron on wrong side only and very light pressure. Brush up on right side if pile is flattened.

Care
Wash.

BRUSHED COTTON

Plain or printed cotton fabric can be slightly brushed on one side to add warmth. This additional warmth makes it very suitable for children's clothes, winter blouses and shirts. An inexpensive fabric, it creases easily but washes well. It does not wear as well as unbrushed cotton. The brushing process may be applied to the right or wrong side of the fabric. Extremely inflammable, so do not use for nightdresses for children or elderly people.

Width
90cm, 114cm (36in, 45in).

Handling
Easy to sew. Use seams appropriate to the garment. Does not fray readily.

BRUSHED DENIM

Thread
Synthetic or mercerized.

Needle
Machine: 80 11. Medium stitch.
Hand: 7.

Pressing
Hot iron or steam iron.

Care
Machine hot wash.

BRUSHED DENIM

Denim weave cloth, usually all cotton, with a brushed finish on the right side. It has a softer appearance than conventional denim, but its use should be confined to shirtwaist dresses, safari-style jackets, trousers and jeans, casual shirts for men and children's clothes. Hard-wearing but not as tough as denim. Usually found only in a limited range of colours such as denim blue, green, red and brown.

Width
114cm (45in).

Handling
Use machine fell seams for strength. Topstitching in matching or contrast colour looks good. Use firm interfacing. Use special jeans zip or strong metal zip.

Thread
Synthetic or mercerized.

Needle
Machine: 90–100 14–16. Medium to large stitch.
Hand: 6. Keep hand-sewing to a minimum.

Pressing
Hot iron and damp cloth or steam iron.

Care
Hot hand or machine wash.
See also Denim, page 139.

BRUSHED NYLON

Jersey nylon brushed on the right side to make it warm. It is strong and hard-wearing. Inclined to build up static more than most nylon due to the brushing. It is much warmer than plain Nylon Jersey but is not a particularly attractive fabric, so its use is confined to nightwear, children's nightwear and sheets. Does not crease. It washes easily and dries quickly due to the inability of nylon fibre to absorb moisture. White fabrics adopt a grey tone unless washed separately.

Width
90cm, 114cm (36in, 45in).

Handling
Brushed nylon does not fray but the edges will tend to curl up as it is cut. This makes it difficult to work open seams, so it is best to use narrow finish or French seams.

Thread
Synthetic. Medium length stitch, slight zigzag.

Needle
Machine: 80 11. Use a ball point needle if necessary.
Hand: 7.

Pressing
Warm iron. Edges will tend to curl after pressing so, if necessary, use a slightly damp cloth, too.

Care
Machine or hand wash. Drip dry or short spin. No ironing necessary.

See also Nylon Jersey, page 202.

BRUSHED VISCOSE

Many plain and printed spun viscose fabrics are brushed. This makes the fabric feel soft and warm, and more attractive. It is not quite as strong as unbrushed viscose but will wash and wear quite well. It is very inflammable. Tends to crease easily.

Used for baby's and children's clothes and for blouses, shirts and nightwear.

Width
90cm, 114cm (36in, 45in).

Handling
Easy to sew. Use open seams. Gathers well. Use soft iron-on interfacing. Use nylon zips. Machine-made or hand-worked buttonholes. Good fabric for beginners.

Thread
Synthetic.

Needle
Machine: 80 11. Medium stitch.
Hand: 7. Easy fabric to hand sew.

Pressing
Medium iron or steam iron.

Care
Machine or hand wash. Iron while slightly damp.

See also Viscose, page 43.

BRUSSELS LACE
This type of lace was originally made with very fine linen threads. The motifs were made as bobbin lace and then appliquéd on to a mesh ground. Now all fibres may be used and the motifs and the mesh are usually machine-made.

BUCKINGHAMSHIRE LACE
A very fine hand-made lace originating in Buckinghamshire. It was characterized by a diamond mesh ground, was often narrow, and was used only for trimming.

BUCKRAM

A cloth made from cheap cotton yarn and heavily impregnated with size to give it a very stiff finish. Sometimes two layers are glued together. Used for stiffening, e.g. in millinery, waistbands and bookbinding. (The size may wash out.)

Width
90cm (36in) or less.

Handling
Very stiff and springy; it may need pressing to remove the curl it adopts on the roll. When cutting, it may be necessary to place objects on the corners of the buckram to hold it flat. Often cut on the cross so that it has 'give'. Do not add seam allowances as it

is too stiff to include in seams. Cut exactly to size and attach to fabric with machining or herring-bone stitch. Will not fray.

Thread
Synthetic or cotton.

Needle
Machine: 100 16. Large stitch.
Hand: 5–6. Very difficult to hand-sew.

Pressing
Hot iron.

Care
Dry clean.

BUCKSKIN
A white or pinky beige leather, which originally came from the elk and deer, but is now also obtained from sheep. It is strong but supple.

Used for clothes, shoes, gloves, belts, etc. Not easy to obtain skins for sewing.

BUNTING

A soft open-weave cotton or woollen fabric used for ceremonial flags; it resembles Scrim. It is dyed and printed. Cheaper short-life flags are made from cotton bunting, a fabric that resembles Cheesecloth in texture. Usually dyed in plain bright colours; colours may not be fixed. Neither type is easy to find. Unsuitable for clothing.

Width
150cm (60in) or less.

Handling
Fabrics fray easily, so all edges must be turned in twice and machined. Cut carefully on the straight grain.

Thread
Synthetic.

Needle
Machine: 90 14. Large stitch.
Hand: 6. Not really suitable for hand-sewing.

Pressing
Medium iron and damp cloth, or steam iron.

Care
Hand wash woollen bunting. Hand or machine wash cottons but do not mix colours.

See also Scrim, page 224.

BURLAP

A heavy fabric made of jute fibre or allied yarns with a coarse plain weave. The name originally meant a cleaning cloth, which implies hard wear. May shrink.

Burlap is used for carpet backing, for upholstery webbing, and when dyed and printed for heavy curtains.

Width
100cm (40in).

Handling
Very tough and difficult to handle. Must be cut exactly on grain. Frays easily, so enclose all raw edges.

Thread
30's cotton.

Needle
Machine: 100 16. Large stitch.
Hand: 4–5. Keep hand-sewing to a minimum.

Pressing
Hot iron and damp cloth.

Care
Hot wash.

BURNT OUT

Specially woven patterned, plain colour fabrics to which acid is applied to remove or burn out some of the fibre. The fibres are mixed so that only certain parts of the design are burnt out and they become transparent while the rest remains opaque, creating very attractive fabric. The fibres used vary but are often polyester and cotton.

The fabrics are often sheer and lightweight and are used for blouses, dresses and curtains.

Width
114cm (45in) or wider for curtains.

Handling
Slightly springy but not difficult to handle. Fabrics do not usually fray very much. Cut one way if design demands it. Will not shrink. Gathers and drapes well. For clothes, use transparent interfacing and, if the fabric is very sheer, avoid deep hems and facings that will show through to the right side. Does not crease easily.

Thread
Synthetic.

Needle
Machine: 80 11. Medium stitch.
Hand: 7.

Pressing
Warm iron.

Care
Warm wash by hand or machine. Drip dry to reduce the necessity of ironing. Iron with a warm iron if necessary.

BUTCHER RAYON

This fabric used to be called Butcher Linen but it no longer contains linen yarns. Now it is not permissible to use the word rayon, so presumably it is Butcher Viscose, although Butcher Cloth is probably more acceptable. Butcher Linen has also been used to describe cotton cloth but this is no longer permissible.

Whatever the fibre, the cloth is plain weave, stiff and heavy. It is used for overalls and protective coats because it wears well, sheds dirt easily in wear and washes well.

Width
90cm (36in) but may be wider.

Handling
Use only for plain straight garments, aprons, etc. Tough to sew. Does not fray readily. Machine-made buttonholes or metal studs to fasten.

Thread
30's cotton or synthetic.

Needle
Machine: 100 16. Large stitch.
Hand: 5–6. Hand-sewing not really appropriate.

Pressing
Hot iron and damp cloth, or steam iron.

Care
Boil and starch. Iron damp.

BUTTER MUSLIN

A cheap open-weave cotton cloth, very soft. Used in the production of dairy products, for straining jelly, etc., but it is also the perfect cloth with which to press. It will shrink when first dampened for use. It is useful to have a couple of pieces, each one metre in length, so that one can be kept dry while the other is damp.

Width
90cm (36in).

Handling
Difficult to cut straight as the weave is so open and movable.

Thread
If you wish to hem the edges, use synthetic thread.

Needle
Machine: 70 9, if used. Large stitch.
Hand: 7, if needed.

Pressing
Hot iron.

Care
Boil or hot wash if necessary. It will gradually become grey with constant use as a pressing cloth, but this does not affect the fabric on which it is used.

See also Pressing Equipment, page 25.

C

CALF FUR
A coarse, flat fur with a sheen, not often used in its natural state, but dyed and cut to imitate other furs, such as pony, leopard, ocelot.

CALF LEATHER
A very soft, pliable leather of top quality. It is used as the basis of good patent leather because it takes a high polish.

Used for gloves and shoes; skins can be purchased.

CALICO

Cheap plain-weave cotton often printed; coarser than Lawn. One of the oldest fabrics, it is named after Calicut in India where it was first produced. In the same grouping as Percale but coarser and poorer quality. Firmly woven and very strong.

Washes and wears well but creases. Used for nightwear and dresses, also sheeting. Unbleached Calico has the characteristic creamy look of a natural fabric, it has darker flecks of fibre in it. Used for under sheets, mattress covers, etc.

Width
90cm, 186cm (36in, 73in).

Handling
Does not fray readily. Easy to sew.

Thread
Synthetic or mercerized.

Needle
Machine: 90 14. Medium stitch.
Hand: 6.

Pressing
Hot iron or steam iron.

Care
Hot wash, some may be boiled. May be starched. Iron with hot iron while damp.

CAMBRIAN TWEED

A rough woollen cloth made in the uplands of Mid-Wales from the local hardy sheep. Plain-weave, hopsack or herringbone weaves are the most usual and the yarns are either dyed with synthetic dyes (for fastness) or, more attractively, left in their natural colours of white, grey and black (although the sheep in the field look brown) and mixed together.

Used for hard-wearing clothes such as men's suits, sports jackets, Norfolk skirts and jackets. The coarser yarn is made into rugs.

Width
140cm (54in).

Handling
A tough cloth, which needs experience to handle. Use plain tailored styles. Clothes need lining. Use firm interfacing.

Thread
Synthetic or mercerized 30's.

Needle
Machine: 100–110 16–18. Large stitch.
Hand: 6.

Pressing
Hot iron, damp cloth, bang steam in after removing cloth.

Care
Hand wash or dry clean.

CAMBRIC

Heavier than Lawn, this is a fine, firm closely woven plain-weave fabric, finished with size to give a slight shine on the right side. At one time it could be made from linen but is now cotton. Mainly in plain colours. Used for children's clothes, baby clothes, nightwear, blouses, handkerchiefs.

Width
90cm, 114cm (36in, 45in).

Handling
Easy to sew, firm and non-slip. Fine fabric which lends itself to hand-sewing and decorative stitching. It creases in wear and may shrink initially. Does not fray. Use lightest interfacing, nylon zips, tiny buttons and hand-worked buttonholes.

Thread
Synthetic or mercerized.

Needle
Machine: 80 11. Small to medium stitch.
Hand: 8.

Pressing
Hot iron or steam iron.

Care
Hot wash. May be boiled and starched. Iron with hot iron while damp.

CAMEL CLOTH

A term now used to describe any camel-coloured coating with a soft feel and slight pile. May be wool, wool and acrylic, or other mixtures. They are cheap imitations of real camel hair, but some are very good quality and expensive. Sometimes made as a reversible cloth with cream colour on the other side. Fabric used for coatings, scarves, rugs.

For handling, etc., see Camel Hair (below).

CAMEL HAIR

The fibre comes from the camel, it is like wool and gives warmth without weight. Very expensive, often mixed with sheep's wool to reduce cost. Colours range from light tan to dark brown.

Used for overcoats, knitwear, rugs.

Width
140cm (54in).

Handling
Cut one-way as it has a slight pile. Does not fray. It is easy to handle as it is soft, but can be bulky. Keep to plain tailored styles. Use firm interfacing, perfectly tailored hand-worked buttonholes. Metal zips. Hand prick-stitch looks good to finish coat edges. Needs lining. To be handled only by the very experienced.

Thread
Silk or mercerized.

Needle
Machine: 100 16. Large stitch.
Hand: 7.

Pressing
Medium hot iron and damp cloth, very light pressure on the wrong side to avoid iron imprints. Place a piece of spare fabric against raw edges to lift all to one level. Brush up right side after pressing. Do not overpress.

Care
Dry clean.

CANDLEWICK

A thick tufted pile fabric imitating an early handicraft when the wicks of candles really were used for decoration. The extra yarns are added to a loosely woven fabric of muslin construction and the thicker yarn is threaded through the backing in straight lines or patterns, leaving spaces between. The loops are then cut leaving thick tufts firmly wedged in the backing.

A warm, cuddly, absorbent fabric, usually with cotton backing and tufting, though viscose may be added. Used for bedspreads, dressing gowns, bathrobes. Does not crease, but robes can lose shape.

Width

Most is made in bedspread widths, but for clothes, 120cm (48in).

Handling

The fabric is thick, so allow additional seam allowances. Backing does not fray, but tufts may become detached when cut. Reduce bulk by removing tufts in seams, etc. Soft and easy to sew, fit loosely. Avoid topstitching and buttonholes.

Thread

Synthetic or mercerized.

Needle

Machine: 90–100 14–16. Large stitch.
Hand: 6–7. Keep hand-sewing to a minimum.

Pressing

Not normally needed, but if necessary a hot iron on the wrong side and light pressure. Cover board with a towel first.

Care

Washes easily by hand or machine in hot water. Short spin, shake vigorously and hang to dry. No ironing needed. When pale colours fade, candlewick re-dyes beautifully.

CANTON CRÊPE

This is a crêpe with filling yarns to produce a pebbly surface, originally a silk from Canton, but now often viscose or polyester. It is durable, due to the high twist yarn, and washes easily. Often in white or may be piece-dyed.

Used for blouses, dresses.

Width

90cm, 114cm (36in, 45in).

Handling

Cut out carefully as it is inclined to slip. Frays, so allow for this. Like all crêpe, it will lend itself to soft styles and gathers. Use light interfacing and nylon zip.

Thread

Synthetic, silk or mercerized.

Needle

Machine: 80 11. Small to medium stitch.
Hand: 8–9.

Pressing

If silk, press lightly on wrong side with medium hot dry iron. Other fibres may be pressed with a steam iron but only on the wrong side.

Care

Wash or dry clean according to instructions on fabric.

CANTON FLANNEL

A medium to heavy cotton fabric in twill weave with a soft filling yarn and a soft flannel-type nap on one or both sides. It is soft and absorbent; may be used unbleached or dyed. Washes well; very inflammable.

Used for lining gardening gloves, driving gloves, and some baby clothes; sometimes used as a warm lining for other clothes.

Width

Various.

CANVAS

Handling
Not often to be found as piece goods, but it is easy to sew and does not fray.

Thread
Mercerized or synthetic.

Needle
Machine: 90 14. Medium stitch.
Hand: 6.

Pressing
Hot iron, pile will become flattened but this is not important.

Care
Hot wash by hand or machine.

CANVAS

Sometimes called Duck, this is rugged, heavy, stiff fabric, made of unbleached coarse cotton or linen yarn, often woven in stripes.

Used for shoes, sails, awnings. It can also be open-weave, in various weights, and in this form it is used for embroidery.

Canvas is not often sewn in the home, but it may have to be tackled for garden chair repairs, rucksacks, tents, etc.

Width
Various.

Handling
Use large, sharp scissors, marking out cutting lines first with tailor's chalk. Cut singly if very heavy. Leave wide seam allowances for hems, etc. Fasten with metal eyelet holes and cord, or with metal studs.

Thread
Synthetic, linen or 30's cotton.

Needle
Machine: 100–110 16–18. Large stitch.
Hand: Not suitable for hand-sewing, but if this has to be done, use a No. 3 or 4, or a large curved, or sailmaker's, needle.

Pressing
Hot iron.

Care
Scrub with soapless detergent in hot water, using a stiff brush.

CANVAS INTERFACING
This is made in various fibres and weights, but is generally heavier than other types of interfacing; may be 'sew-in' or 'iron-on'. It is durable and very malleable under a hot iron with moisture. Most types can be easily shaped to the body and give excellent structure to a tailored garment.

Used in coats and jackets.

For information on types, see under separate names of canvas.

CARRICKMACROSS LACE
An old Irish traditional type of lace made with heavy yarns in an almost crochet type of work. It is characterized by many loops.

CASEMENT CLOTH

As the name implies, this is for casements or curtains. Usually cotton, it is plain-weave fabric in white or cream, with the weft often predominating on the surface. It is soft and drapes well.

The term is now generally used to cover a wide variety of simple weave plain curtaining, made from practically any fibre and in any colour, and in various weights. It is not particularly hard-wearing so is not used for other furnishings. May shrink. Can be lined.

Width
120–150cm (48–60in) or more.

Handling
Machine all hems to control fraying, allowing extra fabric for possible shrinkage.

Thread
Synthetic or mercerized.

Needle
Machine: 90 14. Large stitch.
Hand: 6. Keep hand-sewing to a minimum unless making curtains by hand.

Pressing
Hot or medium hot iron, or steam iron.

Care
Hot wash.

CASHA

A fabric woven of wool with some Cashmere goat's wool; similar to flannel in appearance, but the cashmere adds softness.

Used for overcoats for adults and children.

Width
140cm (54in).

Handling
See Cashmere Cloth, below.

CASHMERE CLOTH

Cashmere is made from the wool of the Cashmere goat. It is warm and soft, silky and lustrous, with a smooth, slippery, luxurious handle. Used for dress fabrics and coatings and suitings.

Sheep's wool is often mixed with the cashmere to make the fabric less expensive and this also makes it harder wearing. Soft botany wool is often made up in imitation of cashmere, but cannot be labelled as such.

Cashmere cloth is most readily available in men's weight overcoating. It is very expensive but when tailored by experts produces results second to none; only to be handled by those who are very experienced. Needs top quality lining; add hand prick-stitch to edges.

Width
140cm (54in).

Handling
Cut one way as the cloth has a slight lustrous nap. Will not fray. Use heavy interfacings and perfectly tailored worked buttonholes.

Thread
Silk.

Needle
Machine: 90–100 14–16. Large stitch.
Hand: 7–8.

Pressing
Hot iron with damp cloth, light pressure to avoid iron marks. Brush up right side after pressing.

Care

Dry clean. Choose a reputable firm who specialize in good finishing.

CAPE LEATHER

Originally this came from Cape of Good Hope sheep, but it now comes mainly from Russia. It is firm and hard-wearing, and is usually given a glacé or shiny finish.

Used mainly for gloves, and skins can be purchased for making gloves.

CAVALRY TWILL

A rugged, very strong, smooth surfaced twill cloth with a clean double twill line. Traditionally, this is a medium-weight worsted or woollen cloth for hard-wearing clothes such as riding breeches and men's trousers. Now it is also made from cotton or viscose for sportswear, but whatever the fibre the cloth is tough and hard-wearing.

Width

114cm, 140cm (45in, 54in).

Handling

Lends itself to topstitching, welt seams, etc., as double stitching strengthens and also reduces fraying.

Needle

Machine: 100 16. Large stitch.
Hand: 6.

Pressing

Hot iron and damp cloth. Cooler iron if viscose.

Care

Dry clean wools, wash other fibres.

CELAFIBRE

Cellulose acetate fibre made in cut staple form by British Celanese Ltd. It is a useful fibre for mixing with wool or cotton to make medium-weight fabrics, blankets, etc. When mixed with other fibres in woven fabrics it may reduce the tendency to creasing.

CELON

Trade name for Courtaulds' nylon fibre. A thicker denier filament than Bri-nylon, it is used in stretch fabrics, quilted materials, upholstery, lingerie, rainwear. Stays white even after repeated washing and is flame-resistant. Often mixed with other fibres.

CHALLIS

  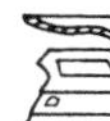 

A soft lightweight fabric in slightly open plain weave with soft handle, similar to voile.

Worsted yarn makes a beautiful dress weight challis; it may also be wool with polyester or polyamide.

Cotton challis has a slight nap to achieve the soft finish. Used for full dresses, blouses, children's clothes, baby dresses. It gathers well and takes unpressed pleats. May be plain or printed; may need lining in paler colours. It crushes in wear but sheds creases overnight.

Width
140cm (54in) if wool.
114cm, 160cm (45in, 60in) if in other fibres.

Handling
Frays, so allow for this when cutting. Avoid heavy finishes such as topstitching. Use light interfacing, nylon zips, small buttons and buttonholes or rouleau loops.

Thread
Synthetic, silk or mercerized.

Needle
Machine: 80 11. Medium stitch.
Hand: 7–8.

Pressing
Press wool or wool blends lightly with medium hot iron and damp muslin, or steam iron. Hotter iron for cotton.

Care
Dry clean wool; other fibres may be washable.

CHAMBRAY

Plain-weave, durable cotton fabric, with the mottled look, similar to denim, of white weft and coloured warp threads. Striped and checked as well as plain.

Used for children's clothes, shirts, pyjamas.

Width
90cm, 114cm (36in, 45in).

Handling
Easy to sew, does not fray too much, a good choice for beginners. Use light to medium-weight interfacing. Can be topstitched.

Thread
Mercerized or synthetic.

Needle
Machine: 80–90 11–14. Medium stitch.
Hand: 6–7.

Pressing
Hot iron and damp cloth, or steam iron.

Care
Hot wash.

CHAMOIS
Originally the skin of the chamois, the small mountain goat, but now also from deer, sheep and goats. The skins are dressed with oil and given a suede finish on both sides. It is very soft and easy to sew.

Used for many types of clothing. Readily available for sewing. Choose soft styles as the leather is limp.

CHANTILLY LACE
Originally a silk bobbin lace with a very fine spidery ground. Well-spaced isolated decorative motifs are applied in a heavier thread and outlined. It is now made by machine in nylon, viscose and mercerized cotton. Often used for bridal veils.

CHARMEUSE

A silk, cotton or viscose satin weave fabric with a dull back and semi-lustrous right side; may sometimes be a mixture of fibres. Not hard-wearing. Will crease.

Used for lingerie, nightwear, soft evening dresses.

'Charmeuse-type' often used to describe other soft silky fabrics.

Width
90cm, 114cm (36in, 45in).

Handling
Frays easily, so allow for this. May be slippery to cut out; pin edges together first, do not fit tightly. Use soft interfacing and nylon zips. Do not topstitch.

Thread
Synthetic or mercerized.

Needle
Machine: 70–80 9–11. Medium stitch.
Hand: 7–8.

Pressing
Warm iron on wrong side only.

Care
Lingerie fabrics will wash, possibly by machine. Dress fabrics may have to be dry cleaned (follow instructions on label).

CHARVET

Soft fabric of silk or acetate in a diagonal rib weave, often with crosswise stripes of alternate dull and satin finish.

Used for making ties.

Width
90cm (36in) or less.

Handling
The fabric has to be cut on the bias so that the tie knots and drapes softly. A join is often necessary to produce sufficient width.

Interface with special tie interfacing, a soft cream plain weave cloth, which should be cut on the cross, too. The fabric frays readily but as it is cut on the bias this will not present a problem. Line the wide end of the tie with matching or contrast fabric.

Thread
Silk or synthetic.

Needle
Machine: 70–80 9–11. Medium stitch, slight zigzag.
Hand: 7–8.

Pressing
Warm iron on wrong side only to open the seams. After making, press the tie very lightly with warm dry iron on a dry muslin. Take care not to flatten the soft edges of the tie.

Care
Dry clean.

CHEESECLOTH

A gauze that is soft and loosely woven cotton of low thread count and therefore sheer; its natural colour is cream but it can be bleached or dyed. It is of a plain weave, sometimes heavily sized, and has a rough finish and wrinkled look. It is not hardwearing but washes well.

Originally used for wrapping cheese and for making polishing cloths, and sometimes as a mounting or underlining fabric.

When it became a fashion fabric, the quality was improved and the texture made slightly closer. Fashion cheesecloth may contain some polyester. Strictly speaking it does not require pressing but this does improve its appearance. Used for blouses, skirts, nightwear, men's shirts.

Width
90cm, 114cm (36in, 45in).

Handling
Soft and easy to sew, but it frays a little. Works well into any soft style, including gathers and frills. Use light interfacing and nylon zips. It creases, but as it has a wrinkled appearance anyway, this is often not noticeable.

Thread
Synthetic.

Needle
Machine: 80 11. Medium stitch.
Hand: 7.

Pressing
Light pressure on wrong side with dry or steam iron.

Care
Hot wash by hand or machine. Steam iron if necessary.

CHENILLE

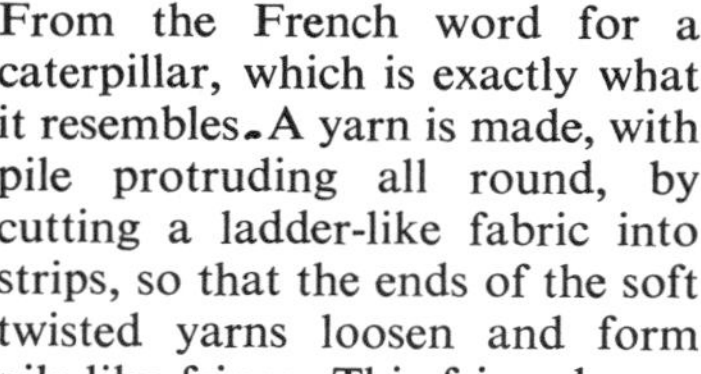

From the French word for a caterpillar, which is exactly what it resembles. A yarn is made, with pile protruding all round, by cutting a ladder-like fabric into strips, so that the ends of the soft twisted yarns loosen and form pile-like fringe. This fringed yarn is then woven in a gauze weave to make a fabric with a pile on one or both sides. Fibres used may be silk, viscose, cotton, wool, or mixtures.

Chenille fabric is made for furnishings, curtains, chair covers, cushion covers and specially finished Chenille is also made for dresses and coats. Very expensive. Does not crease. Frays very readily as the pile drops off as the fabric is cut. Chenille knitting yarns are also made.

Width
150cm (60in). Although dress fabric may be less.

Handling
Choose plain straight styles, avoiding gathers and fine detail. Use heavy interfacing. Fray-check liquid may help to control fraying. Avoid topstitching.

Thread
Synthetic.

Needle
Machine: 100 16. Large stitch.
Hand: 5–6.

Pressing
Light pressure on wrong side only with steam iron. Do not flatten pile.

Care
Dry clean.

CHEVIOT

Rough surfaced wool suiting similar to tweed. The name was originally given to the rough wool from the sheep on the Cheviot

Hills. It is a plain or twill weave, which is very hard-wearing because of the rough, uneven yarn, but loses shape in wear, e.g. trousers lose creases and bag at the knees.

Excellent for men's hard-wearing suits and sporting clothes, golfing skirts, etc.

Width
140cm (54in).

Handling
Use tailoring techniques, heavy interfacing, hair canvas, etc., heavy metal zips. Jackets must be lined and some men find the cloth rough to the legs, so trousers may need to be lined.

Thread
Synthetic or 30's cotton.

Needle
Machine: 100 16. Large stitch.
Hand: 6.

Pressing
Hot iron, damp cloth, heavy pressure on both sides. Use pressing block.

Care
Dry clean.

CHIFFON

A plain-weave, soft, filmy material. It may be made from silk of the finest lightly twisted yarn, woven in gum condition, then degummed after weaving. It is also made in nylon, viscose, cotton and polyester.

Although so thin and sheer it is fairly strong, but it may give at the seams. Used for loose fitting garments, such as blouses, nightwear and as an evening overdress on top of a dress of satin, taffeta, etc. Not expensive. Silk Chiffon is softest, Polyester Chiffon slightly firmer and less transparent. Chiffon may have a satin stripe or spot as decoration.

Width
114cm (45in).

Handling
All chiffon is difficult to sew, but Silk Chiffon is the easiest as the fibre is less slippery. Lay the fabric carefully for cutting out. If the edges will not lie straight, pin the fabric to large sheets of paper. Use very fine pins, or even needles, to avoid making holes in the fabric. Cutting-out scissors must be very sharp. Try to keep the pieces flat on the table for tacking, as once they are lifted they appear to lose shape. Chiffon frays very easily. Use French seams or narrow finish seams, and transparent interfacing. Avoid deep double hems which will show. Confine edge finishing to shell edge, rolled hem, binding, etc. There are many decorative machine stitches that may be used.

Thread
Synthetic.

Needle
Machine: 70–80 9–11. Small stitch, slight zigzag. Place tissue paper under fabric to prevent wrinkling.
Hand: 8–9.

Pressing
Warm dry iron.

Care
Nearly all Chiffons have to be dry cleaned but some synthetics may be labelled washable.

CHIFFON VELVET
A very light, soft velvet with little substance to it. It is floaty and effective but very difficult to sew. It has a short cut pile.

CHINA-GRASS
Sometimes called Grass Linen. An old Chinese fabric woven from vegetable or bast fibres. An uneven weave, but a very fine transparent fabric once used a great deal in China as a basis for embroidered table linen. Launders and starches well. Wears for many years. Very similar in appearance to Pineapple Cloth. Also known as Ramie (page 218) and Rhea (page 221).

CHINA SILK
See Jap Silk, page 175.

CHINCHILLA
A bluish grey fur, with marks and shadings, which comes from a small rodent bred in captivity for the fur. Soft and curly and pearly grey, but rarely found now due to the rarity of the animal and subsequent high cost of the fur.

For handling, see Fur Handling, page 157.

CHINCHILLA CLOTH

This is made to simulate the fur of the chinchilla rodent. It is a wool coating, in thick twill weave with a napped surface rolled into little curly balls by a special rubbing machine. Its chief characteristic is its spongy feel; it is not heavy or dense. Fairly expensive. Used only for coats and capes.

Width
140cm (54in).

Handling
It is a napped fabric, so cut pieces with pattern lying in one direction. Keep to plain tailored styles with no decorative details. Use heavy interfacing. Fabric will not fray unduly but coats require lining.

Thread
Synthetic.

Needle
Machine: 100 16. Large stitch.
Hand: 6–7.

Pressing
Hot iron and damp cloth on wrong side only, with very light pressure. Avoid flattening the curly surface.

Care
Dry clean.

CHINO
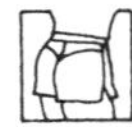

Firm, usually white, cotton fabric, in twill or plain weave, of combed mercerized yarns.

Used for sportswear, as it is hard-wearing, and also for summer uniforms for the armed forces, when it is vat dyed the appropriate colour.

Width
114cm (45in).

Handling
Stiff to handle, it frays a little. Keep to tailored, uncluttered styles. Use

heavy interfacing and waistbanding and strong metal zips. Topstitching looks good.

Thread
Synthetic.

Needle
Machine: 90–100 14–16. Large stitch.
Hand: 6.

Pressing
Hot iron and damp cloth, or steam iron.

Care
Hot wash, boil, starch. Iron when damp with a hot iron.

CHINTZ

Good quality cotton fabric usually with a large printed design of flowers, birds, etc. It is a fine closely woven cloth, sized and calendered in order to resist dirt.

Used for curtains, loose covers etc., and only occasionally for clothes. Allow for shrinkage.

Glazed Chintz
The fabric is given a resin finish, which is more permanent and will not wash out.

Chintz wears well and has good draping qualities, but like most curtain fabrics it needs regular washing to prevent disintegration. Allow for shrinkage.

Width
114cm (45in) and wider.

Handling
Frays a little, so all hems should be turned double and stitched. Neaten all raw edges. Curtains may be lined. Designs are nearly always one-way so cut fabric pieces accordingly. When matching chair covers, cut so that the large main motifs fall centrally on the chairs.

Thread
Synthetic or mercerized.

Needle
Machine: 90 14. Large stitch. Close stitching will cause fabric to split.
Hand: 6.

Pressing
Hot iron or steam iron.

Care
Hot wash, iron damp with hot iron.

CHROME LEATHER
An inexpensive leather that has been tanned with chromium salts. It is used in the shoe industry and is not usually available for sewing.

CIRÉ

The French word for 'waxed', it was originally a waxed fabric used for shrouds. This treatment of the fabric surface makes it very lustrous and smooth; it may be applied to silk. Not readily available now.

Nylon Ciré
The waxing process applied to lightweight plain-weave nylon produces a very attractive, shiny fabric for thin raincoats, anoraks,

protective clothing for cyclists, etc. Made in a limited range of colours, but these include bright ones like red and royal blue which are popular for children's rainwear and aprons. The fabric is showerproof rather than waterproof. To make it warmer and heavier, it may be lined with quilting, or quilted on to wadding.

Width
150cm (60in) or more.

Handling
Easy to handle, does not fray. Seams tend to pucker. Use machine fell or welt seams to reduce the risk of water penetration. Topstiching in contrasting colours looks good. It is firm fabric with no 'give' at all, so choose styles where no easing is required, e.g. raglan sleeve instead of plain set-in sleeve. Fasten with large plastic zip or metal capped studs.

Thread
Synthetic.

Needle
Machine: 80 11. Medium to large stitch.
Hand: 7–8.

Pressing
Cool iron on wrong side only.

Care
Warm wash to sponge down. Drip dry.

CISELE VELVET
The characteristic of Cisele is a pattern formed by cutting only some of the pile; the rest is left uncut.

CLOQUÉ

The French word for blistered. This describes the fabric exactly; the raised figures may be regular or in irregular lines. Once a popular silk fabric for gowns and hats, it was superseded by 'artificial silk' imitations. Now it is produced mainly from acetate and polyester yarns, and the advantage of this development is that the blistering is permanent. Used for evening and cocktail wear, some millinery, negligées. Does not crease.

Width
90cm, 114cm (36in, 45in).

Handling
A soft fabric that drapes well into elaborate styles. Use soft interfacing and nylon zips. Avoid topstitching.

Thread
Synthetic.

Needle
Machine: 80 11. Medium stitch.
Hand: 7.

Pressing
Warm iron and light pressure with the toe of the iron on the wrong side. The use of the iron on the right side may produce shine.

Care
Most Cloqués are to be dry cleaned only.

CLOTH
The word used to describe any type of fabric but perhaps most used in connection with woollens

and worsteds—the suitings and coatings.

CLUNY LACE

A close, heavy bobbin lace made in France and Belgium, often with a wheel design. Its heaviness limited its used to collar decoration in dress but it was much used for mats, doilies and table wear.

CLYDELLA

Trade name for a traditional, soft woven mixture of 81 per cent cotton and 19 per cent wool, in plain or print. It wears well, is soft and warm and washes easily.

Used for shirts, blouses, nightwear, baby's and children's clothes.

Width

114cm (45in).

Handling

Very easy to sew, ideal for beginners. Inclined to fray a little, but the seams will probably be French or machine fell and the hems machined or hemmed. Use light interfacing, nylon zips. Large checks should be matched.

Thread

Synthetic or mercerized.

Needle

Machine: 80 11. Medium stitch.
Hand: 7.

Pressing

Medium hot iron or steam iron.

Care

Hot wash by hand or machine. Iron when very slightly damp.

See also Viyella, page 247.

CONY (RABBIT)

A soft, long-haired cheap fur, often used to imitate more expensive ones. Not hard-wearing.

CORDOVAN

A heavy leather that may sometimes be available for sewing. It is from horsehide and is the most common leather used for coats, jackets, boots and shoes.

CORDUROY

A strong cotton yarn fabric characterized by pile ribs running its length. It is made with three sets of yarns. During the weaving, extra yarns float in lengthwise rows across the ground weave, and are then cut to make the pile. The ground fabric is usually plain weave or twill, and the final finishing lays the pile at a slight slant, in one direction.

Corduroy has about 10–12 wales or ribs per inch and is used for walking gear, jackets, trousers, skirts.

Needlecord is a lighter weight fabric of the same construction, but with 14–16 wales per inch. Used for skirts, dresses, children's clothes, shirts.

Pincord or Babycord is even finer and can be used for softer styles.

Jumbo or Elephant cord is, as the name suggests, a thick, heavy-ribbed fabric used for coats.

In all three types, the ribs may be even or they may be 'High-Low', i.e. wide, high ribs alternating with smaller low ones.

Special Jean Cord is available and also a showerproofed cord. Lightweight cords are often printed.

All corduroy is very hard-wearing, washable and comfortable to wear. The finer ones crease.

Width
90cm, 114cm (36in, 45in).

Handling
Cut all pieces with the pile running upwards or shading will occur. Use welt seams on jeans and trousers. Fabrics will fray easily as the pile becomes detached, but this should not present a problem providing no raw edges are left. Use interfacing and zip of a suitable weight for the cord. Metal capped studs make good-looking fastenings for casual garments.

Thread
Synthetic.

Needle
Machine: 80, 90 or 100. 11, 14, 16. Medium to large stitch.
Hand: 6–7.

Pressing
Place a piece of spare fabric, pile side up, on the pressing surface. Place section to be pressed pile down and press wrong side only, with light pressure, using a steam iron or a hot iron over a damp muslin. Brush up the pile on the right side if it appears flattened.

Care
Hot wash by hand or machine, very short spin or drip dry. Press on wrong side only.

COTTON
A soft, absorbent fibre made into a wide variety of fabric and also mixed with other fibres, e.g. polyester/cotton. Cotton fabrics are easily laundered and are used for all types of clothing.

See also Cotton, page 35.

COTTON BROADCLOTH
A lightly woven cotton, usually mercerized to give a lustrous finish. Handle as for a medium-weight cotton or linen fabric. A mainly American cotton.

Other cotton fabrics appear under their usual name, e.g. Sateen, Denim, Cheesecloth, etc.

COTTON CRÊPE
Lightweight, crinkled fabric. Washable. Used for dresses, blouses, children's clothes.

COTTON FLOUNCING
Plain-weave, fine cotton fabrics, embroidered with cotton or viscose thread, with a scalloped or flounced edge down one side. Creases easily.

COTTON JERSEY

Knitted cotton, plain or printed. It is cool and lightweight, very absorbent and comfortable.

Used for sports and casual wear, summer dresses and blouses, children's clothes.

Width
90cm (36in) or more.

Handling
Very easy to sew and an excellent fabric for beginners. It has 'give' in it, but unless very poor quality it regains its shape immediately. Insert cotton tape into crosswise seams that are not intended to stretch, e.g. shoulder seams. Use light interfacing if any is needed.

Thread
Synthetic.

Needle
Machine: 80 11. Slight zigzag stitch.
Hand: 7.

Pressing
Hot iron.

Care
Hot wash by hand or machine. Iron with hot iron.

COTTON RATINE

A loosely woven plain-weave fabric with a rough surface produced by twisting heavy and fine cotton yarns at various tensions. Usually dyed and polished for use as a furnishing fabric, though it is too loosely woven for use as chair covers.

Width
114cm (45in) or more.

Handling
Fabric will fray so all hems must be double and all edges neatened. Easy to handle and easy to see the grain for accurate cutting of curtains, etc.

Thread
Synthetic or mercerized.

Needle
Machine: 90 14. Large stitch.
Hand: 6.

Pressing
Hot iron and sharp pressure. If the iron tends to flatten the surface, press on a towel.

Care
Hot wash. It may shrink. Iron slightly damp with a hot iron.

See also Ratine, page 219.

COTTON SATIN

Cotton yarn woven in satin weave to produce a soft fabric with a sheen on the right side. Produced in various weights and usually printed. A dress fabric, but also a very popular curtain fabric.

Width
Curtaining: 120–136cm (48–54in).
Dress: 114cm (45in).

Handling
Allow for shrinkage in curtain fabrics. Cut to match patterns. Easy to sew. Suitable for most styles of dress.

Thread
Synthetic or mercerized.

Needle
Machine: 80 11. Medium stitch.
Hand: 7.

Pressing
Hot iron or steam iron.

Care
Hot wash. Iron slightly damp with hot iron or steam iron.

COTTON SHANTUNG

A plain-weave cotton fabric made from irregular cotton yarns. The nubs or slubs are soft and are weak areas.

Used mainly for curtains and bedspreads.

Width
120cm (48in).

Handling
The fabric will fray easily, so all hems must be double. Curtains need not be lined.

Thread
Synthetic or mercerized.

Needle
Machine: 90 14. Large stitch.
Hand: 6.

Pressing
Hot iron or steam iron.

Care
Hot wash. Iron slightly damp.

COTTON VELVET

A short pile cotton fabric that is woven double, with the additional warp interlacing between the two base fabrics. The pile is afterwards cut and the fabrics are separated.

Not as luxurious as other velvet but hard-wearing. Suitable for trousers, for instance.

It is much easier to sew than other velvets, but follow the same rules for handling, see Velvet, page 244.

COURTELLE
Courtaulds' trade name for their acrylic fibre. Used alone for clothes, carpets and blankets. It blends well with other fibres and mixtures are used for all types of clothing and furnishing fabrics. Crease-resistant, strong, washable, unaffected by moths and mildew.

See also Acrylics, page 35.

COUTIL

A strong cotton fabric made in herringbone weave or reverse-twist twill weave. It is a close textured cloth, sometimes patterned and used for corsetry, and sometimes used as a strong lining fabric or tropical suiting.

Width
90cm (36in)

Handling
Does not fray readily and is not difficult to sew, but as it will receive hard wear, use strong finishes, machine fell seams and double stitching.

Thread
Mercerized or synthetic.

COVERT

Needle
Machine: 100 16. Large stitch.
Hand: 6.

Pressing
Hot iron and damp cloth, or steam iron.

Care
Hot wash by hand or machine, scrub, boil. Iron when damp with a hot iron.

COVERT

A twill lightweight men's overcoating in wool or worsted. It is a tightly woven fabric with a smooth finish, traditionally made with two shades of brown yarn, which produce a mottled beige effect.

Covert cloth is also made in cotton, viscose and acetate with the characteristic speckled effect. This is lighter in weight than the overcoating and is used for suits and raincoats.

Width
140cm (54in).

Handling
This firm cloth lends itself to all the tailoring techniques, and is only for experts. Use heavy interfacing and perfectly tailored hand-worked buttonholes. Coats need lining.

Thread
Synthetic or 30's cotton.

Needle
Machine: 100 16. Large stitch.
Hand: 5–6.

Pressing
Hot iron, damp cloth and pressing block, on both right and wrong sides.

Care
Dry clean.

COWHIDE
Occasionally used for ready-made clothes, but not usually available for sewing.

CRASH

Fabric (usually linen) in plain weave or twill, or variations on twill, with a rough texture due to thick uneven yarns used in the weft. Traditionally, it is creamy beige. Brown mercerized cotton, or occasionally wool, may be used for the warp in place of linen. Mainly used for towels, curtains and embroidery.

Width
Various.

Handling
Frays readily so all edges should have double hems. Cut exactly on the straight grain.

Thread
Synthetic or mercerized.

Needle
Machine: 80–90 11–14. Medium stitch.
Hand: 6–7.

Pressing
Hot iron and damp cloth, or steam iron.

Care
Hot wash. Iron while damp.

CRÊPE

The term refers to any type or weight of fabric made with crêpe yarns either twisted or chemically crinkled. Crêpe fabric can be made with any fibre, natural or synthetic, or from mixtures or blends. Various descriptive names are applied to different types of crêpe, but from a sewing point of view they all have similar characteristics.

Width
The width of the fabric varies according to the country of origin and the manufacturer, but the majority are now 114cm (45in), with wool crêpe at its traditional width of 140cm (54in).

Handling
All crêpe is springy to handle, but the softer varieties are easy to sew and gather well. Most crêpe frays readily, due to the nature of its construction, so neaten all raw edges. Use soft or medium sew-in interfacing, according to the weight of the fabric, and nylon zips.

Thread
Synthetic or mercerized.

Needle
Machine: 70–90 9–14. Medium stitch, slight zigzag.
Hand: 7–8.

Pressing
Press lightly, with the utmost care, on the wrong side only to avoid shine. Test a small scrap of fabric to find the most effective pressure. Many crêpes shrink if steam is used, so check this carefully.

Care
A few crêpes, such as cotton, are washable, but the majority will be labelled dry clean.

Alpaca Crêpe, see page 96.
Bark Crêpe, see page 101.
Canton Crêpe, see page 119.
Cotton Crêpe, see page 131.
Crêpe back satin, see below.
Crêpe Charmeuse, see below.
Crêpe de Chine, see page 136.
Crêpe Georgette, see page 136.
Crêpe Marocain, see page 136.
Crêpe Romaine, see page 136.
Crinkle Crêpe, see page 137.
Faille Crêpe, see page 151.
French Crêpe, see page 156.
Indian Crêpe, see page 172.
Moss Crêpe, see page 198.
Polyester Crêpe, see page 212.
Wool Crêpe, see page 251.

CRÊPE BACK SATIN
Satin weave, with crêpe filling yarns which can be used with either side as the right side. Yarns are silk or polyester.

Used for evening wear, wedding-dresses, etc.

CRÊPE CHARMEUSE

Rich, dull lustred smooth silk crêpe, which is fairly stiff, but clings and drapes well. Now usually polyester.

Used for evening wear.

CRÊPE DE CHINE

Soft, sheer crêpe, usually washable, in plain weave, with a lustrous smooth finish. Luxurious to touch. Originally only real silk, but now imitations are made in synthetic fibres.

Used for blouses and lingerie.

CRÊPE GEORGETTE

Sheer, dull-textured fabric like georgette but with a crêpe surface. It may be polyester, cotton, viscose or silk.

Used for blouses and dresses.

CRÊPE MAROCAIN

A heavier type, similar to Canton Crêpe. Fibres include polyamide, polyester, silk.

Used for evening and bride's wear.

CRÊPE ROMAIN

A heavy semi-sheer crêpe in 2/1 basket weave in a dull finish rayon.

Used for evening and bride's wear.

CRÊPON

A crinkled fabric, often cotton, but it may contain some polyester or viscose. It is usually made from chemically crimped yarns, not from crêpe yarns, and is soft and absorbent and comfortable in wear because it 'gives'.

Used for nightwear, blouses, softly gathered summer dresses and men's casual shirts.

Width

114cm (45in).

Handling

Very easy to sew, an ideal fabric for beginners. Use soft sew-in interfacing.

Thread

Synthetic.

Needle

Machine: 80 11. Medium slight zigzag stitch.
Hand: 7.

Pressing

Use the toe of a medium iron on the wrong side only.

Care

Hand wash. Drip dry. May not need ironing, but if it does, do so lightly with a warm iron, or the crêpy appearance may be flattened.

CRETONNE

A printed or plain cotton fabric, woven with a fine cotton warp and a thick weft spun from waste cotton. The weave may be plain or twill. In appearance, Cretonne is similar to Chintz but does not have a glazed treatment. Fairly inexpensive.

Used for curtains, loose covers, bedcovers. Washes well and is hard-wearing, but like most cotton curtain fabrics it will disintegrate if not washed regularly.

Width

120cm (48in) or more.

Handling
If printed, the design is probably one-way, so cut all pieces in one direction. Be sure to match up patterns. Allow for shrinkage. Conceal all raw edges to control fraying.

Thread
Synthetic or mercerized.

Needle
Machine: 90–100 14–16. Large stitch.
Hand: 6.

Pressing
Hot iron or steam iron.

Care
Hot wash. Iron damp. May be starched.

CRIMPED VISCOSE TWILL

Bulked viscose yarn woven into plain colour fabric of medium weight. The bulking adds warmth. The fabric creases slightly. It has a soft feel rather like Flannelette.

Used for children's clothes, nightwear.

Width
90cm (36in).

Handling
The fabric frays as it is twill weave, so enclose or neaten all raw edges. Break up the surface of the fabric with decorative stitching, braid, etc. Use soft interfacing if it is required. Not hard-wearing. Very easy to sew. A good fabric for beginners.

Thread
Synthetic.

Needle
Machine: 80 11. Medium stitch.
Hand: 7.

Pressing
Warm iron.

Care
Warm machine or hand wash. Iron with a warm iron.

CRINKLE CRÊPE
See Plissé, page 210.

CRINOLINE

A loosely woven stiff cotton, similar to Cheesecloth, with hair filling. It may now be produced from synthetic fibre and stiffened. Made in white, grey and black.

Used as an interfacing or stiffening material for hats.

Width
Various.

Handling
Cut without seam allowances. Make sure this fabric is entirely covered as it is stiff and scratchy. Often used on the cross.

Thread
Synthetic.

Needle
Machine: 100 16. Large stitch.
Hand: 6. Rarely hand-sewn.

Pressing
Medium dry iron.

Care
May be hand washable, but is liable to lose its stiffness, so not

often used in articles requiring washing. Hats should be cleaned according to the main fabric used.

CROCHET KNIT

Fancy openwork knit in a variety of colours and patterns, often produced in traditional designs, e.g. Aran. The fabric resembles crochet but is made on a knitting machine. Any man-made fibres may be used but they are mainly acrylic.

Used for sweaters, shirts, dresses.

Width
150cm (60in).

Handling
Some fabrics are bulky but open in design so edges can be finished with close satin stitch in preference to turning double hems. The fabrics are not difficult to handle but care should be taken not to allow them to stretch. Insert tape in crosswise seams such as shoulders and yokes.

Thread
Synthetic.

Needle
Machine: 80 11. Slight zigzag stitch.
Hand: 6.

Pressing
Steam iron or warm iron.

Care
Hand wash. Dry flat to prevent stretching. No ironing needed.

CROCODILE
Crocodile skin is very expensive and only used for top quality shoes and handbags. It is difficult to tan. It can be distinguished from Alligator by the fact that the markings are more uneven.

CUPRO
Now the official designation for rayon produced by the Cuprammonium method. A very soft silky fibre. It is often still referred to as Bemberg, the name of the company first making it.

See also Cupro, page 36.

CURL OR LOOP
A thin basic yarn with a thicker one twisted with it, but fed at a different speed so that regular loops are joined. This type of yarn can be made into a variety of fabrics.

D

DACRON

The trade name for an American polyester fibre. It blends well with other fibres, can be bleached and takes dye well. Used mainly in the manufacture of clothing, curtaining, furnishings, and fillings for pillows and quilts. Washes well, and drips dry as the fibre does not absorb moisture.

See also page 40.

DAMASK

A very old type of fabric first made in silk in Damascus. Elaborately woven on a Jacquard loom, the fabric has satin floats on a warp satin background; the surface design runs in the opposite direction from those in the background. It is now woven in different fibres and different weights, and is mostly used in furnishings, table linen, towels. It is rarely found now as a dress fabric. Most damask is self-toned, that is the warp and weft are in the same colour; the design creates the interest.

Linen makes the most elegant, hard-wearing tablecloths, as it may be boiled, starched and given a high gloss with the iron.

Cotton and viscose damask is not as hard-wearing, a point to bear in mind when choosing fabric for loose covers.

All damask creases readily.

Width
120cm (48in) or more, depending on its use.

Handling
The closer the texture the more hard-wearing it will be. Damask made from soft fibres such as viscose will fray easily. Designs will usually be one-way, so allow for cutting this way when calculating the quantity.

Thread
Synthetic or mercerized.

Needle
Machine: 90 14. Large stitch.
Hand: 6.

Pressing
Linen and cotton: hot iron and damp cloth, or steam iron. Other fibres: medium hot iron and damp cloth, or steam iron.

Care
Hot wash by hand or machine, iron damp with hot or medium hot iron on right side. Starch cotton and linen damask.

DENIM

 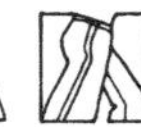   

This fabric has its origin in the traditional blue (indigo-dyed) overall cloth made and worn in Nîmes, hence 'de Nîmes'. It is a twill weave fabric easily recognizable by the white yarn weft and coloured (usually blue) warp. It is stiff and unyielding but softens in wear, and is very strong and hard-wearing, but fades to whitish patches at creases or points of strain, hem edges etc., and creases easily.

Used for casual style clothing, such as jeans, skirts, lightweight jackets and suits, shorts, children's clothes, and for protective clothing.

If made from all cotton, or cotton with polyester: the fabric is firm. Cotton with modal: soft. A mixture of cotton, polyester and viscose: firm. Allow for shrinkage.

Some denims made for dresses and less casual clothes contain more polyester. The colours are different, the fabric sometimes thinner, and it may fray slightly but will crease less.

Width
114cm (45in).

Handling
Choose plain styles, avoid soft effects such as gathers. Machine fell seams and topstitching looks excellent. Use heavy metal zips, metal cap studs for fastening and firm iron-on interfacing. Takes appliqué, badges etc., well.

Thread
Synthetic.

Needle
Machine: 100 16. Large stitch.
Hand: 6.

Pressing
Medium hot iron and damp cloth, or steam iron.

Care
Hot wash by hand or machine, scrub dirty marks. Iron while damp with a hot iron. Wash dark colours separately when new.

See also Brushed Denim, page 112 and Denim Cord (below).

DENIM CORD

A denim-look fabric made from white and a coloured yarn, with a slight Bedford cord effect produced by raised ribs. It is a mixture of polyester and cotton fibres, and creases less than all cotton.

Used for casual jackets, trousers, skirts, children's clothes.

Width
114cm (45in).

Handling
The fabric will fray slightly. Use firm iron-on interfacing, metal zips, stud fastenings. Topstitching looks good.

Thread
Synthetic.

Needle
Machine: 100 16. Large stitch.
Hand: 6.

Pressing
Medium hot iron and damp cloth, or steam iron.

Care
Hot wash. Iron damp.

DICEL
Trade name for Courtaulds' cellulose acetate fibre. Dicel gives a soft, silky feel to fabrics made from it. Colour-fast.

See also page 34.

DIMITY

The name comes from the Greek word meaning 'double thread' and the fabric is made from double or treble yarns, which create ridges in plain areas. It is a fine or medium weight fabric, usually made from cotton, and wears well. It is often in check.

Used for nightwear, children's clothes, curtains.

Width
90cm, 114cm, 120cm (36in, 45in, 48in).

Handling
Easy to sew though inclined to fray, soft to handle.

Thread
Synthetic or mercerized.

Needle
Machine: 80 11. Medium stitch.
Hand: 7.

Pressing
Hot iron and damp cloth, or steam iron.

Care
Hot machine or hand wash. Iron damp with hot iron. May be starched.

DOCTOR'S FLANNEL

A soft, medium weight, inexpensive flannel. The fibres are mixed or wool. In white or red only. It's the type of fabric that could be used for interlining for warmth, lining children's clothes, nurses' cloaks, etc.

Width
68–70cm (27in).

Handling
Easy to handle, does not fray. The grain is easy to see as the surface is only slightly napped.

Thread
Synthetic.

Needle
Machine: 90 14. Medium stitch.
Hand: 6.

Pressing
Steam iron. Allow for shrinkage.

Care
Washable.

DOESKIN (1)

A very close satin-weave fabric from highest quality Merino wool. The cloth is milled and raised and given a napped finish on the right side. It is very soft and luxurious, with a sheen; expensive. Made in dress weight or heavier.

Used for tailored suits and dresses and men's overcoats.

Width
140cm (54in).

Handling
A napped fabric, so cut it one way. It feels more comfortable in wear if the pile runs from top to bottom. Use plain styles. May be topstitched by machine or hand, and prick-stitched for decoration. Make piped or hand-tailored buttonholes. Use firm or medium sew-in interfacing. Coats need lining.

Thread
Silk, synthetic or mercerized.

Needle
Machine: 90 14. Medium to large stitch working with the pile.
Hand: 7–9.

Pressing
Medium hot iron and damp muslin, using light pressure on the wrong side only to avoid iron marks—these appear so easily that, where fabric is double, it is wise to slip strips of paper under the seam edges before pressing. Before pressing hems, place a spare piece of fabric against the hem edge to level the area. Brush on the right side if necessary.

Care
Dry clean only.

DOESKIN (2)
A well known glove-leather from lambs. It is readily available and very soft and easy to sew.

DOMETTE

A very soft open-weave fabric of wool, of wool and fibre or wool and cotton, with a long nap on the surface. Used for interfacing coats and jackets in which hair canvas is to be used. The Domette is placed against the chest area of the coat and the hair canvas on top. The soft Domette prevents hair from penetrating to the right side of the garment and also avoids showing a hard ridge. Domette is also used as padded interlining for quilting.

Width
140cm (54in).

Handling
Easy to cut. Use on the same grain as the garment piece. The fluffy surface enables the Domette to stick and it therefore remains in place if loosely basted.

Thread
Synthetic, or basting thread for hand-sewing.

Needle
Machine: 90 14. Not usually machined until attached to firmer interfacing.
Hand: 5 for basting.

Pressing
Hot iron.

Care
Washable, but the fabric of the garment and other interfacings probably are not.

DONEGAL
Originally a rough woollen, hand-made Irish tweed typified by the use of several colours, and particularly the use of white nubs, in the cloth. The word Donegal is now used to describe almost any plain-weave tweedy looking cloth with white nubs in it. Fibres used include acrylic, cotton, viscose, and mixtures and blends of these.

Handle woollen Donegal as Harris Tweed, page 168. Handle others according to weight and fibre content.

DOTTED SWISS

A sheer cotton fabric with crisp finish. The distinguishing feature is self-colour or contrast woven spots made from soft yarn and brought on to the right side of the fabric. The dull crisp finish is mainly a Swiss textile finish, but the name now applies to many fabrics that are fine and spotted. It is usually cotton but may contain polyester, and is hard-wearing.

Used for blouses, nightwear, children's clothes, sheer curtains.

Width
90cm (36in).

Handling
An easy fabric to handle, it frays little.

Thread
Synthetic or mercerized.

Needle
Machine: 80 11. Small to medium stitch.
Hand: 7–8.

Pressing
Hot iron and damp muslin, or steam iron.

Care
Hot wash by hand or machine. Iron damp with hot iron. May be starched if cotton.

DOUBLE CANVAS
An open embroidery canvas usually made of cotton yarn. It is plain weave but with the warp and weft threads arranged in pairs, allowing quite large holes to alternate with very small ones. It is a rigid canvas stiffened with size, and is available in several weights.

DOUBLECLOTH
Heavy two-sided cloth, often each side of different colour and weave, held together by a loose running thread.

Used for blankets, coats, duffle coats.

Width
140–150cm (54–60in).

For handling, see Reversible Cloth, page 220.

DOUBLE JERSEY

Although traditionally wool, which has become very expensive, this may now be acrylic fibre. It is a heavy fabric in plain colours and is characterized by the fact that both right and wrong sides are identical, i.e. they look like stocking stitch.

Used for women's trousers, jackets, warm dresses, light coats.

Width
150cm (60in).

Handling
Easy to handle, has little 'give', but is too bulky for gathers. Use stretch interfacing and nylon zip. Trousers will 'knee', so either line half-way or re-press to regain shape. Line coats, etc., with nylon jersey.

Thread
Synthetic.

Needle
Machine: 80 11. Possibly ball point. Slight zigzag stitch.
Hand: 7.

Pressing
Medium hot iron and damp cloth, using short, sharp pressure.

Care
Dry clean.

DOUPPION (Doupion)

A fabric with an uneven surface and rough texture made from yarns that are irregular in thickness. It was originally the term used to describe the particular type of silk yarn which was spun from the silk of two cocoons that had nested together. The two silks were not separated in spinning and were therefore uneven.

Douppion may still be made from silk, but it is also made from viscose, acetate and other synthetic yarns which can be manufactured in uneven thickness, and is a firm, medium-weight fabric of plain weave.

Used for women's summer suits, wedding outfits, etc.

Width
90–114cm (36–45in).

Handling
It frays readily so allow for this when planning an outfit. Choose simple styles, avoid gathers except in small amounts. It may lose its shape, so line with silk or acetate lining. Use medium interfacing, nylon zips, piped buttonholes. Topstitching works well, so do decorative finishes such as frog fastening and ball buttons.

Thread
Silk or synthetic.

Needle
Machine: 70–80 9–11. Medium stitch.
Hand: 7–8.

Pressing
Warm to medium iron on wrong side. If pressing the right side, cover fabric with a dry pressing cloth.

Care
Dry clean silk, but synthetics may be labelled hand wash.

DOWN-PROOF CAMBRIC

Cream or white plain weave cotton of cambric weight with a waxed or glazed surface to make it feather- or down-proof.

Used for pillow coverings, cushion covers, duvet covers, mattress covers.

Width
140cm (54in).

Handling
Soft to handle. Allow for shrinkage. Double stitch seams to prevent feathers coming out.

Thread
Synthetic.

Needle
Machine: 80 11. Small stitch.
Hand: 7.

Pressing
Hot iron or steam iron.

Care
Hot wash. Hot iron when damp.

DRALON

Trade name for an acrylic fibre made by Bayer. It is mothproof, has good resistance to acids and alkalis and is unaffected by sunlight. It is washable, but absorbs hardly any moisture and is therefore quick-drying. It does not shrink or felt or pill. It may be blended with other fabrics.

Used for upholstery and furnishings, often as pile fabrics, and for net curtaining.

See also Acrylics, page 35.

DRESDEN POINT LACE
A fine linen fabric with threads withdrawn and embroidered to form a square mesh design.

DRILL

Twill weave fabric, usually cotton, made in various weights. The commonest fabric known as drill is in white or dark working colours, and is a thick hard-wearing fabric.

Used for uniforms, men's summer trousers and suits, overalls and protective clothing.

Width
114–150cm (45–60in).

Handling
A stiff fabric. Use strong machine processes, heavy metal zips, heavy interfacing. It creases easily.

Thread
Synthetic or mercerized.

Needle
Machine: 100 16.
Hand: 5–6.

Pressing
Hot iron and damp muslin.

Care
Hot wash by hand or machine, scrub dirty areas. Boil if white. Iron damp with hot iron.

DUCHESSE LACE
A bar lace with a design of bands or tapes, which is very fine and is worked with fine threads. A very old type of Bobbin Lace.

DUCHESSE SATIN

A thick, heavy twill weave high gloss satin, which may be silk, but is more likely to be viscose.

Used mainly for wedding-gowns and evening dresses.

Width
120cm (46in).

Handling
Difficult to handle. It will fray and is stiff to manipulate. Cut pieces all one way to avoid shading, especially in dark colours. Stitch seams carefully as they are likely to wrinkle, especially those on the straight grain of the fabric. Choose elegant styles that enhance the fabric. Avoid topstitching. Use firm interfacing and concealed zips.

Thread
Synthetic.

Needle
Machine: 70–80 9–11. Medium stitch.
Hand: 8.

Pressing
Warm iron on wrong side. For right side pressing, cover the fabric with dry muslin first to prevent iron marks.

Care
Dry clean.

DUCK
A variety of heavy strong cotton or linen fabrics of canvas appearance in plain weave. The warp yarns are in pairs and form a distinctive effect. Used for sails, awnings, etc.

See also Canvas, page 120.

DUNGAREE

Similar to denim, but the warp and the weft are usually in the same colour. Hard-wearing cotton fabric for dungarees, overalls, jeans, children's clothes.

For handling, see Denim, page 139.

DURACOLOUR

Trade name for a process applied to curtain fabrics which guarantees that they will not fade.

DURAFIL

The trade name for a strong viscose staple fibre made by Courtaulds Ltd.

DUVETYN

Similar to doeskin but more velvety and lighter in weight. The soft, velvet-like surface is made by napping, then shearing and brushing, the right side. The weave is twill and usually wool but may be other fibres.

Used for women's clothes and hats.

Width

140cm (54in).

Handling

Establish the direction of the pile and cut all pieces in one direction. Coats need lining. Use medium weight sew-in interfacing. A fabric for experts to handle.

Thread

Synthetic or mercerized.

Needle

Machine: 100 16. Large stitch.
Hand: 7–8.

Pressing

Press lightly on the wrong side only with a medium hot iron and damp cloth.

Care

Dry clean only.

DYNEL

Trade name for a 'modified' acrylic fibre made by Carbon and Carbide Chemicals Ltd, which has the advantage of being flame-resistant. It has a warm handle and bulks well, and is often used in fur fabrics.

See also Acrylics, page 35.

E

EGYPTIAN COTTON

Fine top quality cotton originally from the Nile region; plain-weave soft cotton made into fabrics, which may be plain or printed. It dyes well, is very strong and hard-wearing but soft to touch.

Used for expensive baby clothes, blouses, summer dresses, nightwear.

Width

90cm (36in).

Handling

Easy to sew, frays very little. If the fabric is very fine the seams may wrinkle, so reduce this tendency by placing tissue paper underneath when machining. A good fabric to hand-sew, it gathers well and takes decorative stitching well, e.g. on baby clothes.

Thread
Mercerized or machine embroidery thread.

Needle
Machine: 70 9. Small stitch.
Hand: 9–10.

Pressing
Hot iron.

Care
Hot wash by hand or machine. Can be starched, and if white may be boiled. Iron damp with hot iron.

EGYPTIAN LACE
An expensive ornamental lace, hand knotted and often elaborated with beads.

ELANCE SUEDE
A lightweight suede suitable for shirts, dresses, etc. Topstitching, tucks, fullness, etc., all work well.

ELASTANE FIBRE
Synthetic fibres, which stretch easily and have a high rate of recovery. They are lighter and longer lasting than rubber, and are easy to wash.

Used for foundation and swimwear fabrics.

See also page 44.

Lycra
Trade name for du Pont elastane fibre.

Spanzelle
Trade name for Courtaulds' elastane fibre.

EMBOSSED SATIN
Any satin-weave fabric that has had a pattern impressed upon it. Usually only heavier satins are treated in this way, and the embossing is now invariably permanent.

This is a popular wedding-gown fabric.

EMBOSSED VELVET
An ordinary pile velvet, but a pattern is introduced by pressing the pile flat in places.

EMBROIDERED CHIFFON
An open lace-effect chiffon often containing viscose with nylon or polyester. The added embroidery may be worked in cotton, viscose or sometimes metal thread.

EMBROIDERED FLOUNCING
Any plain fabric with an embroidered scalloped edge.

EMBROIDERED KNIT
A lightweight synthetic, usually polyester, knit fabric, in plain colours, with gold or silver metal embroidery, often in border designs. It is crease-resistant.

Handle as Knit, see page 179.

EMBROIDERIES

The description came originally from an old English word meaning border, and was used for early decoration on ecclesiastical robes which were, presumably, worked in border designs.

Now it is used for decorative

fabrics, mostly lightweight, on which embroidery is worked in contrasting or matching colours, often in yarn of a different fibre from the fabric, including metal, which may create washing and pressing problems. The fabrics vary considerably in fibre content and weight and also in width. Some may be washable but most are not. If the embroidery has been added to a base fabric, rather than worked in as part of the weaving process, the threads are likely to fray readily when the fabric is cut. Use synthetic thread and machine and hand needles of a size suitable for the general weight of the fabric.

Uses are confined mainly to *saris* and evening wear. All embroideries should be pressed lightly on the wrong side with a warm dry iron or a steam iron. It is essential to try out pressing methods first. If the fabric has a pronounced raised pattern, cover the pressing surface first with a towel to avoid flattening the design.

ENGINEER'S CLOTH

Term used to describe the entire group of cloth used for working and protective clothing, including Dungaree, Denim, Drill, Moleskin.

ENGLISH GUM TWILL

A silk fabric made from low twist yarns in a diagonal rib weave. When printed it is called Foulard. It varies in weight.

For uses, handling, etc., see Foulard, page 155.

ENKALON

Trade name for the polyamide fibre nylon yarn made by the Enkalon Company, used in upholstery and dress fabrics. It has good resistance to wear and, with the exception of some brighter shades, is colour fast. The fabric washes and dries easily as the fibre does not absorb moisture.

See also Polyamides, page 39.

ENSIGN CLOTH

Plain-weave cotton used for flags.

See Bunting, page 114.

ÉPINGE

Very lightweight fabric in a plain close weave, traditionally worsted but may now contain other fibres.

Used for women's tailored dresses and suits.

Width

140cm (54in).

Handling

Thin and springy, inclined to fray readily. Choose only tailored styles, although pleats work well if correctly pressed. To be avoided by anyone without considerable experience. Use firm interfacing, hand-worked tailored buttonholes. Requires lining for comfort.

Thread

Synthetic or mercerized.

Needle

Machine: 90 14. Medium to large stitch.
Hand: 6.

Pressing
Hot iron and damp cloth, firm pressure. Use pressing block. Press on both right and wrong sides. Leave to cool and harden before moving on.

Care
Dry clean.

ÉPONGE

A woollen or cotton fabric. It is sometimes open-textured, and as the name implies, spongy to feel, and is light in weight in comparison with its thickness.

Used for dresses, children's dresses, robes, sports shirts.

Width
140cm (54in).

Handling
Soft and easy to sew, not springy, frays little. A good fabric for a beginner who is handling wool for the first time. Choose loose, drapy styles that do not strain the cloth. Test for shrinkage before cutting out. Use soft sew-in interfacing and nylon zips.

Thread
Synthetic or mercerized.

Needle
Machine: 90 14. Medium stitch.
Hand: 7.

Pressing
Medium hot iron and damp muslin, or steam iron, and light pressure to avoid iron imprints.

Care
Dry clean.

ERMINE
A soft, fine white fur from a type of weasel, with a distinctive black tail tip. It will discolour after time.

Used as trimming on ceremonial gowns.

ETAMINE
Phrase used to describe porous or open cloth, e.g. leno weave. Similar cloths to Éponge in character, but in thinner varieties.

EVENWEAVE LINEN
Fine linen cloth of fairly open construction in plain weave.

Used for many types of embroidery.

EVLAN
Courtaulds' cellulosic modified viscose fibre. Developed for the carpet industry for its resistance to dirt. Often blended with nylon, wool, and acrylics.

See Viscose, page 43.

EYELETTING
Similar to Broderie Anglaise but the embroidery is usually confined to round holes and surface embroidery round them. This description is used in the United States in preference to Broderie Anglaise.

F

FACE-CLOTH

The term used to describe a smooth, plain-weave cloth that is luxurious looking with a nap on one side. Best quality face-cloth is wool but others may be acrylic or viscose. The fabrics are made in various weights.

Used mainly for coats and jackets, but inexpensive fabrics may be used for robes and dressing gowns.

Width
140–150cm (54–60in).

Handling
Establish the direction of the pile or nap and cut pieces all one way; it is usually more pleasant to wear if the pile runs down the garment. It will not fray. May be top-stitched by machine, or by hand if it is good quality wool. Use medium sew-in interfacing. Coats need lining.

Thread
Synthetic.

Needle
Machine: 80–90 11–14. Medium stitch.
Hand: 6–7.

Pressing
Press lightly on the wrong side only with a medium hot iron and damp muslin. Avoid iron marks by placing spare pieces of fabric against hem edges, etc.

Care
Dry clean wool. Acrylics will probably be washable.

FACONNÉ

This is the French for 'fancy weave', but has come to describe the plain colour fabrics of soft floppy crêpe with satin or taffeta effect patterns. Designs are always small, often shiny on dull background. Popular in the thirties when it was made of silk or 'artificial silk', it returned to popularity in the late seventies, made from viscose, acetate, polyester or mixtures.

Used for blouses, soft dresses, evening wear.

Width
114cm (45in).

Handling
Frays readily and is very slippery to handle. Cutting out must be carefully executed or pieces will be out of shape. To be avoided by beginners. Creases very easily. Use transparent interfacing, nylon zips, rouleau loops and covered buttons for fastenings. Do not fit too closely. Hemline may become uneven in wear.

Thread
Synthetic.

Needle
Machine: 70–80 9–11. Small to medium stitch.
Hand: 8.

Pressing
Warm iron and light pressure.

Care
Most are for dry cleaning only, but some are labelled washable.

FACONNÉ VELVET
A patterned velvet of various fibres, with the pattern produced by the burnt-out method of design.

See Burnt Out, page 115.

FAILLE

This is characterized by a crosswise rib in the fabric caused by a thicker yarn. The ribs are finer than in Grosgrain (see page 54), but the fibres used are much the same, i.e. occasionally silk, but more likely to be acetate, viscose or polyester. It creases easily.

Used for dresses, light coats, hats, bags, wedding-gowns.

Width

114cm (45in).

Handling

The softer fabrics drape well, but faille is essentially for formal clothes that are not subjected to hard wear. If the style is fitted closely, the fabric should be mounted to prevent pulling at the seams; it will fray very readily. Use light interfacing and nylon zips.

Thread

Synthetic.

Needle

Machine: 70–80 9–11. Medium stitch.
Hand: 8.

Pressing

Warm iron and light pressure on wrong side only. Easily marked by the iron, so if touching up on the right side, it is necessary to cover with a dry muslin first.

Care

Dry clean only.

FAILLE CRÊPE

A smooth, rich fabric resembling Crêpe de Chine, but heavier. The fibre may be silk, but is more usually synthetic.

Used for blouses, evening wear, negligées.

FAILLE TAFFETA

A taffeta weave fabric made from silk or synthetic fibres but with a pronounced crosswise rib effect that resembles Faille.

See Taffeta, page 236.

FAIR ISLE KNIT

Knitted fabric with coloured patterns resembling Fair Isle. The fibre is usually acrylic and the fabric has a great deal of elasticity. It may be inclined to 'seat' or lose its shape under strain, so garments should not be tight.

Handle as Crochet Knit, page 138.

FAKE FUR

See Fur Fabric, page 156.

FELT

Wool fibres are milled while wet and soapy until they are interlocked and matted and then pressure is applied. The fabric is rigid and does not drape so it is not very useful. It does not wear well, and it loses shape as it has no elasticity.

Best quality felt is made from good quality wool but other qualities are made by using viscose, cotton and kapok, and waste as well. The result is more brittle than wool.

Used for hats, protective coverings, etc., and is useful because it has no grain. For clothes, however, confine its use to appliqué decoration, and small articles, such as boleros, that will not have to withstand strain.

Width

150cm (60in)
80cm (30in)
45cm (18in)
Or often only in small squares.

Handling

Cut pieces in any direction. Fabric will not fray, but welt seams look good. Topstitching, embroidery, etc., improves the rather flat, dull texture. Will probably shrink badly.

Thread

Synthetic.

Needle

Machine: 90 14. Long stitch.
Hand: 6.

Pressing

Hot iron and slightly damp cloth, or a steam iron, but if shrinkage has to be avoided use no moisture.

Care

Cannot be washed successfully, loses substance and colour.

FELT FABRIC

This is an ordinary woven fabric, usually cotton or wool, but may be other fibres, that have been milled on the surface to produce a felt-like appearance which disguises the weave beneath. The fabric may be of any weight, and the process is sometimes applied to cheap base fabric to give it more warmth and interest.

Treat as a normal woven fabric, cutting pieces one way if the felting has been flattened in one direction. Use a size of needle and stitch suitable for the thickness of the fabric and press according to the fibre. Remember that it will be liable to shrink if it is of wool or unshrunk cotton.

FIBRO

The trade name for the viscose staple fibre made by Courtaulds.

FIGURED VELVET

A patterned velvet with some pile cut and some uncut, but also with areas of backing fabric visible.

FILET LACE

A mesh fabric of square design with some squares blocked in to form a design.

FISHEYE CLOTH

A fabric with a woven diamond-effect pattern, constructed in a similar way to bird's eye, but larger. It is often a woollen cloth, but may contain other fibres such as polyester.

Treat according to weight.
See Bird's Eye, page 103.

FLANNEL

The term may be used to describe the old woollen underwear material which was rather coarse and scratchy, but it is more likely now to conjure up a picture of a plain, dull-surfaced, slightly fuzzy cloth. In all-wool or worsted fibre, top class flannel, well tailored, makes super clothes; it is soft, warm and elastic with all the properties of woollen cloth. A small percentage of nylon or other synthetic fibre may be added, but if viscose is included it makes it a cheap material that will not shape or wear well.

Used for blazers, trousers, women's suits, men's suits.

Width
140cm (54in).

Handling
It's a lightweight cloth, which will not fray, and would be a good choice for someone working on wool for the first time. Top-stitching looks good. Pleats well. Use firm, or coat weight, or stretch interfacing, and metal zips.

Thread
Synthetic or mercerized.

Needle
Machine: 90–100 14–16. Large stitch.
Hand: 6–7.

Pressing
Hot iron, damp cloth, sharp heavy pressure, and use the pressing block afterwards. Cheaper flannels may mark so use lighter pressure.

Care
Dry clean.

FLANNELETTE

A lightweight imitation of wool Flannel, Flannelette is made from cotton, viscose, modal or mixtures. Soft yarns are used so that the fuzzy, warm surface is easily achieved. In plain colours or stripes and prints. Wears fairly well. Creases easily.

Used for nightwear and sheets although highly inflammable.

Width
90cm, 114cm (36in, 45in).

Handling
Easy to sew, frays little, does not slip, a good fabric for beginners. Use machine fell seams for strength.

Thread
Synthetic.

Needle
Machine: 80 11. Medium stitch.
Hand: 7.

Pressing
Hot iron or steam iron.

Care
Hot wash by hand or machine. Cotton may be boiled. Iron slightly damp with a hot iron.

FLANNELETTE SHEETING
Made of cotton and slightly brushed for warmth. Highly inflammable.

Handle as Sheeting, page 227.

FLAX
The name of the basic bast fibre from the flax plant. Linen is made from flax. Some tailoring and embroidery canvases are referred to as Flax Canvas.

See also pages 37 and 186.

FLAX CANVAS
See Canvas, page 120.

FLEECE (1)

A heavy wool, or wool mixture, with a long soft nap. The cloth may be woven or knitted, or woven on the pile principle. The long nap or pile provides air spaces which make the fabric very warm and the basic weave is not visible from the right side. The nap wears out on cheaper cloth.

The fabrics vary in quality and weight, but are mainly used for coats.

Width
140cm (54in).

Handling
Always a thick cloth and so difficult to handle except by those with experience. Use plain styles and make capes, etc., to reduce the manipulation required. Need not be lined if loose fitting. Cut one way.

Thread
Synthetic or mercerized.

Needle
Machine: 100 16. Large stitch.
Hand: 5–6.

Pressing
Cover the pressing board with a spare piece of fabric and press the garment lightly with a hot iron and damp cloth. Brush up the fleece on the right side afterwards.

Care
Dry clean.

FLEECE (2)
The skin of an animal, e.g. sheep, goat, to be used for making clothes.

FLEECED
A term applied to fabric that has a napped surface. The process is often applied to knit fabrics.

FLEECY
A word used to describe the feel and implied warmth of any fuzzy surfaced fabric. The fabric may be cheap cotton, or acrylic, or it may be wool. Often used as a lining fabric and therefore the term 'fleecy lining' is often heard.

FLOCK
Many fabrics may be flocked and their characteristic is that the right side of the fabric has tufts of fibres added in dots or patterns. The fabrics are usually light and floaty, the flocking may be in contrast or self colour and it may be worked in a different type of fibre. The flocks are normally stuck on with an adhesive which is applied to the fabric in a pattern. The surplus flock fibres are afterwards blown off.

Flocked nylon is a common fabric for *saris*, etc. Handle according to the weight and fibre content of the base fabric. If a small percentage of a different fibre is mentioned on the label, this is probably the flocking, so consider this when setting the iron temperature.

FLOSS
1 Very short tangled fibre of waste silk.
2 A silky embroidery yarn.

FLOUNCING
Fabric of any type or fibre which has one selvedge shaped in

scallops. The edge is finished off, usually with embroidery.

FLUFLENE

The trade name for a polyester fibre made by I.C.I. Modified Terylene yarn used in the manufacture of socks, stockings, underwear and clothes.

FLUFLON

A stretch nylon filament yarn used in outer garments, knitted fabrics and furnishing fabrics. Made by Frost and Sons, UK.

FOLKWEAVE

Coarse yarn, loosely woven fabrics with a woven pattern often including several colours. Fabrics are woven on dobby or Jacquard looms. Yarns used are cotton, viscose, acrylic. Patterns are usually striped with possibly diamonds or other small patterns between them. These fabrics do not crease easily and are used for bedcovers, curtains, loose covers and cushion covers.

Width

114cm (45in)—or more.

Handling

Soft and easy to handle but the fabrics fray so all hems must be double and all raw seams finished off.

Thread

Synthetic or mercerized.

Needle

Machine: 100 16. Large stitch.
Hand: 6.

Pressing

Medium hot iron or steam iron.

Care

Hot wash by hand or machine if cotton, use cooler water if synthetic. Cotton may shrink. Iron slightly damp with medium hot iron.

FOULARD

A soft, printed, lightweight plain or twill-weave fabric, which can be made of silk, acetate, viscose, polyester or triacetate. The printed patterns usually take the form of small figures on contrasting background colours. Used for soft-styled dresses and blouses, robes, scarves and men's light dressing gowns.

Width

114cm (45in).

Handling

Soft and floppy and quite difficult to handle. Take care with cutting out as the fabric may move from the straight position. Use very sharp scissors. Foulard frays very readily so all raw edges must be enclosed or neatened. It drapes and gathers well. Avoid top-stitching. Place tissue paper under seams if fabric wrinkles. Use soft interfacing.

Thread

Synthetic.

Needle

Machine: 70–80 9–11. Small to medium.
Hand: 8–9.

Pressing
Warm iron and light pressure.

Care
Most fabrics are dry clean only, but if labelled washable, wash gently by hand in warm water, do not squeeze or wring. Drip dry. Iron when slightly damp on the wrong side with a warm iron.

FOX
This fur is blue-grey in colour, the tail is used as trimming and an interesting effect can be achieved by adding the fur from the paws.

FRENCH CRÊPE
A very soft lightweight, inexpensive fabric for lingerie, now usually made from polyamide.

FRENCH SERGE

A very superior quality serge used for women's tailored clothes.

For handling, see Serge, page 225.

FRINGED EMBROIDERY
A base fabric, usually synthetic, with fringing on one edge. For draping, the fringe is often viscose yarn.

FRISE

A pile fabric, but the loops are not cut. It is often made in two colours, and wires are used to lift the pile yarns above the surface, giving the effect of a patterned doublecloth.

The fibre used may be cotton or cotton with acrylic, viscose or modal. All-cotton fabric is often called cotton frieze. Allow for shrinkage.

Used for curtains and furnishing. Does not crease.

Width
114cm (45in)—or more.

Handling
A heavy cloth that frays. The design will invariably be one-way and will need matching if widths have to be joined for curtains.

Thread
Synthetic or 30's cotton.

Needle
Machine: 100 16. Large stitch.
Hand: 6.

Pressing
Hot iron or steam iron.

Care
Warm or hot wash. Iron with a medium-hot iron.

FUJI
Fuji should be pure silk (see page 41), but may be imitated in viscose, acetate, triacetate yarn. The only difference in use and handling between these and pure silk would be the necessity for a cooler iron and moisture if necessary.

FUR FABRIC

Imitation fur is made from synthetic fibre, usually acrylic or nylon pile, on a firm jersey or woven backing. It is fairly expensive, available in a wide range of colours and types, some deliberately imitating real fur, some blatantly unreal.

Used for coats, jackets, children's coats, hats, collars, cuffs.

Width

150cm (60in) or more, or in narrow strips for trimming.

Handling

Use simple patterns with few pieces. Cut with the pile lying in one direction. Spread out a sheet or newspaper before cutting to catch the ends of pile. Stitch seams but trim away excess pile from seam allowances to reduce bulk; if pile is caught in the stitching on the right side pull out with a pin or a teasel brush. Avoid top-stitching. A less bulky look can be achieved by the use of knitted cuffs, collars, pocket welts. Use firm interfacing and heavy zips stitched so that fabric pile is well away from the teeth.

Thread

Synthetic.

Needle

Machine: 90–100 14–16. Large stitch.
Hand: 5–6.

Pressing

Press lightly on the wrong side with a warm iron. Brush up the right side.

Care

Some fur fabric is washable, but be guided by the label.

FUR FELT

Sometimes rabbit, rat and beaver hairs are added to felt to give a sheen and surface texture. These felts are expensive and usually only used for millinery.

FUR HANDLING

Patterns and direction of fur should be matched. Mark out the required shape on the reverse side with tailors chalk. Cut carefully by splitting the skin only with a guarded razor blade or a trimming knife. Mount the pieces on to domette, muslin, etc., leaving the stitches in place after making up.

Join the seams by oversewing on the wrong side, using a leather needle and waxed synthetic or linen thread. If any edges of fur are thin, or if repairing a seam, first hem a piece of tailor's stay tape along the edge to strengthen it, then oversew through tape and skin.

Hems should be trimmed to a small amount and herringboned, then a wide strip of lining fabric placed on top, raw edges trimmed in, the lower one slightly above the bottom of the garment and hemmed all round. Garments must be lined. Fasten with fur hooks or tie belt, or a heavyweight zip sewn in so that the zip is visible and the fur does not become caught in the teeth. Use firm interfacing. Avoid topstitching.

Pressing is not usually necessary.

Care

Store at an even temperature uncrushed by other clothes. Do not cover with polythene covers. Have fur cleaned by expert furriers who undertake this work.

For individual descriptions, see under name of fur.

FUR TRIMMING

Fur fabric and also real fur can be purchased in strips normally from about 6–20cm in width. The strips may be cut in lengths or taken from a roll according to your requirements. The fur is usually backed with a thin layer of synthetic foam and edged with cotton tape. Real furs will have been joined before being backed.

This edging may be used for hats, cuffs, collars, etc., and is applied to existing detail. It is useful for lengthening coats, but in this case it must be backed with lining, or the coat first lengthened with cloth before the fur strip is applied on top.

For handling, see Fur Fabric, page 156.

FUSED FABRIC

See Laminates, page 181.

FUSTIAN

An old Egyptian cotton or linen fabric supposed to date from Roman times. Fustian is now used as a general term to describe a range of cotton fabrics, including pile fabrics.

G

GABARDINE

A steep sloping twill fabric with a prominent rib. It always has more warp than filling. Long floats make the diagonal lines, and there are short floats between the wales.

This fabric is lightweight and, due to the close weave and steep slope of the rib, gabardine (especially gabardine worsted) is amazingly water repellant. Other fibres used include cotton, viscose, wool, silk, polyester and cotton.

Used for outerwear, including raincoats, anoraks and trousers, and for women's skirts and suits. Very hard-wearing.

Width

140cm (54in) or 114cm (45in), depending on fibre.

Handling

A difficult springy fabric to be avoided by beginners, although the softer cotton and viscose types are slightly easier. Use firm interfacing. Topstitching breaks up the surface of the fabric very well. Frays very readily. Coats need lining.

Thread

Machine: 90 14. Medium to large stitch.
Hand: 7.

Pressing

Hot iron and damp cloth with short, sharp pressure. Gabardine marks very easily with the iron so place strips of spare fabric against hems, etc., before pressing.

Care

Worsted must be dry cleaned, other fibres may be washed according to the label.

GALATEA

A cotton fabric in twill weave, made plain, or in simple stripe patterns, for nurses' uniforms, children's clothes, linings. It is given a hard lustrous finish which repels dirt.

Width
114cm (45in).

Handling
A stiff fabric — it is not difficult to handle, but avoid soft styles and gathers. Use topstitching, firm interfacing, metal zips.

Thread
Synthetic or mercerized.

Needle
Machine: 90 14. Medium stitch.
Hand: 6.

Pressing
Hot iron or steam iron.

Care
Hot wash by hand or machine. Boil. Starch. Iron damp with a hot iron.

GALLOON
A narrow braid, often metallic, used to decorate uniforms.

GALLOON LACE
Any lace fabric with a finished scalloped edge on both sides.

GAUZE

A sheer, loosely woven, plain-weave fabric, made from cotton, silk, viscose, acetate. It may be soft and unfinished in appearance or it may be sized to add stiffness.

Often used as a mounting fabric. Some open lacy gauze is made for curtains.

Width
Various.

Handling
A fine fabric that frays, but it is soft and lends itself to gathers. Avoid interfacing.

Thread
Synthetic.

Needle
Machine: 80 11. Small to medium stitch.
Hand: 8.

Pressing
Dry iron or steam iron, set according to fibre.

Care
Most gauzes are washable. Cotton gauze will probably shrink. Iron slightly damp.

GENOA VELVET
An elaborate velvet of satin ground fabric with a multi-coloured pile. The pile is sometimes left uncut.

GEORGETTE

A filmy fabric with a crêpe appearance, woven with very hard twisted threads. It is a springy fabric, plain or printed, and made from a variety of yarns including wool, silk, polyester, nylon. Georgette does not crease readily, and polyester Georgette will hardly crease at all.

Used for blouses, dresses (must be lined), evening wear, over-dresses with opaque fabric beneath.

Width
114cm (45in).

Handling
Cut carefully as the fabric is inclined to move. It frays readily so enclose all edges. Use soft, full floaty styles, gathers, soft ties, rouleaux, etc. Use transparent interfacing, nylon zips. It is easier to handle than chiffon but not a fabric for a beginner.

Thread
Synthetic.

Needle
Machine: 70 9. Small stitch.
Hand: 8–9.

Pressing
Warm iron and light pressure. Wool will shrink if moisture is used.

Care
Synthetic Georgette may be hand washed in warm water. Drip dry. Iron with a warm iron if necessary. Silk and Wool Georgette should be dry cleaned.

GINGHAM

A yarn dyed, plain-weave fabric, with the yarns balanced in strength and usually cotton or polyester and cotton. A firm, very hard-wearing cloth, with stripes or checks woven in; white is always used with a colour.

Used for blouses, shirts, dresses, children's clothes, tablecloths, napkins, curtains.

Width
90cm, 114cm (36in, 45in).

Handling
Easy to handle, it frays little, and is ideal for beginners. It looks attractive if parts are cut on the cross. Good in plain or soft styles.

Thread
Synthetic.

Needle
Machine: 80 11. Small to medium stitch.
Hand: 7.

Pressing
Hot iron or steam iron.

Care
Hot wash by hand or machine. Cheap cotton gingham may shrink. Iron damp with a hot iron. May be starched.

GIVRENE
Silk, acetate or polyester fabric very similar in appearance to Grosgrain, see page 165.

GLACÉ LEATHER
This is goatskin. It is soft and glossy. If available in skin form, it is not difficult to sew.

Used mainly for shoes.

GLASS CLOTH

A plain-weave cloth made from twisted linen yarns, often woven in stripes or checks, but sometimes printed. The fabric is made without any surface fuzz, yet it readily absorbs moisture because it is of medium weight. It is very durable.

Used to make tea towels for drying glass and china.

Cotton glass cloth is cheaper, but is not quite so effective for drying up as it becomes damp sooner, and does not wear as long as linen.

Width
Various, often narrow, made specially for towels.

Handling
Because of the hard wear the towels will receive, all non-selvedges must have double hems turned and finished by machine.

Thread
Mercerized, cotton or synthetic.

Needle
Machine: 90 14. Medium stitch.
Hand: 6.

Pressing
Hot iron or steam iron.

Care
Hot wash by hand or machine. Boil. Iron slightly damp with hot iron. Colours of printed towels will fade with wear.

GLENSHEE
A plain-weave mercerized cotton or linen made in a wide variety of weights and used for all types of embroidery.

GLENSHEE CRASH

A rough, uneven plain-weave fabric of equal quantities of cotton and linen fibre.

Used mainly for curtains and loose covers and as a base for embroidery.

Width
114cm (45in) for furnishing.

Handling
Cut exactly on the straight grain. It frays readily so all edges must be neatened or enclosed.

Thread
Synthetic or mercerized.

Needle
Machine: 90 14. Medium stitch.
Hand: 6.

Pressing
Hot iron and damp cloth, or steam iron.

Care
Hot wash by hand or machine. Iron damp with a hot iron.

GLEN URQUHART PLAID
The name comes from a Scottish clan. This cloth is also sometimes called overplaid, because the blocks of check weave are arranged at right angles, and then there is a larger outline check effect over this, often in another colour. It may be wool or worsted and is made in various weights, from light suiting to overcoating.

An ornate plaid, used for golfing clothes, cloaks, men's sporting hats and overcoats.

Handle according to weight, matching checks carefully.

GLISSADE

A closely woven satin-weave cotton fabric that is polished in finishing. It is made in plain colours, an uninteresting fabric used only where cotton lining is needed.

Width
90cm (36in).

Handling
This fabric will not fray, but the lining has to withstand strain and satin weave tends to pull at points of strain. Sew strongly.

Thread
Synthetic or mercerized.

Needle
Machine: 90 14. Medium stitch.
Hand: 6.

Pressing
Hot iron.

Care
Hot wash by hand or machine. Iron slightly damp with hot iron. Remember however that this applies only to the lining, follow care instructions for the main fabric of the garment.

GLORIA

A strong, firm, plain-weave cotton, silk or nylon fabric. It is very closely woven and very lightweight, in plain, twill or satin weave.

Used for covering umbrellas as when stretched taut it is water repellant.

GLORIA SUEDE
A firm heavy suede for jackets and coats.

GLOVE SILK

A fine warp knit silk fabric made in basic colours and used mainly for glove lining, although it was once also used for lingerie.

It is difficult to obtain as piece goods. If it is available, sew as any fine pure silk, but using a slight zigzag machine stitch for 'ease'.

GOLD TISSUE

Transparent metal cloth — very soft and luxurious — consisting of metal warp in gold colour and silk or synthetic weft.

Used mainly for evening dresses, *saris*, etc.

Width
90cm (36in).

Handling
This fabric frays easily as the metal threads detach when cut. Drapes well. Needs lining. Use transparent interfacing.

Thread
Silk or synthetic.

Needle
Machine: 70 9. Small stitch.
Hand: 9.

Pressing
Warm iron and light pressure on wrong side only.

Care
Dry clean.

GOSSAMER

A very soft fine silk gauze used for veils.

Width
Varies, but usually wide.

Handling
Sew by hand if possible.

Thread
Silk.

Needle
Machine: 70 9. Small stitch.
Hand: 10.

Pressing
Warm iron and light pressure.

Care
Dry clean. Store in tissue paper, sealed in a box when not in use.

GRAIN LEATHER
The term used to describe all leather that has had a finish applied to the right side. Most leather skins available for sewing are referred to as grain leathers.

GRANADA

An old term meaning 'grained'; the fabric is a fine worsted cloth with a face finish on the right side. The weave has a broken appearance. The cloth is normally black.

Used for women's coats, men's lightweight overcoats.

Width
140cm (54in).

Handling
Cut one way with face finish running downwards on the garment. Soft and easy to handle compared with many worsteds, but to be avoided by beginners. Lends itself only to tailoring processes. Use firm interfacing.

Thread
Mercerized.

Needle
Machine: 100 16. Large stitch.
Hand: 6.

Pressing
Hot iron and damp cloth on wrong side, but take care not to leave iron impressions. Brush up the right side if necessary after pressing.

Care
Dry clean.

GRENADINE (1)

This description was once used to describe an outer garment, such as a cloak, but it now refers to a loosely woven gauze-type fabric. It may be cotton, polyester, nylon or mixtures, including acrylic fibre. It may also occasionally be produced as a filmy dress or blouse fabric.

Width
114cm (45in).

Handling
A springy net-like fabric best finished by machine. Drapes well. Allow plenty of width in curtains.

Thread
Synthetic.

Needle
Machine: 80 11. Medium stitch. Straight or zigzag.
Hand: 7.

Pressing
Warm or medium iron depending on fibre content.

Care
Wash frequently in hot water. Drip dry, often no ironing required. Cotton grenadine may shrink. White nylon grenadine may go yellow, but it can be restored with nylon-whitener.

GRENADINE (2)
This term applies also to a yarn made from three very highly twisted basic yarns. The fibre may be silk, cotton or synthetic. The yarn is woven into a variety of fabrics of varying weights, including voile, organdie and satin.

The word Grenadine was once used to describe a hard-wearing, close silk fabric with a dull surface created by the highly twisted yarns.

GRENFELL CLOTH
Closely woven reversible twill fabric, mainly used for raincoats, because the close twill weave causes it to be water-repellant. The fibres used may be worsted or polyester or blends. Similar to Gabardine in appearance.

Handling
See Gabardine, page 158.

GREY GOODS
This term refers to any fabric, regardless of colour or fibre content, that has been woven, but has not yet undergone any finishing treatment either wet or dry. Many companies produce only grey goods, sending them to specialists to be finished.

GROS DE LONDRES

A cross-ribbed fabric with alternating heavy and fine ribs, or ribs of different colours. Made in plain weave and plain-weave variations. A glossy finish is applied and it is fairly stiff to handle. The fibres used are viscose, acetate, triacetate, polyester or silk.

Used for millinery and also for evening dresses.

Width
90–114cm (36–45in).

Handling
Avoid gathers and other soft processes. It will not pleat. Frays easily, so neaten all edges. Use medium interfacing and nylon zips.

Thread
Synthetic.

Needle
Machine: 80 11. Medium stitch.
Hand: 8–9.

Pressing
Warm iron and light pressure on wrong side. The fabric is easily marked by an iron, so cover with dry muslin if right side pressing is necessary.

Care
Dry clean unless labelled washable.

GROSGRAIN

A plain weave cloth with a prominent rib effect. The fibres may be silk, worsted, cotton, or viscose, acetate, nylon. The cords are heavier than those in Poplin and rounder than those in Faille, and it is a fairly stiff fabric, made only in plain colours.

Used for formal clothes, such as ceremonial gowns and church vestments, but also (in synthetic fibres) for ribbons. Grosgrain fabrics are hard-wearing due to the weave, but clothes made from it rarely receive hard wear.

Width
Mainly 114cm (45in).

Handling
It will fray readily, due to the slippery fibres used, so neaten all raw edges. Will not gather but will take unpressed pleats as fullness. Use firm interfacing. Avoid buttonholes.

Thread
Silk or synthetic.

Needle
Machine: 80 11. Medium stitch.
Hand: 7.

Pressing
Warm iron and light pressure on the wrong side.

Care
Dry clean silk, but some synthetic Grosgrain will be labelled hand washable.

GUANACO
A small, wild deer-like animal, with big brown eyes, from the llama group of animals found in the Andes. The hair of fifteen-day-old animals was once used for spinning, but the Guanaco is now a protected species.

GUIPURE LACE
Although now entirely made by machine, this was once a hand-made Italian type of lace. It is composed of thick, heavy patterns, often with quite large motifs, joined together with bars or brides. The ground fabric is made from nylon acetate or sometimes cotton; the thick embroidery is worked and then the ground fabric is dissolved with chemicals that will not affect the embroidery.

GUNCLUB CHECK

Description of a distinctive, sporty-looking check wool fabric. The checks are usually woven in greens, browns and sometimes blue, sometimes with an over-check.

Worn by sports enthusiasts as jackets, plus fours, golfing skirts — makes rather natty outfits.

Handle as medium-weight wool, such as Flannel, see page 152.

H

HABIT CLOTH
A woollen, medium-weight suiting material in satin weave, with a fine warp, a thicker weft and a dress face finish.

HABUTAI (1)

Used for suits and winter-weight dresses.

Handle as Face-cloth, see page 149.

HABUTAI (1)

The term means soft and light—and was originally used for Japanese waste silk. It is now made in many Far Eastern countries on power looms in plain or twill weave; it is heavier than traditional Chinese silk, and is usually in natural écru colour.

Used for men's jackets, women's shirtwaisters and skirts.

Width
90cm, 114cm (36in, 45in).

Handling
Beginners should avoid silk fabrics as they are usually slippery and sometimes the seams wrinkle. This fabric frays, so neaten seams. Jackets can be lined, but if they are not, then raw edges must be bound. Use medium interfacing.

Thread
Silk or synthetic.

Needle
Machine: 80 11. Medium stitch.
Hand: 7.

Pressing
Medium hot iron. Use a slightly damp muslin if necessary.

Care
Usually this must be dry cleaned, but may be washable.

HABUTAI (2)

Not to be confused with the thicker fabric, there is a cheap silk Habutai which is excellent as a soft, lightweight lining fabric for evening dresses, wedding-dresses, etc., especially for those who find synthetic lining uncomfortable to wear.

Width
90cm (36in).

Handling
The fabric frays very little, but all edges must be neatened. Narrow finish seams are suitable. Gathers well, but not hard-wearing so allow the necessary ease in the lining.

Thread
Silk or synthetic.

Needle
Machine: 80 11. Medium stitch. Zigzag or embroidery stitch on hems, etc.
Hand: 7–8.

Pressing
Warm iron.

Care
Hand wash only in warm water. Iron with a warm iron. Be sure the fabric of the garment is also a 'hand wash' material.

HAIRCLOTH
Cotton, polyester, linen or other fibre with which horsehair has been mixed to make it strong and inflexible.

Used in upholstery, and also as a chest canvas in tailoring.

See also Woven Interfacings, page 251.

HAIR CANVAS

A woven interfacing material in various weights. Coarse goat hair combined with wool, cotton or rayon is used in the filling.

Used in coats and jackets made from suitings and coatings.

See below for various types.

Types of Hair Canvas

There are several to choose from, according to the weight of the fabric being used.

1 60cm (24in). Dry clean.

Cotton canvas, fairly stiff, 45 per cent cotton with hair.

2 60cm (24in). Dry clean.

A more expensive, softer canvas made from wool, viscose and hair. A better quality and a good choice for expensive coatings and suitings.

3 70cm (28in). Dry clean.

Canvas made from a heavier yarn and hair, a good choice for coat-weight fabrics.

4 80cm (32in). Dry clean.

A grey canvas with a thin white stripe. More expensive than those above. Made from viscose, goat hair and polyester yarn. Available in two weights.

5 90cm (36in). Dry clean.

A stiff grey canvas of leno weave construction, made of cotton, viscose and goat hair. Use with coatings.

HANDKERCHIEF LINEN

This is known as handkerchief lawn, and it describes the finest cotton or linen lawn, or cambric, used for handkerchiefs. Made in plain colours or printed; it can be boiled and hot-washed, and wears very well.

In addition to handkerchiefs it is used for baby clothes, christening gowns and table linen.

Handling

See Cambric, page 117.

HARDANGER CLOTH

A plain-weave cotton fabric of coarse construction, so that the weave is easily visible.

Used for embroidery, especially the types where threads have to be counted. The threads are usually arranged in pairs.

HARE

This is greatly used in the United States. The hair texture of hare is soft and woolly and can be spun with wool, producing a similar result to a wool and rabbit mixture.

HARRIS TWEED

A rough, very hard-wearing tweed in mixed natural colours with a distinctive close weave and hairy finish. Harris Tweed comes only from the Outer Hebrides, where it was once made from hand-spun yarn. It is now more often made from machine-spun yarn and the cloth is labelled accordingly, but it is a very exclusive and expensive cloth and anyone possessing it is usually proud of it, with good reason.

Used only for tailored coats and suits.

Width
Once only 71cm (28in) but now may be more.

Handling
To be used only by experts who can shape, mould and finish the garment as the cloth deserves. It responds well to all tailoring processes. Choose classic styles. Use firm interfacing. Jackets need lining.

Thread
30's cotton.

Needle
Machine: 100 16. Large stitch.
Hand: 6.

Pressing
Hot iron and damp cloth. Use pressing block to put creases in trousers.

Care
Dry clean.

HEATHER MIXTURES
This phrase describes a combination of greens and purples, or Scottish heather colours, found in both woollen cloth and knitting wool. The colours are often used in equal amounts so that no one colour predominates.

HELANCA

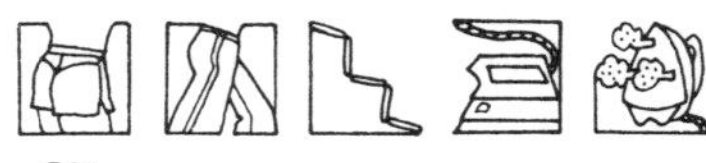

A Swiss elastic fibre made from nylon and polyester. Fabrics made from it have two-way stretch and are very hard-wearing and washable.

Used for sportswear, ski-wear, swimsuits, trousers, panels in maternity clothes.

Width
150cm (60in).

Handling
Choose patterns designed for stretch fabrics. Cut out, and fit before sewing as invariably the garment will have to be made tighter. Use double-stitched narrow finish seams. If seams are to be kept rigid, add cotton tape when stitching. Use nylon or concealed zips. Helanca will not fray or crease.

Thread
Synthetic.

Needle
Machine: 80 11. Slight zigzag stitch.
Hand: 8.

Pressing
Warm iron or steam iron. Press in trouser creases with hot iron, damp cloth, and pressing block.

Care
Hot wash by hand or machine. No ironing needed.

HEMP

A plant similar to Jute, grown in many countries. When spun, it is rather like flax but thicker and coarser.

It is a very strong fibre and is used in the manufacture of carpets, rugs, ropes, etc., but has limited use because bleaching is difficult.

HENRIETTA

Fine diagonal twilled dress fabric made with silk warp and fine worsted filling which makes it resemble cashmere cloth. Once in great demand, but it has not been much in evidence for some years.

HERRINGBONE

Strictly speaking herringbone is a weave, but the name is often applied to any woollen cloth made in a herringbone design, that is with a broken twill effect in two colours producing an up and down striped effect. (See page 50 for structure.) Any fibres can be used to make herringbone cloth.

Handle according to fibre content and weight, e.g. handle heavy wool as Cashmere Cloth, see page 121; handle Acrylic Herringbone as medium-weight Acrylic, see page 93.

HESSIAN

Coarse jute, or sometimes jute and hemp, yarns are used to make this coarse, even, plain weave, which is then plain dyed.

Used for sacking and in upholstery, but it can also be a well finished smooth cloth, dyed in a wide variety of colours, and used for wall-covering, notice-board covering, curtains and blinds.

Width

Various.

Handling

Hessian frays easily so allow for this if it is to be handled excessively. Before cutting, make sure the grain is exactly straight. It may be dampened and pulled to shape. Use adhesive when covering large areas.

Thread

Synthetic or 30's cotton.

Needle

Machine: 100 16. Large stitch.
Hand: 5.

Pressing

Hot iron.

Care

Usually washable, but check when buying that it is pre-shrunk and colour-fast.

HICKORY CLOTH

This resembles ticking, but is lighter in weight and not so firmly woven. It is made from cotton, or polyester and cotton.

Used for protective clothing, overalls, etc.

Width

114cm (45in) or more.

Handling
Not difficult to sew, but an uninteresting fabric to handle. Use double-stitched welt seams for strength and metal zips or metal capped studs to fasten.

Thread
Synthetic.

Needle
Machine: 100 16. Large stitch.
Hand: 6.

Pressing
Hot iron and damp cloth, or steam iron.

Care
Hot wash. Can be boiled. Iron damp with hot iron.

HIMALAYA
Like shantung in appearance and weight, but made from slub cotton yarns. Easier to sew than Silk Shantung, but handle in a similar way, see page 231.

HOLLAND

Medium-weight plain-weave cloth made from linen or cotton yarn. It has a finish of size and oil applied to stiffen it.

Mainly used in upholstery for an undercovering, as it is firm and hard-wearing.

Handle as Hessian, see page 169.

Holland is also a canvas interfacing, see Woven Interfacing, page 251.

HOMESPUN
A rather coarse, plain-weave woollen fabric with a hand-woven appearance, which was once actually woven in the home in all countries. It has always been a hard-wearing, serviceable cloth, but is now entirely machine-made, although sometimes labelled Homespun to indicate its good qualities. It may be made from any fibre now, and in any weight.

Similar to Harris Tweed. See pages 167 and 168.

HONAN
Silk fabric made from silk yarn obtained from the Honan area of China, which is the only type of wild silk that accepts dye evenly. The fabric is light and rough textured.

Handle as for Pongee, page 213.

Honan is also used to describe a viscose fabric which has a checked effect.

HONEYCOMB

The threads in this fabric form ridges and hollows giving a cell-like appearance to both sides. Warp and weft threads float on both sides and the rough structure makes the cloth absorbent. It may be printed or woven in patterns.

Once made only from worsted yarn, but that type of fabric is now so rare that it is not worth considering as a dress fabric. Cotton Honeycomb (sometimes called Waffle Cloth), however, is very common and, plain or printed, is used for children's clothes, dresses, kitchen curtains.

tablecloths. It often contains some polyester fibre.

Width
90cm, 114cm (36in, 45in).

Handling
It is fairly stiff but does not fray. A good fabric for a beginner. Does not gather well. Use medium interfacing. Due to the way it is made, fabric cut on the cross will not have much 'give' and may not be successful as binding, etc.

Thread
Synthetic or mercerized.

Needle
Machine: 80 11. Medium stitch.
Hand: 7.

Pressing
Hot iron and light pressure.

Care
Hot wash by hand or machine. Press with a hot iron lightly, although the honeycomb effect should not be impaired by laundering.

HONITON LACE
A hand-made lace that originated in Devonshire. It is characterized by designs of flowers and leaves on a very fine mesh ground.

HOPSACK
Originally hopsack was a coarse double yarn sacking, made from jute or hemp, and used as sacking by hopgrowers. Now the name is given to a plain-weave suiting weight cloth made by using two yarns in each direction (see page 48). This may be made from any natural or synthetic fibre, but if synthetic, the fibres are usually bulked to produce the traditional cloth. It may also be produced as a furnishing and curtain fabric.

All hopsack fabrics will fray fairly readily. Handle according to the weight and fibre content.

HORSE HAIR
Long, very coarse hair from manes and tails of horses. At one time it made a cheap, strong material used widely for upholstery, carpets and interfacing fabrics, but it is now becoming scarce and very expensive. The hair is being replaced by man-made fibre, but the resulting fabric is referred to as Hair Canvas, not Horse Hair Canvas. See Canvas, page 120.

HOUNDSTOOTH CHECK

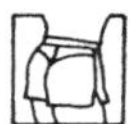

A four-pointed star check design in a broken twill weave; the checks are medium-sized and one of the colours is often white.

Used for men's sports suiting.

HUCKABACK

A linen or cotton cloth with a square weave, in which the yarns are twisted to add to its absorption qualities as it is used almost exclusively for towels in hotels, schools etc. It is made in white or plain colours, sometimes with a woven contrast stripe or name included. Very hard-wearing, and fairly stiff and heavy.

Width
According to width of towel required.

Handling
Firm and not easy to manipulate, but in the normal way there will be a selvedge down both sides, so only ends have to be hemmed. The even squares provide a good base for embroidery stitches such as cross-stitch.

Thread
Mercerized.

Needle
Machine: 90 14. Medium stitch.
Hand: 6.

Pressing
Hot iron.

Care
Hot wash, boil. Iron damp with a hot iron.

I

IMPERIAL CLOTH

A coating fabric of fine worsted in twill weave. Imperial serge is similar, but softer and looser woven. Both are firm, durable cloths, usually dyed navy blue, and used for coats, capes, and raincoats if showerproofed.

Width
140cm (54in).

Handling
The serge is softer and easier to handle than the cloth. Choose plain styles. Use firm interfacing, piped or worked buttonholes. Requires lining except in the case of capes. Topstitching looks attractive.

Thread
Synthetic or mercerized.

Needle
Machine: 100 16. Large stitch.
Hand: 6.

Pressing
Hot iron and damp cloth.

Care
Dry clean.

INDIAN CRÊPE
A cotton crêpe of rough unfinished appearance, used for blouses, men's shirts.

INDIAN SILK

A hand-loomed silk, not always made in India. This fabric has a slightly wrinkled impressed appearance, but it is a crisp fabric. Made in plain colours.

Used for *saris*, evening wear and for some furnishing items such as cushion covers.

Width
112cm (44in).

Handling
Drapes fairly well, but do not fit closely or use soft finishes such as gathers. Fabric will fray easily, so all edges must be neatened.

Avoid topstitching. Use medium sew-in interfacing. Fabric will crease easily in wear.

Thread
Silk or synthetic.

Needle
Machine: 80 11. Medium stitch.
Hand: 7.

Pressing
Warm iron.

Care
Dry clean.

INDUSTRIAL NYLON

A heavy-duty plain-weave nylon fabric made in a limited range of colours. It is fairly stiff and does not crease.

Used for overalls and protective clothing, but it is also useful for the bags of men's trouser pockets as it is extremely hard-wearing.

Width
136cm (54in).

Handling
As the yarn is slippery there is an inclination for seams to give way under strain, so stitch twice, e.g. machine fell seams. Stitch twice round pocket bags. Neaten all raw edges to control fraying.

Thread
Synthetic.

Needle
Machine: 90 14. Ball point may be needed. Large stitch.
Hand: 6.

Pressing
Warm iron.

Care
Hot wash, drip dry. No ironing required especially when new. White nylon may go yellow in time but it can be restored with a nylon whitener.

INSERTION LACE
This is usually narrow and often with slits for threading ribbon through, but it always has two straight edges. It is inserted as decoration, and the backing fabric is usually cut away afterwards.

INTERFACING
Woven or non-woven fabric used to give body to certain areas of a garment. It adds to the outward appearance of the garment if some areas are reinforced, e.g. collars, buttoned openings, cuffs, pocket flaps, and this structuring also makes the garment last longer.

Interfacing has always been a vital and integral part of tailoring, but until comparatively recently was regarded as less important in dressmaking. Now, however, we have a very wide range of types and weights of interfacing so it is not difficult to interface correctly and improve the garment. Choice depends entirely on the fabric being sewn. In general, the interfacing used in dressmaking should be lighter and softer than the fabric, otherwise the interfacing will take over and make the area where it is used appear different.

See also Choosing Interfacings, page 18.

INTERFACINGS
Non-woven, see pages 18 and 60.
Woven, see page 251.
Canvas, see page 120 and below.

INTERLOCK

A closely knitted cotton, viscose or modal jersey, plain or with a small pattern in the knitting. It is a warm fabric, which washes and wears well.

Used for ready-made underwear and not usually available as piece goods.

IRISH LACE
The term used to describe a heavy crochet lace with looped edges. Made in Ireland; Carrickmacross and Limerick are two places of origin. See also Limerick Lace, page 186.

IRISH LINEN

The fine quality linen cloth woven in Ireland from Irish flax.

Used for handkerchiefs and table linen; coarser grades used for tea towels and glass cloths. As nearly all that is made goes into this industry, it is not usually available as dress piece goods.

Washes in hot water and boils. May be starched. Iron damp with a hot iron.

IRON-ON CANVAS INTERFACING
An iron-on woven canvas does not give the shaping advantages of the sew-in varieties. However, it is quick to use and is effective on flat areas such as coat fronts, pocket flaps, hemlines, (where added body is needed), etc. Choose the weight according to the fabric being used.

1 74cm (29in). Dry clean.
A thick, soft canvas made from a mixture of linen and cotton.

2 90cm (36in). Dry clean.
A very soft cotton canvas that would be suitable for the lightweight cloths used for women's coats and jackets.

IRON-ON COTTON
90cm (36in).
A soft cotton, almost like muslin, with adhesive granules on the wrong side. It would add slight stiffness to soft fabrics. Not cheap.

Wash or dry clean.

J

JACONET

A thin, plain weave cotton fabric, heavier than cambric but similar in type, it is glazed on the right side to produce a high lustre. May be plain or have a stripe or check pattern. May now contain a proportion of polyester fibre.

Used for men's shirts, children's clothes and pyjamas.

Width
114cm (45in).

Handling
An easy fabric to handle; a good choice for beginners if a simple pattern is chosen. Most processes

can be used on the fabric. Use medium-weight iron-on interfacing, machine-made buttonholes.

Thread
Synthetic or mercerized.

Needle
Machine: 80 11. Medium stitch.
Hand: 7.

Pressing
Hot iron or steam iron.

Care
Hot wash. Iron damp with hot iron.

JAP SILK

Also called China Silk, made in Northern China. This is a thin almost papery silk fabric, in plain weave and in plain colours. It has insufficient weight or durability for outer clothes, and is used mainly for lining lightweight garments.

Width
90cm (36in).

Handling
Very light and slippery, anchor firmly with the cut pieces of the garment you are lining, to prevent the silk from moving. Use sharp scissors. Tack all seams.

Thread
Silk or synthetic.

Needle
Machine: 70–80 9–11. Small to medium stitch.
Hand: 9.

Pressing
Cool iron and light pressure, no moisture.

Care
May be hand washed, but this will depend upon the care instructions for the outer fabric.

JASPÉ

A hard-wearing cotton stripe fabric using either multi-coloured threads or different shades of one colour. Small matching dots are sometimes woven into the fabric.

Used for curtains, chaircovers, bedspreads.

Width
120cm (48in).

Handling
Make sure the stripes run in the same direction. An easy fabric to handle, but for durability all raw edges should be bound or concealed by turning under. Curtains are often not lined in order to see the effect of light through the stripes.

Thread
Synthetic or 30's cotton.

Needle
Machine: 100 16. Large stitch.
Hand: 6.

Pressing
Hot iron or steam iron.

Care
Hot wash, iron slightly damp with a hot iron.

JASPÉ CLOTH

A hard-wearing cotton cloth made on a dobby loom, usually in a narrow striped pattern. Colours are either mixed or shades of one colour creating a shadow effect.

Used for curtains, bedcovers and chair covers. Allow for shrinkage.

Width
120cm (48in).

Handling
Cut exactly on the grain to ensure stripes are straight. An easy fabric to sew.

Thread
Synthetic or mercerized.

Needle
Machine: 90 14. Large stitch, straight or zigzag.
Hand: 6.

Pressing
Hot iron or steam iron.

Care
Hot wash. Iron damp with a hot iron.

JEAN

A very hard-wearing cotton fabric, similar to drill but softer to handle. Made in plain colours only, sometimes in herringbone weave.

Used for overalls, dungarees, protective clothing, children's clothes.

Width
90–114cm (36–45in).

Handling
Easy to handle; a good fabric for beginners. Lends itself to top-stitching to break up the plain surface. Use double-stitched seams for strength on working clothes.

Thread
Synthetic (for strength).

Needle
Machine: 90 14. Medium straight or zigzag stitch.
Hand: 6.

Pressing
Hot iron or steam iron.

Care
Hot wash. Iron damp with hot iron.

JERSEY

Knitted fabric, usually stocking stitch, made from any fibre, including cotton, wool, silk, polyester, acrylic, modal. It has give and elasticity and is comfortable to wear. There are many types and these will be found under the fabric or fibre name. It may be warp or weft knitted. See page 56.

JERSEY GABARDINE

Although Gabardine is strictly speaking a woven cloth, many of the old terms have to be used to describe new-effect fabrics. Jersey Gabardine is a twill-effect closely knitted polyester. It is usually in plain colours.

Used for trousers, jackets, etc. Very hard-wearing, will not lose its shape or show any deterioration with time.

Width
150cm (60in).

Handling
Firm but not difficult to handle. The knit does not move in cutting. Use stretch interfacing, nylon zips.

Thread
Synthetic.

Needle
Machine: 80 11. Possibly ball point.
Hand: 11.

Pressing
Medium hot iron, damp cloth and heavy pressure.

Care
Hot wash. Drip dry. No ironing.

JERSEY VELOUR

A plushy surface knit fabric with a velvety attractive appearance. The back of the fabric is a smooth knit, fairly stable fabric, while the pile on the right side is short and soft. The fibre is polyester with viscose (Viloft) pile. Made in attractive plain colours.

Used for soft dresses, blouson tops, jumpsuits, T shirts, etc.

Width
From 150cm (60in).

Handling
The pile tends to drop off when cut but it will not fray any further. Edges will curl up so must be neatened. Cut all pieces in one direction of pile — whether for pale or dark effect is a matter of choice. Very easy to sew and a good fabric for a beginner, once she has understood the one-way rules.

Thread
Synthetic.

Needle
Machine: 80 11. Slight zigzag.
Hand: 11.

Pressing
Steam iron or medium iron on wrong side only. Place spare fabric on pressing board to avoid flattening the pile.

Care
Hand wash. Warm iron on wrong side.

JUTE

A hard-wearing coarse fibre from a plant grown in India.

Used in heavy textiles and in upholstery.

K

KAPOK
A fibre resembling cotton but silkier, it is a seed fibre which is round, smooth and light. It is only used as a bulky soft filling in upholstery, cushions, mattresses, toys, etc., and can be purchased in bags of various sizes. It has been superseded to a certain extent by the cheaper synthetic foam as a filler. Both are highly inflammable.

KASHA

1 This may be fine wool and Tibet goat hair, a softly napped fabric with a crosswise streak caused by darker hairs.

Used for soft jackets and dresses. Handle as for a soft napped wool, such as Face-cloth, page 149.

2 Kasha may also be a cotton flannel, with a napped right side, slightly écru in colour and made as sheeting. See Sheeting, page 227.

Needle

Machine: 90 14. Medium to large stitch.
Hand: 7.

Pressing

Hot iron and damp cloth, but use light pressure to avoid marking the surface. Brush up on the right side if necessary.

Care

Dry clean.

KERSEY

A woollen cloth that originated in Kersey, Suffolk. It has a lustre caused by the use of cross-bred wool, and is a very heavy, thick wool coating fabric which has been fulled and also felted. Often a twill weave, although the face finish that is applied conceals this. It is a conventional cloth in appearance and not much used now except for classic overcoats, or in lighter weight for a classic black dress. It may now contain some acrylic fibre.

Width

140cm (54in).

Handling

An easy soft fabric to handle that does not fray. Cut one way with the nap running downwards. Coats need lining. Confine styles to classics and avoid effects such as gathers.

Thread

Synthetic or mercerized.

KETTLECLOTH

A fairly stiff plain-weave fabric, with a dull surface and a slight slub in the weave which may be coloured. Made from cotton and polyester yarns.

Ideal for men's light summer jackets, for trousers for men and women, and other casual but crisp effect clothes.

Width

112cm (44in).

Handling

Easy to handle. Use crisp interfacing and metal zips. Will topstitch well. Trouser creases will press in well. Will fray, so neaten all seams.

Thread

Synthetic.

Needle

Machine: 90 14. Medium stitch.
Hand: 6.

Pressing

Medium hot iron and damp muslin, firm pressure. Use pressing block if necessary on trouser creases.

Care
Hot wash. Iron with medium hot iron.

KID (1)
The coat of the young deer. Usually marked grey, white and black. Very soft, but hard-wearing.

KID (2)
The skin of the young goat. Easy to sew.

It is readily available for making gloves. Heavy varieties are used for shoes.

KNIT
A knit fabric is generally accepted as looser than jersey and with more stretch in both directions. All fibres may be used, including cotton, wool, silk, polyester, acrylic, and the fabrics may be of any thickness from fine to coat weight.

Many patterns are now designed specifically for use with knit fabrics and care should be taken to use these, as often darts, zips, etc., have been omitted, and the pattern has been cut slightly smaller.

To test a true knit fabric, hold a length of 10cm across the width of the fabric and if it will stretch up to 15cm or more it can safely be used as a knit fabric.

There is a variety of different types and they can be found under the name of the fibre or fabric.

It may be warp or weft knitted. See page 57.

L

LACE

(See also page 62.)
Open-work fabrics of various construction and elaborate designs. Any fibre may be used but the most common are now nylon, viscose and cotton. Made as edgings as well as wide-width fabric, it is with few exceptions, machine-made. There has been a great revival in hand-made bobbin or pillow lace, but as a leisure-time craft interest, not for commercial purposes.

Narrow lace is used flat, pleated or gathered as decoration; wide lace is used for lingerie, nightwear, formal dresses, such as wedding outfits; cheaper varieties are used as curtains and bedspreads. Lace often has an underlay, either matching or contrasting.

Width
Edgings from 3mm ($\frac{1}{8}$in).
Piece lace from 90cm (36in).

Handling
Most lace in the piece is fairly crisp, so choose styles with limited fullness. Designs are elaborate so keep to classic styles. Lace is expensive, but plain garments can be decorated by cutting motifs from piece lace and attaching them as appliqué. Lace garments may be mounted or lined. Use narrow finish seams. To avoid heavy looking hemlines, either bind with another fabric, such as Satin or Crêpe de Chine, or face

the edges with Net or Organdie. To join lace invisibly, overlap the pieces, matching the outline of the design as closely as possible and oversew by hand, or zigzag by machine. Cut away surplus lace on both sides afterwards.

Thread
Synthetic.

Needle
Machine: 70–80 9–11. Medium straight or zigzag stitch.
Hand: 8–9.

Pressing
Set iron at temperature suitable for the fibre content. Cover board with a towel and press lace lightly on the wrong side only.

Care
Lace is usually machine washable, but if it is very fine or expensive or even antique, put it in a pillow case and hand wash in warm water and liquid soapless detergent. After rinsing, roll it in a towel to absorb excess moisture before leaving it to dry.

Types
There are many types of lace with different descriptive names, often taken from the area in which they were first developed. The following list includes a selection. For details of how to identify each, look for the name in its alphabetical position.

Alençon; All-over; Aloe; Antique; Antwerp; Appliqué; Arabian; Armenian edging; Baby lace; Barman; Battenberg; Beading; Binche; Blonde; Bobbin; Bobbin net; Breton; Broderie anglaise; Bruges; Brussels; Buckinghamshire; Carrickmacross; Chantilly; Cluny; Dresden point; Duchesse; Egyptian; Filet; Flouncing; Galloon; Guipure; Honiton; Insertion; Irish; Leavers; Lille; Limerick; Macramé; Malines; Maltese; Mechlin; Medallion; Milan; Needlepoint; Nottingham; Paraguay; Picot; Princess; Ratine; Re-embroidered; Renaissance; Rose-point; St Gall; Schiffli; Shadow; Spanish; Suiting; Tatting; Teneriffe; Torchon; Val; Valenciennes; Venetian.

LAMÉ

Any fabric containing metal yarns. The metal may be added as decoration or it may exist as the warp or weft thread. The main fibre of the fabric can be silk, viscose, acetate, triacetate, nylon or polyester, and the weave is usually plain. The fabrics are thin and drape well.

Used for evening dresses, capes, boleros and fancy dress. Requires lining.

Width
90–114cm (30–45in).

Handling
A one-way fabric. Cut all pieces in one direction. The fabric will fray very easily and may be inclined to crease if the garment is tightly fitting. Allow for fraying by adding extra seam allowances and use fray-check liquid if necessary. Neaten all raw edges; net is an appropriate binding material. Line with a soft silk or

acetate lining as the metal threads will be scratchy to the skin. Use soft sew-in interfacing, nylon zips. Avoid buttonholes if possible.

Thread
Synthetic.

Needle
Machine: 70 9. Medium stitch.
Hand: 9.

Pressing
Use the tip of a warm iron on the wrong side only.

Care
Dry clean.

See also Lamé Jersey, below.

LAMÉ JERSEY

A knitted fabric, usually acetate, viscose or polyester, with metallic yarn included as an extra thread in the knitting. Usually lightweight and often almost transparent. Very soft and drapes beautifully for evening wear.

Width
150cm (60in).

Handling
Hold the fabric vertically to see which way you prefer to use it. It is a one-way fabric with a light silver or gold (or coloured) effect one way, but when held up the other way less shine will be visible and more of the basic colour. Cut all pieces in one direction. Choose full, gathered styles. Use light sew-in interfacing.

Thread
Synthetic.

Needle
Machine: 80 11. Slight zigzag stitch. Ball point needle may be needed.
Hand: 7.

Pressing
Warm iron, light pressure.

Care
Dry clean.

LAMINATES

Laminates or foam-backed fabrics are constructed of a layer of fabric, usually an inexpensive acrylic jersey, a nylon or acetate jersey backing and, sandwiched between the two, a thin layer of synthetic foam. The layers may be stuck together with adhesive or, more usually, all three are passed through a machine which applies flame to both sides of the foam to melt it. The three layers are then pressed together. The fabrics are not hard-wearing, nor are they very warm but the foam adds body to the fabric. Used for children's clothes, women's jackets and trousers and inexpensive coats.

Width
150cm (60in) or more.

Handling
Slightly springy, but easy to handle and a good fabric for beginners. The fabric is already lined and it does not fray at all. Lends itself to adhesive strip in hems, etc. Use firm interfacing. Choose plain styles without gathers or pleats as the fabric does

not shape to the body. Break up the surface with top stitching.

Thread
Synthetic.

Needle
Machine: 90 14. Large stitch.
Hand: 6.

Pressing
Press with a hot iron and damp cloth on both sides, but with sharp pressure to avoid iron marks. The fabric may well spring up again, but adhesive strip or top stitching can be employed to hold the edges down.

Care
Some laminates are dry cleanable only, and some can only be washed, so be guided by the label.

LAMPAS

 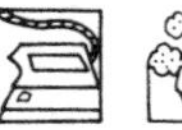 

A fabric similar to brocade, originally an East Indian printed silk, but now a woven fabric with a rep ground and a satin-like pattern formed by the warp yarns. A contrasting effect is achieved, too, with the weft yarns so that the same colour appears in the pattern as in the background. Very elaborate designs are produced. It is a heavy fabric, usually made now of cotton, viscose, acrylic or mixtures.

Used for curtains and furnishings. Allow for shrinkage.

Width
120cm (48in).

Handling
Heavy to handle, match patterns carefully. It will fray readily so all hems must be double and all raw edges neatened. Curtains may be lined, although the wrong side is often attractive enough not to need lining.

Thread
Synthetic.

Needle
Machine: 90 14. Large stitch.
Hand: 6.

Pressing
Medium iron or steam iron. Take care not to flatten the design.

Care
Probably dry clean only, but check the label.

LAPPET
A type of weave in which floating threads are carried on the surface of the fabric and introduced at intervals to form the pattern. The floats are not long and the patterns are usually geometric, i.e. zigzag stripes in white yarn on a coloured plain-weave ground. The technique can also be introduced to form woven spots. In this case, the floating yarns between the spots are cut. Almost any fibre or mixture of fibres can be used.

Handle the fabric according to the weight and the fibre content.

LATEX
This is the raw material from which rubber is made. It is used by various companies, made into stretch yarns with a variety of

names, and incorporated into various fabrics to make corsetry, swimwear, ski-wear, lace and elastic.

LAWN

A very fine smooth fabric. It is lighter in weight than cambric, may be plain or printed, and has a slightly stiff finish which may be permanent. It is a plain-weave fabric made from cotton or linen and is very cool and absorbent and hard-wearing.

Used for baby clothes, blouses, nightwear, underwear. Creases easily.

Width
90–114cm (36–45in).

Handling
Easy to handle but rather fine for beginners. Lends itself to decorative hand work such as smocking. Use fine finishes, French seams, hand-worked hems.

Thread
Mercerized or machine embroidery.

Needle
Machine: 70 9. Small stitch.
Hand: 9.

Pressing
Hot iron.

Care
Hot wash. Boil. Starch. Iron damp with hot iron.

See also Handkerchief Linen, page 167.

LEATHER

The hide or skin of animals. The thickness and type varies according to its source. There is a variety of types and these will be found listed under the appropriate name. Handling is the same for all types of leather.

Width
Leathers are all skin-shaped as they come from the animal, so they vary in size. It may be necessary to take the paper pattern to the supplier and lay it out in order to calculate how many skins are required. Most leathers used for clothes are from sheep and the following is a guide:

Skirt	3 skins
Waistcoat	3–4 skins
Jacket	5–6 skins
Coat	8–9 skins
Trousers (Join at knee)	5–6 skins

Handling
Choose a simple pattern but one with small pieces, i.e. panelled skirt for economy. It is an advantage to choose a pattern that has been used previously and adjusted, as it is not easy to fit leather garments before stitching, and unpicking leaves holes. Cut out with large cutting-out scissors, laying the skins singly right side up, in order to avoid flaws or thin areas of skin. Lay the pattern pieces on the skin and secure with a few pieces of Sellotape. Either chalk round the pattern and cut, or cut beside the paper pattern. Remember to reverse each

pattern piece in order to cut the other piece of the garment. Hold pieces together with paper clips or clothes pegs for fitting—do not tack. Seam edges and hems can be secured with an adhesive such as Copydex, although top stitching looks very effective on leather. Use metal zips or metal capped fasteners. The zip can be secured for stitching with adhesive and Sellotape. Outer garments need lining so that they will slip over other clothes.

Thread
Synthetic or mercerized.

Needle
Machine: 80–90 11–14. Spear point needle. Large stitch. Use roller foot.
Hand: 6–8. Spear point needle, but hand-sewing should be kept to the minimum.

Pressing
Warm iron on wrong side only, no steam. If the iron sticks, cover the leather with a piece of brown paper.

Care
Dry clean. Take a cleaner that specializes in cleaning leather. To improve the appearance between visits to the dry cleaner, leather can be lightly sponged with warm water and a little soap or washing-up liquid. Wipe with a damp cloth and dry off with a soft dry duster.

LEAVERS LACE
A trade name which has developed into a generic term for describing laces made on a Leavers machine. See page 62.

LENO
A type of weave in which one yarn moves alternately from side to side producing a cellular hole. This process can be used to produce a fancy effect or for more practical reasons. For example, the crossed yarn will introduce stability into a fine fabric. Any fibre can be used to make leno weave cloth.

See page 52.

LENO CRÊPON

A fabric comprising a cotton crêpon background cloth with leno-weave style embroidery on the surface. The embroidery may be white or in a contrasting colour and it is usually worked in striped formation.

Used for blouses, shirts, dresses.

Width
114cm (45in).

Handling
Cut pieces all one way if the embroidery is one-way. Choose plain styles as the fabric is fairly elaborate. Use medium-weight interfacing. Embroidery ends will fray so neaten edges.

Thread
Synthetic or mercerized.

Needle
Machine: 80 11. Medium stitch.
Hand: 7.

Pressing
Hot iron and light pressure on wrong side.

Care
Hot wash. Iron slightly damp with hot iron and light pressure.

See also Crêpon, page 136.

LENO VOILE

A plain-weave cotton voile fabric with an open, leno weave stripe in it. A soft drapy fabric.

Used for children's clothes, blouses, nightwear.

Width
114cm (45in).

Handling
Easy to handle, but the stripes are tougher to sew than the voile areas. Use transparent interfacing.

Thread
Synthetic or mercerized.

Needle
Machine: 80 11. Medium stitch.
Hand: 7.

Pressing
Hot iron.

Care
Hot wash. Iron slightly damp with hot iron.

See also Voile, page 247.

LEOPARD
A buff-coloured, short-haired, flat fur, with black rosette markings. Very hard-wearing.

LIBERTY PRINTS
Exclusively designed prints usually incorporating many colours and applied to fine cotton lawn, silk or fine wool challis (Veruna wool), sold by Liberty and Co. of London.

Handle according to weight of fabric and fibre content.

LIBERTY SATIN

Trade name for a very soft piece-dyed satin fabric, with raw silk warp and single spun-silk filling, made by Liberty and Co.

Used for lingerie, robes, dresses, wedding gowns, etc.

Width
90cm (36in) or more.

Handling
Very soft, so it will gather easily into soft drapy styles. Slippery to handle so not a fabric to be used by beginners. Frays readily so neaten all edges. Lends itself to hand-sewing and decorative work.

Thread
Silk.

Needle
Machine: 70 9. Small stitch.
Hand: 9.

Pressing
Warm dry iron on wrong side only.

Care
Dry clean.

LILLE LACE
A very fine textured bobbin lace, with patterns outlined in thicker threads, characterized by a dotted design. It resembles Mechlin Lace.

LIMERICK LACE

An Irish hand- or machine-made lace, in which the patterns are embroidered on to net with a darning stitch. This is a fine lace and not to be confused with Irish Lace. See page 174.

LINEN

A very strong yarn of high lustre made from flax fibres. The resulting fabric is also called linen. The yarn can be used for all types of weave and all weights of fabric from fine lawn to suiting and household furnishings. An expensive but attractive fibre, it mixes very well with other fibres such as cotton and wool. It is often called flax when mixed in small quantities. See also pages 37 and 153.

LINEN CANVAS

Linen Canvas

Tailor's close, even weave, beige coloured canvas of excellent quality. Used in men's coats in conjunction with hair canvas. It is also called Holland or Flax Canvas.

Width

60cm (24in). Dry clean.

Collar Canvas

An open weave, plain dark brown canvas, best made of linen, but sometimes cotton. It is very stiff and is used cut on the cross to interface coat and jacket collars. Does not fray.

Width

38cm (15in). Cut on the cross. Dry clean.
60cm (24in). Cut on the straight. Dry clean.

White Canvas

An open weave, slightly stiff fabric made of cotton or, for better quality, of linen.

Used for white and pale coloured coats and jackets.

Width

114cm (45in). Dry clean.

LINEN-LOOK

Fabrics made to resemble plain weave linen suiting, which were developed when linen became very expensive for dress wear. They have the typical uneven slub yarn and a crisp even finish. Most have a crease-resist or crease-recovery finish applied to them. Fibre content may be 50 per cent cotton with the remainder polyester, or they may be mainly viscose fibre.

Used for shirt-waister dresses, trousers for men and women.

Width

114cm (45in).

Handling

These fabrics fray readily so neaten all edges. They pleat well. Use firm iron-on interfacing. Adhesive strip for hems works very well. Avoid gathers. Use topstitching as decoration.

Thread

Synthetic.

Needle

Machine: 90 14. Medium to large stitch.
Hand: 6.

Pressing
Medium hot iron and damp cloth, or steam iron.

Care
Hot wash, short spin or drip dry. Press with medium iron or steam iron.

LINEN TWILL
As the name implies, a twill weave linen fabric light in weight and used mainly for embroidery.

LINING

A lining fabric may be made from silk, viscose, acetate, triacetate, polyester, cupro. The fabrics suitable for lining are either plain weave, satin or twill and they are usually slippery to enable the garment to be put on and off with ease. The wearing quality varies with the price. An inexpensive acetate satin will wear for only a short time, but a silk or polyester satin or pongee will give long service. Choose the weight of lining to suit the weight of the fabric and choose the quality according to the type of garment and its prospective life. For example, a cheap taffeta can be used to line an evening dress.

Width
90–140cm (36–54in).

Handling
All slippery lining will fray, so do not cut it until ready to use it. Always make the lining slightly bigger than the garment to avoid strain on lining seams and to avoid a pulled appearance on the right side of the garment. If the lining hem is to be sewn to the garment hem, make quite sure the lining is slightly longer to avoid pulling.

Thread
Synthetic.

Needle
Machine: 70–80 9–11. Medium stitch. Edges can be decorated with machine embroidery.
Hand: 8–9.

Pressing
Cool iron and light pressure to avoid imprints of seams.

Care
This will depend on the garment fabric. It is sensible to put a washable lining with washable fabrics, and a dry cleanable lining with dry cleanable fabrics.

LINSEY (1)
A term once used to describe any waste or rags containing wool.

LINSEY (2)
A coarse fabric with a cotton warp and a blended yarn of cotton and waste wool for the weft. The weave is plain twill, usually in stripes across the width.

Used for aprons and overalls. Handle as for Butcher Rayon, see page 115.

LINSEY-WOOLSEY
A fabric no longer made or used; it was a cheap, coarse cloth of wool and cotton or linen.

LIRELLE
Trade name for a polyester fibre developed by Courtaulds for its high degree of wet strength. It is used on its own to make all types of fabric and it also blends well with fibres such as cotton.

LISLE
This fabric, now superseded by finer synthetics, was a knitted material made from mercerized cotton yarns. Originally made in France, it was used in large quantities for women's stockings before the invention of nylon.

LIZARD
A rigid snake skin, not usually available for sewing, except sometimes as a trimming. Mainly used for shoes and handbags.

LLAMA
The hair of the fleece of various animals found in South America. Types of hair include alpaca, vicuna and guanaco. For more information, see under those headings.

LOCK THREAD CANVAS
A lattice-effect embroidery canvas, very rigid and kept flat by warp threads locked round the weft threads to avoid movement.

LODEN CLOTH

From Austria and still associated with the country, this is a heavy cloth woven from the fleeces of mountain sheep. It is soft and thick and characteristically dark green in colour. The fabric is also waterproof, because the rough wool used is oily and coarse and prevents water penetration. Used a great deal in mountainous countries for warmth, and in all countries for coats, capes, duffle coats.

Width
140cm (54in).

Handling
This fabric is thick, but does not fray. Use welt seams and heavy interfacing. If the garment is full there is no need to line it. Keep to plain styles. Use topstitching.

Thread
Synthetic or 30's cotton.

Needle
Machine: 100 16. Large stitch.
Hand: 5–6.

Pressing
Hot iron and damp cloth.

Care
Dry clean.

LONGCLOTH
An old-fashioned term referring to the first fabric to be produced in long lengths and rolled. If this term is used now, it simply means a plain-weave cotton, mainly used for handkerchiefs.

LOUISINE

A plain silk with a glossy texture, and a coarse surface like a very small basket weave. It now often contains synthetic fibres rather than silk.

Used for dresses and coat linings. Hard-wearing.

Width
90–114cm (36–45in).

Handling
Frays easily, so even raw edges of lining seams must be neatened.

Thread
Synthetic.

Needle
Machine: 90 14. Medium stitch.
Hand: 7.

Pressing
Warm iron, no moisture.

Care
Dry clean unless labelled washable.

LOVAT
Although this really describes a colour, it is often used for woollen overcoating of good quality in typical lovat colour, which is greeny-grey.

LUREX
Trade name for a United States metallic yarn, produced in various colours by coating thin sheets of aluminium on both sides, using a thermoplastic resin. The yarn is slippery and breaks easily but will not tarnish. It can be incorporated into a variety of woven and knitted fabrics; it is used for embroidering fabrics and it is also made into a sewing thread.

LYNX
Silky, soft long fur of the wild cat; colours vary from fawn to grey.

LYONS VELVET
A fine quality thick velvet with a stiff, erect, high pile. The backing may be visible through the pile but it is a good quality fabric. The backing is made from silk or sometimes linen, viscose or cotton. The pile is silk.

M

MACCLESFIELD SILK

A high-textured, hard-wearing spun silk. The silk yarn is twisted to give a crêpy texture, and it is traditionally striped or small-patterned.

Used for men's ties and women's classic shirts.

Width
90cm (36in) or less.

Handling
It will fray. Fairly crisp so choose plain styles. Use medium interfacing. If making ties, cut on the bias and interface with tie interfacing, sew by hand and line ends with firm silk or satin. Avoid top-stitching.

Thread
Silk.

Needle
Machine: 80 11. Medium stitch.
Hand: 8.

Pressing
Warm iron on wrong side only.

Care
Dry clean.

MACKINAW

Sometimes called Mackinac, this is a heavy woollen fabric, heavily felted and napped on both sides, so that no weave is apparent on the surface. The construction is similar to Melton, except that Mackinaw is often woven in large checks and in coarser woollen yarns. Used in cold climates for blankets, cloaks, lumber jackets. In addition to cheaper woollen yarn, other fibres such as cotton and waste yarns may be included.

Width
140cm (54in) or more.

Handling
Thick but easy to handle as it does not fray. Not often lined unless fleece is used for extra warmth. Use topstitching, heavy interfacing, heavy metal zips. Knitted or fur cuffs, collars, etc., may be added.

Thread
Synthetic.

Needle
Machine: 100 16. Large stitch.
Hand: 6.

Pressing
Hot iron and damp cloth.

Care
Dry clean.

MACKINTOSH

A waterproof coating no longer in use, which was named after its inventor. It was rubber on cotton with an adhesive to join the two. The rubber perished in a short time and the fabric could not 'breathe' and so caused condensation.

Now the name mackintosh has become generic to a waterproof coat, whatever the fabric.

MACRAMÉ LACE
A revived craft with modern application, this was originally a Spanish knotted lace in geometric patterns, often with fringed ends. Any thread, yarn, wool or string may be used to produce fine or coarse designs. The threads are anchored to a board which may have a paper pattern on it. Motifs may be made or complete items such as mats, bags etc.

MADRAS COTTON
A soft cotton, rather like gingham, but including more colours. It is often rough and unfinished and colours bleed when washed. It is also inclined to fade.

Handling
See Gingham, page 160.

MADRAS MUSLIN

Imported from the Far East, this has a fine and open gauze foundation of cotton, with figured textures and design in thick, soft spun, weft threads. In better quality fabric, two or more different colours are introduced.

An inexpensive fabric, used for *saris*, blouses, nightwear. Creases easily. Often in border designs.

Width
114cm (45in) or more.

Handling
Soft and easy to sew but the open weave of the base fabric tends to move in cutting. Gathers and drapes well in full styles.

Thread
Machine: 80 11. Small stitch.
Hand: 8.

Pressing
Medium hot iron.

Care
Warm wash. Iron with medium hot iron when slightly damp.

MADRAS SHIRTING

A fine, lightweight, often colourful, cotton material of better quality than Madras Cotton. The fabric is plain with woven stripes in satin weave, which may be in another fibre such as viscose, or in an expensive fabric, like silk.

Used for men's shirts, women's dresses. Often a one-way stripe.

Width
114cm (45in).

Handling
Easy to sew as it is soft and manageable, but fairly expensive so not a good choice for beginners. Also its design demands classic collars, etc., which are difficult to handle. If stripes are used horizontally they must be matched. Use firm iron-on interfacing and metal or nylon zips.

Thread
Synthetic or mercerized.

Needle
Machine: 80 11. Medium stitch.
Hand: 7.

Pressing
Hot iron or steam iron.

Care
Hot wash. Iron damp with a hot iron.

MALABAR

An East Indian cotton fabric made in very bright colours, used almost entirely in the manufacture of handkerchiefs. It creases easily.

Handle as for Cotton Lawn. See page 183.

MALIMO

A type of fabric constructed and made in East Germany and produced at a great speed using three sets of yarns: warp yarns, filling yarns laid across the warp and a third system which stitches them together. Technically this fabric is neither woven nor knitted. It is very stable, and does not move or 'give'. It is often ribbed in appearance. It is mainly acrylic but other fibre may be used.

Used for curtains, tablecloths for indoors and out, bedspreads, chair covers. As yet, it is not attractive as a dress fabric.

Width
150cm (60in) or more.

Handling
Easy to sew. Does not fray at all. Inclined to 'pill' if subjected to constant wear.

Thread
Synthetic.

Needle
Machine: 90 14, or ball point. Large stitch.
Hand: 6.

Pressing
Warm iron.

Care
Hot wash. Little ironing needed.

Also known as Stitch Bonded Fabric (see page 233).

MALINES
One of the very oldest types of fabric. The term is used to describe a variety of fine diaphanous silk, lace and net fabrics.

MALTESE LACE
Similar in appearance to Cluny Lace, Maltese Lace is heavy and often incorporates regular wheel designs and squares. Used mainly in small areas such as corners of handkerchiefs and table linen.

MARABOUT
A delicate thin silk fabric made from twisted raw silk.

Used for blouses, linings and lampshades. Handle as Jap Silk, page 175.

MARBLE SILK
A soft lightweight silk fabric with a mottled appearance. This effect may be achieved by the use of multi-coloured yarns or by warp printing.

Used for blouses, as a lining fabric, and for lampshades. Handle as Jap Silk, page 175.

MARCELINE
(Also Merceline). A light, thin silk fabric that is almost transparent.

Used for lining hats and lightweight clothes. Handle as Jap Silk, page 175.

MARLED YARN
Two different coloured threads are woven together, not necessarily in equal quantities, to form a marled yarn.

MARMOT
A cheap fur from a small rodent. It is not used in its original state, but dyed to imitate more expensive furs, such as mink.

MARQUISETTE
 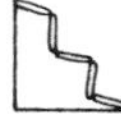  

An open, loose fabric woven in a leno construction, sometimes with spots or other designs included. It can be made from cotton, silk or wool, but is now mainly glass-fibre nylon or polyester and made as a curtain fabric.

Width
120cm (48in).

Handling
Cut exactly on the grain. This is easy to do by following the squares of the weave. Does not fray but ends of yarn will be left protruding. Not really suitable for hand-sewing. Allow for shrinkage.

Thread
Synthetic. See also Woven Interfacing, page 251.

Needle
Machine: 90 14. Large straight or zigzag stitch.
Hand: 7.

Pressing
Set iron according to fibre content.

Care
Hot wash, machine or hand. Short spin and press with warm iron or drip dry. If nylon becomes yellow it may be restored with a whitening agent. Cotton Marquisette may be starched.

MATELASSÉ
A pouching or quilted effect fabric — the word means 'quilted' in French. It is a double or compound cloth. In one type, the cloth consists of warp and weft with an extra weft, used as padding and held in place by an extra stitching warp. The raised effect is achieved by the weaves. The back of the cloth is a fine, loosely woven web of warp and weft interlacing. The fabric is often made on a dobby or Jacquard loom.

The fibres used may be silk, viscose, acetate, nylon, polyester or combinations. The fabric may also contain metallic threads. These are dress fabrics. Others may be made from cotton yarn and used for curtains and bedspreads.

Dress Fabrics

Width
90–114cm (36–45in).

Handling
The designs are usually elaborate and the fabric may be fairly stiff so keep to simple styles, avoiding soft finishes such as gathers. The floating yarns on the wrong side will easily catch and tear so line all garments. Neaten edges. Use fray check. Use firm sew-in interfacing.

Thread
Synthetic.

Needle
Machine: 80 11. Medium stitch.
Hand: 7.

Pressing
Warm iron on wrong side only and light pressure to avoid crushing the surface.

Care
Probably dry clean only.

Furnishing Fabrics

Width
120cm (48in).

Handling
Easy to sew, but usually heavy in weight and thick to sew. All hems to be double and machined. Line curtains at the wrong side, floats may catch when handled. Allow for shrinkage.

Thread
Synthetic or mercerized.

Needle
Machine: 90 14. Large stitch.
Hand: 6.

Pressing
Hot iron, light pressure.

Care
Hot wash. Iron with hot iron but not too heavy pressure.

MATT JERSEY
A jersey fabric of almost any weight with a dull surface due to the fact that it is knitted from crêpe yarns.

Handle according to weight and fibre content.

MAUD
This term has now fallen into disuse, but it used to describe checked woollen travelling rugs woven in different shades of grey.

MECHLIN LACE
A soft, filmy lace in which even the denser decoration is filmy. Often used for bridal veils.

MEDALLION LACE
Motifs are made or cut from a piece of heavy lace and inserted into cloth. Used in lingerie, table linen.

MEISEN
A plain-weave, lightweight Japanese Silk, with a blurred pattern achieved by colouring the yarns before weaving them.

Used for blouses, dresses. Handle as Silk Shantung, page 231.

MELTON

A firm medium-weight wool cloth in a close plain weave, with a felted nap but not a one-way nap. It is dull in appearance and comes in white and all men's suiting colours.

It used to be a coating fabric, but it is now mainly used as an aid to tailoring. Because it does not fray, it is useful for backing collars, as the raw edges can be used to reduce bulk.

Width
90cm (36in) or narrow.

Handling
Cut on the cross the same size as the collar canvas. Baste the two fabrics together and pad stitch. Press and shape with hot iron; the melton, like all good wool, will take on its new shape.

Thread
Synthetic or mercerized.

Needle
Machine: 100 16. Not much machining needed. Large stitch.
Hand: 7.

Pressing
Hot iron and damp cloth.

Care
Dry clean.

MERCERIZED
A finish, involving caustic soda, which is applied to cotton yarn to soften it and increase its lustre. Mercerized yarns are used for many cotton fabrics and sewing threads.

See also page 71.

MERINO
A type of sheep which provides the finest grade, soft, expensive wool fleece. The wool is used in good quality cloth, blankets, etc., often in small quantities with

other wool to reduce the price. The word Merino is now also used for a good quality woollen cloth. It is not possible to give handling instructions, as the variety of so-called Merino cloth is so wide.

MESSALINE

 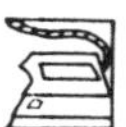 

Messalina, wife of Emperor Claudius, wore a great deal of plain soft silk and this type of fabric was named after her. It is a lustrous, soft silky fabric in a satin weave, usually in plain colours. It may now be polyester, acetate, triacetate as well as silk fibre. This is an expensive silk, which drapes well, and is perfect in black for special occasion dresses.

Width
114cm (45in).

Handling
It frays easily as it is a satin weave. Choose full, soft styles and use gathers, bindings, etc. Avoid buttonholes and topstitching. Use soft sew-in interfacing and nylon zips sewn in by hand. Neaten all edges. Lining is an asset.

Thread
Synthetic.

Needle
Machine: 70 9. Small stitch.
Hand: 9.

Pressing
Warm iron on the wrong side.

Care
Dry clean.

METAL EMBROIDERED LACE
A lace fabric as base, usually of viscose, with embroidery worked in nylon and metal yarns.

METAL THREAD FABRICS
There are a few fabrics, for example silk from the East, which have real silver or gold threads woven into them. The problem with these is that the thread tarnishes. Keep the fabric or garment in tissue paper to slow this process down. No moisture should be used (for example a steam iron) as this will also tarnish the metal thread.

See also Lamé, page 180; Lamé Jersey, page 181.

MIGNONETTE
A knitted silk or viscose fabric used for underwear. It is finer than Tricot but handle in the same way, see page 241.

MILAN POINT
A needlepoint tape lace with a picot edge. Once hand-made, but the simplicity of the design is easy to imitate by machine.

MILIUM

The trade name for a fabric which is insulated by applying aluminium flakes to its back. The fibre of the fabric may be cotton, acetate, viscose, nylon polyester. The insulation keeps out cold in winter and heat in summer. It was once a common coat lining, but, possibly because the seams pull and split easily under pressure, it is now mainly confined to curtain lining.

Width
120cm (48in).

Handling
This fabric quickly blunts scissors. It frays a little. Make up by placing Milium with the metal side against the wrong side curtain. Very stiff to handle.

Thread
Synthetic.

Needle
Machine: 80 11. Large stitch. Can be zigzag for hems.
Hand: 6.

Pressing
Warm iron on both sides.

Care
Follow care instructions on label.

MINK
A very distinctive long pale brown fur from an animal which can be ranch bred or wild. There are also Chinese Mink or Kolinsky Mink, a creamy beige fur which is often dyed; Jap Mink, which is yellow; and Mutation Mink, which is of unusual colourings, e.g. silvery blue and black. Mink is luxurious, but it is also hard-wearing. It is often used for hats.

MIRALENE
Polyester fibre, crinkle or bouclé type yarn based on Terylene.

MIRALON
The name given to a bulking process which can be applied to nylon yarn. The bulking makes the fibre warmer, as air is introduced, and also softer to feel.

MIRROR VELVET
Velvet produced in the normal way, but with a pattern made by pressing the pile flat in different directions and giving a shimmery or mirror effect.

MISTRAL
The name given to a crêpe-effect worsted cloth. Twisted warp and weft yarns are used.

Handle as Crêpe, page 135.

MOCHA LEATHER
Fine, soft sheepskin leather from Africa and the Middle East. If available, it is easy to sew.

MOGADOR
This was the name of the silk used for men's cravats, but it is now used for an acetate fabric resembling faille. It is still mainly used for men's ties.

For handling, see Faille, page 151.

MOHAIR
A white hair up to 10in long, from the angora goat (found in Turkey, South Africa and U.S.A.). Unlike sheep's wool, it is not curly. It is stronger than wool and produces hard-wearing fabrics; it dyes well and has an attractive lustre; but it is very expensive and is difficult to spin. The hair can be used for knitting yarn, and can be mixed

with other fibres to make warm, lightweight fabrics.

MOHAIR SUITING

Mohair can be combined with worsted yarn, or woven alone, to produce a very lightweight shiny, attractive suiting.

Used for lightweight men's suits, dinner jackets, etc.

Width

140cm (54in).

Handling

See Worsted, page 251.

MOHAIR/WOOL

A thick, spongy open fabric, in plain weave, with a very hairy texture. Its composition is usually 70 per cent mohair and 30 per cent wool. It is very bulky and can be used for warm, lightweight lined coats, but is best for simple wrap-over jackets, sleeveless waistcoats, etc., which are unlined, and is excellent for shawls and stoles.

Width

125–150cm (50–60in).

Handling

This is often too thick to fold double, so cut with the fabric single, reversing pattern for the second piece. Very thick to sew by hand. Use plastic-headed pins that will be easily visible. Reduce bulk where possible by using top stitching on edges, etc. It is soft and may 'seat', so line coats. It fringes easily at hems of jackets, shawls, etc.

Thread

Synthetic.

Needle

Machine: 90 14. Large stitch. Use quilting foot with short toes to prevent it being caught in the fabric.
Hand: 7.

Pressing

Medium hot iron and damp muslin. Hold iron above fabric, not on it.

Care

Dry clean.

MOIRÉ

A finish with a wavy, watermark effect that can be applied to a variety of fabrics of almost any fibre, but is most used on silk, acetate, triacetate. The fabric is passed through engraved cylinders which press the watermark on to the fabric. The finish is not necessarily permanent.

Handle the fabric according to weight and fibre content.

The word 'Moreen' is also sometimes used to describe the watermark effect, particularly on cotton fabric.

MOIRÉ TAFFETA

Taffeta weave fabric made from silk or synthetic fibres and then embossed with a moiré pattern. The embossing may or may not be permanent depending on the fibre and the processing.

See Taffeta, page 236 and Moiré, above.

MOLESKIN

A strong, fine cotton fabric lightly napped and sheared on the wrong side. Once only a cloth for protective clothing, particularly dungarees and trousers, because of its durability and additional warmth on the inside, but other fibres such as worsted may be used to produce good quality cloth for men's suits, and it is also made as a lining fabric.

The term now refers to any cloth with a short mole-like nap. Handle according to weight and fibre content, for example, handle cotton moleskin like denim; handle suiting like worsted.

MONKEY FUR

A long-haired fur used in small amounts mainly as trimming. It can be cut and made into fur fringe.

MOQUETTE

One of the best known and hardest wearing furnishing fabrics, used for covering chairs, upholstery, curtains, tablecloths, etc., and probably the most popular until the advent of the more luxurious Dralon velvet.

Moquette can be made in three types, one with cut pile, another uncut, and one combining both cut and uncut. The pile is worsted, mohair or nylon, the backing wool or cotton. Its great advantage is that, although a pile cloth, it does not become flattened by pressure, e.g. sitting on it.

Width

120cm (48in) or more.

Handling

Very tough and heavy; pile will shed from cut edges while sewing on it.

Thread

Synthetic.

Needle

Machine: 100–110 16–18. Large stitch.
Hand: 4–5.

Pressing

Warm iron and light pressure on wrong side.

Care

Dry clean.

MOROCCO LEATHER

The term now refers to leather that has been tanned chemically, although it once referred to leather only from Morocco.

MOSS CRÊPE

(Or Sand Crêpe.) A combination of crêpe yarn and crêpe weave, made in acetate, cotton, wool, polyester or viscose.

MOUFFLIN

A double-faced thick coating fabric which is soft and has an open, airy surface. The yarns used are mainly wool, or wool mixed with acrylic or mohair.

Used for coats and capes. If loose styles are chosen they may not require lining.

If the fabric is very light and airy, handle as Mohair Wool, page 197. If it is dense and firm, handle as Camel Hair, page 118

MOUSSELINE

The French word literally means muslin, but we use it to describe a better quality wool or silk fabric of this nature.

When made from silk, Mousseline is firmer than chiffon, and is cool and comfortable, but it does not wear well as laundering spoils it and dry cleaning is not always satisfactory. Used for evening dresses. Handle as for any chiffon.

Wool Mousseline is made from worsted yarn into a plain or printed lightweight wool. Excellent for dresses. Handle as for Challis, page 122.

Cotton Mousseline — see Butter Muslin, page 116.

MUGA SILK

Also called Assam Silk. It is obtained from a species of Indian moth, and is a wild silk producing a rough surfaced lightweight fabric.

Handle as Pongee, page 213.

MULL

A type of lightweight cotton voile which was once a dress fabric but is now almost entirely confined to use as an underlining fabric, and for experimenting in draping styles, e.g. toiles. It is also used for Eastern turbans. Lawn, voile and cambric give better service in wear as dresses and shirts, but if sewing on mull, handle as for Cotton Voile, page 247.

MUMMY CANVAS

Similar to Mummy Cloth (below), but with a coarse mesh and an irregular, rather than crêpy, surface. Used for embroidery.

MUMMY CLOTH

Also called Granite Cloth and Momie Cloth.

A fabric with a crinkled surface like crêpe, but made with non-crêpe yarns and woven on a dobby loom. It can be bleached, dyed or printed. The fibres include silk warp and woollen filling or cotton with silk. The fabric lacks lustre, and has been a traditional mourning fabric, but is not much used now.

The name is also used for the fine linen fabric used in Ancient Egypt for wrapping mummies.

MUNGO (1)

Also called Shoddy.

A cheap, poor quality wool cloth made from mill wastes. Because of this the fibre staple is short and it does not wear well. Colours are often poor and drab. It should not be used for clothes, but may be used for some types of stage costume.

MUNGO (2)

Waste yarn from woollen mills which is mixed with other yarn, such as cotton, to produce cheap cloth for specialist use such as backing fabric.

MUSQUASH

The coat of the musk-rat. It is a long, downy, grey fur with darker brown, but is often dyed to various colours, including pale honey.

N

NACRÉ VELVET
A velvet in which the backing is woven in a different colour from the pile, giving an interesting, changeable appearance in wear.

NAINSOOK
A soft, fine, light cotton fabric, in plain weave, often mercerized, similar to Batiste in the piece.

Mainly used as ready-to-apply soft cotton bias binding.

If making garments, handle as Batiste, see page 101.

NAPPA LEATHER
This is the skin of sheep or goats that has been tanned by a Californian process using oil.

NARROW FABRICS
See page 55.

NEEDLECORD
A dress fabric, usually cotton, with very fine cords the length of the fabric, and very short pile. It may be printed or plain, and is hard-wearing and usually washable, with one way pile.

Handle as for Corduroy, see page 130.

NEEDLEPOINT
This was originally a type of fine drawn thread work, but it has developed into a craft in which satin stitch and buttonhole stitch are worked over a basic thread.

NET

A transparent fabric that is neither woven nor knitted, but rather the yarns are knotted to form a mesh. Net may be made from cotton, viscose, nylon, polyester and other fibres, according to its ultimate use. Made in varying sizes of mesh and used for curtains, dance dresses, veiling and trimmings.

Width
90–150cm (36–60in).

Handling
There is no grain on net but it tends to 'give' under strain in any direction. It is therefore usually draped and full and not tightly pulled. Bodices and sleeves of dresses that are to be fitted tightly must be mounted on to a firmer backing. Net will not fray when cut and need not have the raw edges neatened, nor need hems necessarily be turned. If edges need finishing for effect, then binding with satin is effective.

Thread
Synthetic.

Needle
Machine: 80 11. Medium slight zigzag stitch.
Hand: 7.

Pressing
Warm to medium iron, depending upon the fibre.

Care
Most net will be labelled dry clean only, especially if the stiffening is not permanent.

NINON

A fabric sometimes called triple voile, which is plain weave and sheer. It is usually viscose or acetate but may be polyester. Because of the similarity of its name to the word 'nylon', it is often confused with it.

Used mainly for sheer curtains.

Width
120cm (48in) or more.

Handling
It is fairly slippery, so cut carefully on the straight grain. It frays easily, so all hems should be double.

Thread
Synthetic.

Needle
Machine: 80 11. Medium straight or zigzag stitch.
Hand: 7.

Pressing
Warm iron.

Care
Hot wash. Drip dry, do not spin. Iron slightly damp.

NON-WOVEN FABRIC
Any manufactured sheet or web of random fibre held together by physical or chemical means or both. Excluded from this definition are woven, knitted, stitch-bonded, felt and paper fabrics.

See also page 58.

NOTTINGHAM LACE
The term is often used to describe a flat, coarse lace used for curtains, bedspreads and tablecloths, but Nottingham is the home of the machine-lace industry, so the word is also used to describe any lace made on a Nottingham-type machine.

NOVELTY TWEED
A description indicating that the cloth is tweed-like, but that it is not one of the conventional tweeds that are easy to recognize. Usually a cloth with some decoration or distinguishing feature.

Handle as Harris Tweed, pages 167 and 168.

NUB YARN
An irregular thread containing small spots or nubs, very similar to Slub but the irregularities are definitely nubs.

NUN'S VEILING

A fine, lightweight plain-weave, plain coloured, worsted or silk fabric, which is very soft and thin. It is now used for dresses, but was at one time used only for religious gowns. Originally dyed only black, brown and grey, but as a dress fabric it is produced in fashion colours.

Used for dresses, blouses, nightwear.

Width
90–114cm (36–45in).

Handling
A soft, attractive fabric that drapes and gathers well and is warm. Tends to fray. Use fine processes such as French seams. Use lightweight interfacing.

Thread
Synthetic or mercerized.

Needle
Machine: 80 11. Small to medium stitch.
Hand: 7.

Pressing
Steam iron or medium hot iron and damp muslin, light pressure.

Care
Hand wash in warm water. Press with steam iron or iron slightly damp.

NUTRIA FUR
This comes from a small South American animal and is similar to beaver.

NYLON
The accepted name for polyamide fibre which is produced from mineral sources. Although resistant to most chemicals, nylon is damaged by strong oxidizing bleaches and concentrated acids; it is easy to dye and is colour fast; melts at a low temperature but does not catch light. Nylon fibre is non-absorbent, hard-wearing and blends well with most other fibres.

See also page 39.

NYLON JERSEY
Similar to Tricot but heavier. A very useful lining and mounting fabric. Although in many other linings polyester fibre has superseded nylon, this is not the case with nylon jersey. It is hard-wearing and has a limited amount of 'give' which will prevent the outer fabric from losing its shape. Nylon jersey may be anti-static.

For handling, see Tricot, page 241.

O

OATMEAL CLOTH
An old-fashioned term which was used to describe any fabric, usually wool, that had a coloured, pebbled effect resembling oatmeal.

OCELOT
This is a fairly coarse textured thin fur, but it is very hard-wearing. Like leopard, it has spots, but they are more oval in shape.

OILCLOTH

One of the early waterproof fabrics, this was a material, usually cotton, treated with linseed oil varnish to give it a shiny effect. It was mainly used as table and shelf covering, before laminated plastics appeared, and for bags and raincoats. The surface wore off easily and it was inclined to tear.

Oiled Silk was another fabric produced in a similar manner and used for rainwear and as waterproof covers for dressing wounds.

Oilcloth has been completely superseded by modern coated fabrics, see pages 73, 228 and 229.

OILSKIN
Fabric of practically any natural or synthetic fibre that has been treated with linseed oil varnish.

Used for protective clothing but not readily available as piece goods fabric.

OMBRÉ

The French word for 'shaded', used to describe any fabric in which the colour shades gradually from light to dark; sometimes a striped effect is achieved, sometimes an attractive all-over shading. Fabric printed in this way may be of any type or fibre. Handle according to the weight of the fabric and the fibre content.

ONDULE

This is similar in appearance to Ombré and also of French derivation, but close examination reveals that the cloth is woven in wavy stripes, achieved by groups of warp threads being forced from side to side. The process is often used in curtain and furnishing fabrics of all fibres. Handle according to the weight and fibre content.

ORGANDIE

The sheerest cotton fabric made of very fine 100 per cent cotton yarn. It is usually Swiss made, and its crisp finish is due to the application of an acid process — when purchasing, it is as well to enquire whether this finish is permanent.

Organdie creases very easily and is mainly used in small areas, such as collars, cuffs, bows, sashes and cummerbunds, rather than for complete garments. It can be used as an interfacing fabric in lightweight garments and also as a mounting material. It is sometimes used for hats.

Width

90cm (36in) or more.

Handling

Very springy and inclined to bubble and lose its shape under pressure. Easier to handle once it is attached to another fabric or when used double, as in cuffs. Does not fray.

Thread

Synthetic or mercerized.

Needle

Machine: 80 11. Small to medium stitch.
Hand: 8.

Pressing

Hot iron.

Care

Hot hand wash, do not squeeze too much. Roll in a towel to remove excess water, pull to shape and leave to dry. Iron damp with a hot iron. May be starched if not permanently stiffened.

ORGANZA

Similar in appearance to Organdie, but made from silk viscose or polyester fibre. It is fine, stiff and wiry and creases very easily.

Used for evening wear and trimming and may also be used as interfacing in fine fabrics.

Width

90–114cm (36–45in).

Handling
Very wiry and springy and difficult to control. It tends to curl up when cut or pressed. Does not fray. Trim all raw edges very narrowly, and keep hems narrow and neat as double layers show through to the right side. Avoid topstitching as this also causes the fabric to curl.

Thread
Synthetic.

Needle
Machine: 70 9. Small stitch.
Hand: 9.

Pressing
Warm iron.

Care
Viscose Organza is hand washable, press slightly damp with warm to medium iron. Polyester Organza, dry clean only. Silk Organza is hand washable unless labelled dry clean.

ORLON
One of the first acrylic fibres made by du Pont. It melts at high heat, but does not catch light. It is warm and absorbent, blends very well with wool and other fibres, and is used extensively in knitwear and dress fabrics. Some 100 per cent Orlon fabric tends to lose its shape in wear.

See also pages 35 and 93.

OSNABURG
A traditional coarse cotton cloth, woven with uneven yarns and often incorporating cotton waste. It is plain weave, resembles crash in appearance and is the basic fabric from which Cretonne may be made.

For handling see Cretonne, page 136.

OTTOMAN

A heavy fabric with broad, flat crosswise ribs of even size. Some Ottomans have small ribs, and Ottoman cord has alternating wide and narrow ribs.

The basic yarn used may be silk or wool, but is now more likely to be acetate, viscose, triacetate or cotton. The weft cords are usually cotton yarn covered by the warp yarns. It is a stiff, unyielding fabric.

Used for plain dresses, coats and curtains. It creases easily across the width of the fabric so garments should not be tight fitting.

Width
114–120cm (45–48in).

Handling
When cutting, the cotton cord may tend to pull out easily, so take care with garment pieces. Fabric in the silky yarns will fray. Avoid gathers and soft finishes. The fabric weight varies so use suitable interfacing.

Thread
Synthetic.

Needle
Machine: 80–90 11–14. Medium to large stitch.
Hand: 6.

Pressing
Light pressure to avoid flattening ribs. Set iron according to fibre content. Steam iron is suitable.

Care
Cotton and viscose Ottomans will be machine washable, but others may be labelled dry clean only.

OUTING CLOTH

An old-fashioned term which was used to describe a variety of flannel-type woollen fabrics. They are plain or striped and often used for blazers, cricket trousers, etc.

Handle as for Flannel, see page 152.

OXFORD CLOTH

A cotton viscose or modal mixture cloth, usually in basket weave and often with a white filling yarn. It is an inexpensive fabric, more expensive if mercerized cotton is used.

Mainly used for shirts, light suits, dresses. Not a sensible choice for children's clothes as it is soft and readily absorbs dirt, and is not particularly hard-wearing.

Width
90–114cm (36–45in).

Handling
A soft, easy fabric to handle; a good choice for beginners, but it tends to fray readily. Keep to classic styles. Use medium iron-on interfacing, machine-made buttonholes. Neaten all edges. Use machine fell seams and top-stitching.

Thread
Synthetic or mercerized.

Needle
Machine: 80 11. Medium stitch.
Hand: 7.

Pressing
Hot iron or steam iron.

Care
Hot wash frequently by hand or machine. Iron slightly damp with a hot iron.

P

PADDOCK

Commonly seen at race meetings, Paddock is really only a term describing a worsted cloth which resembles gabardine in weight and moisture repellancy.

Handle as for Gabardine, see page 158.

PAISLEY
A fine fabric always with scroll designs. Originally only from Scotland, 'a paisley' meant a shawl made in fine soft woollen yarn, with a woven pattern. The original designs were derived from Indian patterns. Real Paisley Cloth is very expensive, but anything of any fibre or mixture printed with the traditional elaborate multi-coloured scrolls is described as paisley design. Handle

according to weight and fibre content. Most Paisley fabrics will be of dress weight.

PANAMA

A very lightweight cloth used for men's summer and tropical wear and women's dresses. The yarns used are cotton and worsted in the traditional Panama Cloth, although other fibres such as polyester and viscose are sometimes used. The cloth has a recognizable square-weave effect, and is usually in plain colours.

Width
114cm (45in).

Handling
A crisp fabric for tailored clothes. Use medium-weight interfacing. Fabric frays easily and creases readily.

Thread
Synthetic.

Needle
Machine: 90 14. Medium to large stitch.
Hand: 6.

Pressing
Medium hot iron and damp cloth on worsted; steam iron, or cooler iron with cloth, on synthetic. Press firmly.

Care
Dress fabrics will be washable by hand or machine. Iron slightly damp. Suiting will probably dry clean only.

PANNE VELVET

Usually nylon jersey-backed velvet, in triacetate yarn with nylon, with the short pile pressed flat in one direction, so producing a very shiny fabric. It may be plain or printed, and is soft and drapes well.

PAPER TAFFETA
A fine-weave, lightweight taffeta which has been treated to make it crisper than usual. The crispness is usually a permanent finish.

PARAGUAY LACE
Single threads are used to produce spider's web effects, which are then woven together.

PATENT LEATHER
A varnished leather that is very expensive. Used mainly for shoes and handbags, and not available for sewing.

PEAU DE CYGNE

As the name implies, a very soft satin, woven in fine soft yarns with a lustrous finish. Used mainly for expensive lingerie.

See Satin, page 223.

PEAU DE SOIE

Originally made from silk, the term is now also used to describe fabrics made from synthetic fibres, such as polyester and acetate, that have the typical look of Peau de Soie. It is a satin weave with matt finish on both sides, and is usually a firm, heavy fabric in plain colours.

Used for formal dresses.

Width
90cm (36in) if silk;
114cm (45in) if synthetic.

Handling
Fabric tends to fray readily and marks easily, so take care when sewing. Avoid pleats. Use gathers only if fabric is soft. Use firm sew-in interfacing, nylon or concealed zips. Cut seams on the bias where possible as they may wrinkle.

Thread
Synthetic.

Needle
Machine: 80 11. Medium stitch.
Hand: 8.

Pressing
Warm iron on wrong side only.

Care
Probably dry clean only.

PECCARY LEATHER
A lightweight pigskin leather, not normally available for sewing. Used for gloves.

PERCALE

Close plain-weave cotton fabric with firm smooth surface and compact texture, plain or printed. It is sometimes called Broadcloth, especially in the United States. It is similar in weight to poplin, is hard-wearing and launders well.

Used for blouses, shirts, children's clothes, sheets and duvet covers.

Width
90–220cm (36in–2½yds).

Handling
Frays little and is easy to handle.

Thread
Synthetic or mercerized.

Needle
Machine: 90 14. Medium stitch.
Hand: 6.

Pressing
Hot iron.

Care
Hot machine or hand wash. May be boiled. Iron slightly damp with hot iron.

PERCALINE
Lightweight cotton print cloth similar to lawn, with a bright soft finish. Usually the yarn is mercerized.

Used for lining fur garments. For handling, see Percale, above.

PERLON
The polyamide fibre produced in Germany. It has the same properties as nylon. See also page 39.

PERMANENT PLEATING

There is a wide variety of permanently pleated fabric available. It is usually knife pleated —

narrow pleats on fine fabric, wider ones on thicker fabrics. The fabric may be of almost any weave, including knit, and may be closely woven or have a lacy pattern. If the fibre is synthetic the pleating will be permanent and therefore probably washable, but if natural fibres are included the pleating cannot be heat set and is therefore not permanent. Many fabrics are sold in matching colours, one plain cloth the other pleated so that garments combining both can be made. The fabrics vary from chiffon and georgette, to fine knits and quite heavy skirt and dress fabrics.

If you are adapting a pattern, work out carefully how much pleating you will need. Some of it is sold flat with the pleats removed, some is sold with a paper backing and measured with the pleats folded. It is all fairly expensive, so it is worth working out the cost of each method of measuring before buying.

Handle the pleating according to the weight and fibre of the fabric. Press according to the fibre but use only the toe of the iron to avoid spoiling the surrounding pleats.

PETERSHAM (1)

Narrow and ribbed belting used for tops of skirts, stiffening waistbands, etc. It is in plain weave; the warp is fine and a thick weft gives a warp rib structure. In various widths, from about 2–5cm ($\frac{3}{4}$–2in). It may be cotton, viscose or polyester. Some Petershams may shrink. Some have bones or elastic inserted.

PETERSHAM (2)

Originally a thick napped overcoating fabric associated with Lord Petersham, but rarely found now.

PICOLAY

Compact cotton fabric with a plain weave, embossed with a diamond pattern to resemble diamond piqué.

Used for children's clothes, tablecloths.

Width

90cm (36in).

Handling

Handle as for Cotton Piqué, page 210.

Thread

Synthetic or mercerized.

Needle

Machine: 70 9. Small stitch.
Hand: 7–8.

Care

Hot wash. Drip dry. Do not iron or iron lightly to preserve the embossed effect.

PICOT

The term used to describe a loop edge. This may be found on many types of lace and edging.

PIGMENT TAFFETA

The only taffeta fabric without shine. Dull pigmented yarns lacking lustre are used, but the fibres are usually silk or man-made.

See Taffeta, page 236.

PIGSKIN

This is easily recognized by the little holes or pores where once the bristles of the pig grew. Very hard-wearing.

Used for gloves, coats, belts, handbags. Available in skins for sewing.

PILE FABRIC

Any cloth of any fibre that has a raised surface of individual fibres, making a furry surface. Pile may be uncut in manufacture, e.g. Terry Towelling, or cut, e.g. Velour. The direction of the pile on the cloth may be felt or it can sometimes be observed by holding the length of cloth vertically. Where the pile is running upwards, the cloth will look a different shade from where it is running downwards. The cloth can be made with the pile in either direction but all pattern pieces must be cut lying in the same direction.

For handling, see individual fabric names.

PILE KNIT

Any fabric with a knitted construction as the base and a looped or cut pile on the surface. Examples are Stretch Towelling, Jersey Velour.

PIN CHECK

Worsted suiting made with different coloured yarns, which produce a figured effect the size of a pin head, and give the appearance of a fine check. A cheaper imitation is made from viscose but this is not hard-wearing. Use worsted type for men's suits, women's skirts.

Width

140cm (54in).

Handling

Tends to fray as all worsted suiting. Springy and not easy to handle. To be avoided by the beginner as it must be carefully tailored. Use firm interfacing, metal zips, hand-tailored buttonholes. It pleats well. Jackets require lining.

Thread

Synthetic or mercerized.

Needle

Machine: 90–100 14–16. Large stitch.
Hand: 7.

Pressing

Hot iron and damp cloth followed by pressing block. Do not move it until cloth is dry and cold.

Care

Dry clean.

PIÑA-CLOTH

A fine plain woven fabric for which the yarns are produced from fibres of the leaves of the pineapple tree. It is a stiff, wiry fabric and makes a good base for embroidery.

PIN CORD

A very fine needlecord fabric.

Handle as Corduroy, see page 130.

PIN STRIPE

The name given to any cloth with very fine pin-width stripes. Usually associated with men's worsted suiting.

PIQUÉ

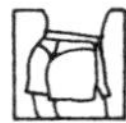 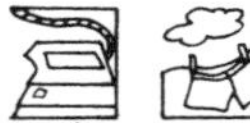

A fabric with a raised surface in ribs, squares, diamonds, etc. Once always in cotton and made in white, but now small amounts of other fibres may be included, or piqué-effect fabric may be made from other fibres.

Cotton Piqué is stiff and absorbent. Used for tennis clothes, etc. Very hard-wearing and washes well.

Width
90cm, 114cm (36in, 45in).

Handling
Easy to sew, but most types would be a little too stiff for beginners to cope with. Cut out with grain exactly correct as the cords will be parallel with the selvedge. Avoid full or gathered styles.

Thread
Mercerized.

Needle
Machine: 90 14. Medium stitch.
Hand: 6.

Pressing
Hot iron.

Care
Hot wash, boil. Iron damp with a hot iron. May be starched.

PLAID
Plaids are basically in a checked design, either square or rectangular. The checks are often simple, sometimes produced by only two or three colours. The word plaid was originally used only for the Scottish tartan shawl worn by Highland women.

PLASTIC
See P.V.C., page 216.

PLISSÉ

A fabric consisting of alternating wrinkled and plain stripes, often in different colours. The fibre content is usually polyester with cotton. Caustic soda is applied to specific sections, causing bubbles to form in the fabric. This is a semi-permanent finish which is liable to lessen with constant washing and particularly with ironing.

It is a soft, cool summer fabric and is used for casual blouses and skirts, beach wear and children's clothes. Will not crease readily.

Width
114cm (45in).

Handling
Very easy to sew, an excellent choice for beginners. Use soft sew-in interfacing.

Thread
Synthetic.

Needle
Machine: 80 11. Medium slight zigzag stitch.
Hand: 7.

Pressing

Use the toe of the iron only, at medium heat.

Care

Wash by hand or machine and drip dry. No ironing needed.

PLUSH

Any cut pile fabric that has a pile length of more than 3mm. The yarns can be almost any natural or synthetic, and many of the fabrics are now washable. Made in various weights for dresses, curtains and upholstery. As for pile fabrics, all pieces of pattern must be laid in the same direction for cutting.

For handling, see Pile Fabrics, page 209 and under individual fabric names.

POIRET TWILL

Named after Poiret, the French designer. This is a firm, twilled worsted material, but its twill is pronounced, like gabardine, and steeply angled. It is not much used now but is an excellent tailoring cloth.

Handle as for Gabardine, see page 158.

POLISHED COTTON

A plain-weave cotton fabric, often inexpensive, that has been calendered to give it an attractive shine. The calendering does not survive laundering so garments have to be starched, unless a resin finish is added, when the finish is permanent.

Many weights of cotton may be polished and used for curtains, loose covers, dresses, etc. Handle as for the weight of the cotton, e.g. Lawn, Cambric, Poplin, etc.

POLO CLOTH

The name given to top quality highly napped fabric that is made into sportswear, and polo caps and coats, jackets etc., for spectators. Mainly produced in expensive-looking shades of brown. Made from wool, it may be woven or knitted in construction.

Handle as thick napped fabric, such as Beaver Cloth, page 101.

POLYAMIDE

Although not strictly chemically true because other fibres come under this heading, polyamide has come to be accepted as the word referring to nylon filament yarn.

POLYESTER

A man-made fibre of great strength. It is treated in various ways and mixes well with fibres such as cotton.

See page 40.

POLYESTER CHIFFON

See Chiffon, page 126.

POLYESTER COTTON

The correct term should be polyester and cotton. The two fibres are mixed in varying percentages according to the weight and type of fabric produced. Polyester and cotton mixtures can be made into any weight of fabric from Voile to Gabardine, but for the purposes of identification in this section, these notes refer only to the medium-weight fabric that resembles a plain-weave all cotton material.

The advantage over 100 per cent cotton is that the polyester reduces creasing and provides good draping qualities. It also makes the fabric even more hard-wearing. It may be plain or printed or woven in patterns.

Used for blouses, shirts, nightwear, children's clothes.

Width

90cm, 114cm (36in, 45in).

Handling

Easy to sew if the percentage of polyester is not too high. A good fabric for beginners. Frays very little. Lends itself to tucks, gathers, soft styles and plain styles. Use soft sew-in or iron-on interfacing. Experiment with machine stitch as seams may pucker.

Thread

Synthetic.

Needle

Machine: 80 11. Medium stitch. *Hand:* 7.

Pressing

Warm iron or steam iron.

Care

Hot wash by hand or machine. Dirt comes out easily. If drip dried, it may need no ironing.

POLYESTER CRÊPE

A soft synthetic crêpe in a wide range of plain colours, which has largely replaced other types for blouses, dresses, evening wear, lounging pyjamas, negligées. Hard-wearing, does not lose its shape and is reasonably priced.

POLYESTER GEORGETTE

See Georgette, page 159.

POLYESTER SATIN

A satin that creases very little, due to its fibre content, and is soft and comfortable to wear and drapes well. It is made in various weights suitable for lingerie, blouses and evening wear. It has less lustre than satins made from shiny fibres such as silk or acetate.

See Satin, page 223.

POLYESTER SHEER

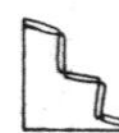  

Firm vision net used for curtains. Fibres vary but polyester is mainly used because it does not lose its colour. Fibre combinations include polyester and silk, and polyester, acrylic and nylon.

Width

120cm (48in).

Handling
Cut exactly on the straight grain. The finer the net the more has to be allowed for fullness. Machine all edges as it is springy.

Thread
Synthetic.

Needle
Machine: 80 11. Large straight stitch or zigzag.
Hand: 7.

Pressing
Warm iron.

Care
Hot wash. May need no ironing if re-hung when damp.

POLYESTER VOILE

Very fine polyester curtain net made in various widths. It is soft, drapes well and keeps its colour.

Width
90cm up to 420cm (36in up to about 10¾ft).

Handling
Allow plenty of fullness. Cut on the straight grain. Machine all hems.

Thread
Synthetic.

Needle
Machine: 80 11. Large stitch, straight or zigzag.
Hand: 7.

Pressing
Warm iron.

Care
Hot wash. May not need ironing.

POLYNOSIC
This is a manufactured cellulose fibre with properties similar to cotton, but the fibre is softer. The fibre is more difficult to dye than cotton. Polynosics are often mixed with cotton and other fibres. Names of two well known polynosics are Vincel and Modal.

See also page 38.

PONGEE

Originally a light silk fabric of slightly rough feel with excellent draping qualities, but it may now be acetate, triacetate, nylon or other fibres, all resembling the silk fabric in weight and handling. It is in plain weave and may be printed or plain.

Used for blouses, soft dresses, nightwear, and in plain colours as a lining fabric.

Width
114cm (45in).

Handling
These fabrics will fray a little. Cut out carefully as all Pongee is slippery. Do not fit tightly or seams may pull. Use fullness in the form of gathers, etc. Use soft sew-in or transparent interfacing.

Thread
Synthetic.

Needle
Machine: 70–80 9–11. Small to medium stitch.
Hand: 8.

Pressing
Warm iron.

Care
Hand wash. Drip dry. Iron with warm iron.

POODLE CLOTH

A medium or heavy fabric characterized by loops of yarn on the surface. It may be wool, acrylic or other yarns or mixtures. Mohair is also sometimes included. It is in plain colours or random effects.

Used for jackets, coats and warm dresses.

Width
140cm (54in).

Handling
A thick cloth to sew, but soft and yielding. Choose plain styles and keep bulky processes to the minimum. Avoid patch pockets. Use firm interfacing, piped buttonholes, and if a zip is used, make sure the fabric is pulled back off the teeth to avoid catching. Garments need not necessarily be lined. Avoid topstitching.

Thread
Synthetic.

Needle
Machine: 100 16. Large stitch.
Hand: 6.

Pressing
Medium hot iron and damp cloth, but very light pressure. It may be necessary to place a piece of spare cloth or a towel on the board first to avoid spoiling the surface.

Care
Dry clean unless labelled washable.

POPLIN

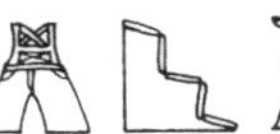

A medium-weight fabric made from mercerized cotton yarns. It has a characteristic crosswise rib effect produced by extra yarns, and has a sheen. It creases in wear, although less so if some polyester yarn has been included. It is in plain colours or prints, and is very hard-wearing, comfortable and absorbent.

Used for shirts, blouses, pyjamas, children's clothes, dresses.

Width
90cm, 114cm (36in, 45in).

Handling
Not an easy fabric to handle. Seams tend to wrinkle when stitched and the fabric can be difficult to press well, due to the additional crosswise yarns. Topstitching looks good. Machine fell seams can be used with effect. Use medium sew-in or iron-on interfacing.

Thread
Synthetic.

Needle
Machine: 80 11. Medium stitch, slight zigzag may reduce puckering.
Hand: 7–8.

Pressing
Hot iron or steam iron.

Care
Hot wash. Iron slightly damp if all cotton.

POULT

A fabric similar to Taffeta but usually heavier and with a more pronounced rib. The fibres used are acetate, triacetate, polyester or mixtures or even silk. It is made in plain colours. A stiff fabric liable to crease.

Used only for formal dresses, coats, wedding gowns, millinery.

Width
114cm (45in).

Handling
Fabric will fray readily, so neaten all raw edges. Seams could be bound with net. Fit the pattern carefully before cutting as the needle may leave holes in the fabric after unpicking. Use firm interfacing. Hems may have interfacing inserted for good effect. Avoid topstitching. Use nylon or concealed zips.

Thread
Synthetic.

Needle
Machine: 80 11. Medium stitch.
Hand: 8.

Pressing
Warm iron on wrong side and very light pressure. Seam edges will make ridges on the right side if too much pressure is applied. Use no moisture.

Care
Dry clean.

PRINCESS LACE
An imitation of the luxurious Duchesse Lace.

PROOFED POPLIN

This is usually heavier weight than dress poplin but constructed in the same way. It may be cotton or polyester and cotton. The fabric has been treated to make it showerproof. See page 228.

Used for raincoats, anoraks.

Width
114–150cm (45–60in).

Handling
Use machine fell seams. Top stitching looks good. Use medium interfacing and heavy zips. Use buttons or metal capped studs to fasten. Keep to uncluttered styles.

Thread
Synthetic.

Needle
Machine: 90 14. Large stitch.
Hand: 6.

Pressing
Hot or medium-hot iron and damp cloth, or steam iron.

Care
Probably hot machine or hand wash. Press with medium-hot iron. Check label in case washing will impair the finish. If to be dry cleaned, state that it is proofed fabric.

PRUNELLA

A fine worsted cloth that has largely gone out of use. It was twill weave and light in weight, made in plain colours only. Often used for children's clothes, but also for clergymen's wear.

P.V.C.

Its full name is polyvinyl chloride and it is a chemically produced thermoplastic material. Most fabrics referred to as P.V.C. are base fabrics, such as plain knitting or plain or printed cotton, that have been sprayed with coloured or colourless polyvinyl chloride. Some are stiff and heavy, some are softer.

Used for aprons, protective wear, raincoats, hats, etc., and for curtains. Upholstery fabric is made from expanded vinyl and a knitted backing cloth.

Width
150cm (60in) or more.

Handling
P.V.C. does not fray and edges may be left cut, although this may encourage tearing. Seams may be open or welt seams, although they are no longer entirely waterproof after stitching. Use metal eyelets, stud fastenings, large plastic zips and stick hems with adhesive. There is no 'give', so choose simple styles.

Thread
Synthetic.

Needle
Machine: 90 14, or spear pointed. If the foot sticks to the right side, try a roller foot and rub a little oil on the needle for easier penetration. If the P.V.C. sticks to the machine, sprinkle talcum powder sparingly on the fabric.
Hand: 8, but hand-sewing is not really suitable for the fabric.

Pressing
Medium hot iron on the back of the fabric only.

Care
Sponge with hot water and soapless detergent.

PYJAMA CLOTH
A hard-wearing cotton (once silk) fabric with a close warp and woven in stripes of varing widths and colours. The fabric is often brushed on the right side. Highly inflammable.

Handle as for Brushed Cotton, see page 111.

Q

QUILTING

Plain or printed cotton, polyester/cotton, viscose, or nylon fabric mounted on to a layer of 2oz wadding (usually polyester) and held with rows of machining in diamond pattern or parallel rows. A backing is usually added before quilting — this may be a thin layer of plain-coloured knitted nylon or another fabric to contrast with or match the outer material. This is referred to as double-sided quilting. All quilting is warm but light.

Used for robes, dressing gowns, bed jackets, anoraks, children's clothes, snow suits, jackets, boleros, belts, and also small pieces of quilting can be used for collars, pockets, yokes, lining hoods.

Width
90–150cm (36–60in).

Handling
Although bulky, quilting is not difficult to handle. The stitching prevents fraying. Avoid gathers and bulky processes. Bind edges where possible and make collars from a single layer. If interfacing is required it should be medium weight. Choose a type of zip to suit the garment. Use machine fell seams, pulling out the wadding and trimming before working the second row of stitching to reduce bulk.

Thread
Synthetic.

Needle
Machine: 90 14. Large stitch. Zigzag on right side to hold down a layer area.
Hand: 6.

Pressing
Warm or medium hot iron.

Care
Hand or machine wash. Pressing may not be needed.

R

RABBIT HAIR
Long rabbit hair is used in combination with other fibres, such as wool, to add softness and interest to a fabric. The percentage of rabbit included should be specified on the fabric label. Fabrics containing rabbit may be one-way and this should be checked before cutting out.

RADIUM

A plain-weave lustrous fabric, that has the draping quality of Crêpe but the crispness of Taffeta. The fibres used include silk, viscose, acetate, triacetate.

Used for lingerie, robes, blouses, and as a lining fabric.

Width
90–114cm (36–45in).

Handling
Slippery to handle, not for beginners. Neaten all raw edges as the fabric frays. Choose soft gathered styles and fine finishes, such as binding, lace edging, etc.

Thread
Synthetic.

Needle
Machine: 70 9. Small stitch, medium if using fabric for lining.
Hand: 8.

Pressing
Warm, dry iron.

Care
Hand wash in warm water. Roll in a towel for a moment to absorb excess moisture then hang to dry. Iron when almost dry with a warm iron.

RAINCOAT FABRIC
See Proofed Poplin, page 215.

RAISED JERSEY

A term used to describe a medium-weight knit fabric of fairly open texture, that has been brushed on the right side to add warmth and give an attractive fuzzy effect. Often made in random colour co-ordinating yarns. The fibre is usually acrylic as it lends itself particularly well to this kind of treatment.

Used for soft suits, dresses, coats.

Width
150cm (60in).

Handling
Use soft styles. Suitable fabric for patterns specifying 'knit fabrics only'. Falls well into cowl necks, flared skirts, etc. Use stretch interfacing, nylon zips. Avoid top-stitching.

Thread
Synthetic.

Needle
Machine: 80 11. Medium, slight zigzag stitch.
Hand: 7.

Pressing
Medium hot iron and damp cloth, or steam iron and very light pressure.

Care
Probably washable but check the label.

RAJAH
A soft, strong, plain-weave silk fabric with rough texture. It was first made, not in the Far East, but in the United States. Tussah Silk was normally used, but it is now made from acetate, tri-acetate, nylon, polyester. It is very similar in appearance and weight to Pongee.

RAMIE

A strong vegetable fibre, also known as China-Grass. Ramie is expensive to produce and is usually mixed with other fibres, particularly for upholstery fabrics.

See also page 127.

RASCHEL KNIT

Raschel is a name of a machine invented to produce this type of fabric. It is not of conventional knit construction but appears to be partly woven in texture. These fabrics are often printed, and some are very transparent; they have some 'give', but only a little, are attractive, wear well and do not crease. The fibre content is polyester.

Used for blouses, dresses, curtains, bedspreads, depending on design.

Width
90cm (36in) or more, according to use.

Handling
Raschel Knit does not fray but, when cut, short ends of fibre may drop off. It is very easy to sew and an excellent fabric for beginners.

It drapes well and will gather, but it will not pleat.

Thread
Synthetic.

Needle
Machine: 80 11. Ball point needle may be required.
Hand: 6.

Pressing
Steam iron or warm iron.

Care
Hand or machine wash. No ironing required.

RATINE
A French word meaning fuzzy, this is a rough, pebbly woollen fabric made of novelty yarns with a fancy twist, and similar in finished appearance to Chinchilla.

Used for men's overcoats. For handling, see Chinchilla Cloth, page 127.

RATINE LACE
A machine-made lace, the groundwork of which consists of heavy loops rather than mesh.

RAYON
The earliest man-made fibre, from cellulose such as wood or cotton. In the United Kingdom this term is no longer used, as the specific cellulose fibre must be mentioned on the fabric label, e.g. viscose, modal, acetate, cupro, etc. For more information, see Fibres section, page 27.

RE-EMBROIDERED LACE
A flat lace that has been re-worked with another intricate design using a variety of threads. An elaborate and expensive fabric, due to the two operations involved.

RENAISSANCE LACE
Motifs joined by a variety of stitches.

REP(P)

Usually a heavy or medium fabric with a very pronounced rib. It is made from a variety of fibres, including cotton, viscose and blends of fibres and occasionally from worsted yarn. It is stiff and unyielding but also very hard-wearing.

Used for curtains, loose covers, bedspreads, etc.

Width
120cm (48in).

Handling
Make sure the ribs are all running in the same direction. It tends to fray, especially if an entire rib is inadvertently pulled away, so handle carefully after cutting. Neaten all seams with binding. Curtains need not be lined if made from heavy rep.

Thread
Synthetic or 30's cotton.

Needle
Machine: 100 16. Large stitch.
Hand: 5.

Pressing
Hot or medium hot iron.

Care
Wash or dry clean. Iron slightly damp with hot or medium hot iron.

REPROCESSED WOOL
Woollen fibres obtained from existing knitted or woven garments. It should be indicated on the fabric label that the wool has undergone this processing and is not pure new wool. These fabrics are usually inexpensive.

RETICELLA LACE
A very early type of needlepoint lace. It was a combination of drawn-thread lace work and cut work.

REVERSIBLE FABRIC
A fabric that can be made up and worn with either side as the right side, the two sides contrasting in either colour or design or both. The cloth is thick, made from wool, acrylic, mohair or blends.

Used for coats, capes, duffle coats, etc. Choose simple, loose fitting styles, wrap-over coats, etc. The fabric should not be lined.

There are two main types of reversible cloth, both requiring different treatment.

(1) The two fabrics joined by a loose thread running at random between the two layers.

Width
140cm (54in).

Handling
To make it truly reversible, cut each piece singly including the collar. There should be no facings to the garment. Join seams by carefully opening the two layers of fabric and snipping the threads. When parted, join two layers of fabric, press open. Complete seam by turning remaining edges to meet each other and slipstitching. Collar edges, front edges and hems should be parted in the same way, and edges turned in and slipstitched. Finish with topstitching. Use patch pockets, attached to both sides of the garment.

Thread
Synthetic.

Needle
Machine: 100 16. Large stitch.
Hand: 6.

Pressing
Hot or medium hot iron and damp cloth.

Care
The fabric will probably be labelled dry clean only.

(2) The two fabrics joined by adhesive. These are less expensive and are often made from poorer quality cloth. The adhesive adds additional body but the fabrics cannot be parted.

Width
140cm (54in).

Handling
Either make up as a normal wool coating, choosing one fabric as the right side, or to make it reversible, use welt seams, patch pockets, and bind all edges including collar, front edges and hems with a matching or contrasting braid.

Thread
Synthetic.

Needle
Machine: 100 16. Large stitch.
Hand: 6.

Pressing
Medium hot iron and damp cloth, using little moisture if acrylic content is high.

Care
May be washable but check the instructions.

RHEA
A fibre better known as Ramie or China-Grass.

RHYTHM CRÊPE
The name given to a fabric with regularly spaced puckering. It is made from viscose and resembles Seersucker.

Handle as Seersucker, see page 225.

RIB VELVET
A rarely used name for Corduroy.

RIBBON
See page 52.

RIBBON EMBROIDERED LACE
A very elaborate fabric of lace background with matching narrow ribbon ruched and stitched in scroll designs on the right side of the lace. The ribbon is likely to be nylon or polyester to avoid crushing. The lace could be almost any fibre.

RICE NET
Woven of coarse cotton thread stiffened by sizing and used as hat foundations.

RICHELIEU

An open-work fabric made in imitation of hand embroidery of the same name. The designs are geometric, the embroidery may be in a yarn which matches or contrasts with the backing fabric. The fibres used may be cotton, viscose, polyester, modal or a mixture of fibres. It is a medium-weight crisp fabric.

Used for blouses, dresses, children's dresses. Also used effectively in small areas, such as yokes or pockets, with a plain matching or contrasting fabric.

Width
114cm (45in).

Handling
Choose simple styles with few gathers. Allow slightly wider seam allowances than usual as the embroidered areas will tend to fray when cut. Use soft or medium sew-in interfacing and nylon zips. If using buttons to fasten, try to plan the area when cutting out so that buttonholes will not have to be made on an embroidered area. Avoid top-stitching.

Thread
Synthetic.

Needle
Machine: 80 11. Medium stitch.
Hand: 7.

Pressing
Steam iron or dry iron set to temperature suitable for fibre content.

Care
Wash by hand or machine. Iron slightly damp.

RIPPLE CLOTH

An inexpensive plain-weave fabric that has been slightly brushed on both sides and then forcibly wrinkled to give it a wavy or rippled surface. Both treatments add warmth. The fabric may be made from wool, but is more likely to be acrylic or from cotton and therefore inflammable; in plain colours only.

Used for dressing gowns and bed jackets.

Width
114–150cm (45–60in).

Handling
Very easy to sew; it does not fray and as it is of medium weight and soft it is easy for beginners to handle. Use a soft sew-in interfacing and nylon zip.

Thread
Synthetic.

Needle
Machine: 90 14. Medium stitch.
Hand: 6. Keep stitches loose to avoid making visible indentations.

Pressing
Warm iron and very light pressure.

Care
The ripple effect may not be permanent in which case the fabric will be labelled dry clean.

ROBIA VOILE
Robia is the trade name of the wide variety of voile fabrics made by Tootal. In 100 per cent cotton, the voiles vary from satin stripes in various widths and colours to plain square-effect weave with self-colour woven spots.

Handle as Cotton Voile, see page 247.

ROSE-POINT LACE
A Venetian needlepoint lace with designs connected by a thick thread. It is characterized, as the name suggests, by delicate close flower or leaf designs.

S

ST GALL LACE
A machine-made imitation of Venetian Lace, copying the texture and designs.

SABLE
A dark brown luxury fur which is very hard-wearing.

SAILCLOTH

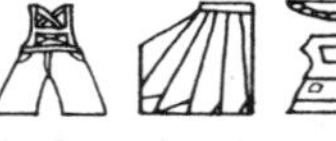  

A firm fabric in plain colours in plain or basket weave. It is made from cotton, or polyester and cotton, and is stiff and hard-wearing.

Used for trousers, dresses, children's clothes, men's summer jackets.

Width
114cm (45in).

Handling
Not difficult to handle but does not drape well, and creases easily. It pleats well. Choose plain styles. Topstitching, machine fell seams, shoulder yokes, pockets all help to break up the plain surface of the fabric. Use firm iron-on interfacing and metal zips. Adhesive strip works well in hems.

Thread
Synthetic.

Needle
Machine: 90 14. Medium stitch.
Hand: 6.

Pressing
Steam iron or medium hot iron.

Care
Hot wash, iron slightly damp. Keep strong colours separate.

SANFORIZED
The trademark of a shrinking process applied to cottons and other fabrics liable to be washed a great deal. Used mainly on shirt fabrics.

See Finishes, page 69.

SARILLE
Trade name of a Courtaulds fibre. Soft cellulosic fibre. Developed from viscose and used to produce warm fabrics. Mainly used in dress fabrics, household textiles such as blankets, and often mixed with other fibres, such as wool, to reduce the cost.

SARSONET
Originally a fine silk Arabic fabric, it is now a net or veiling fabric used in millinery. Made from silk, nylon, or polyester.

SATEEN

This is similar in construction to satin but made from cotton. It is soft and has a sheen and is often of loose construction. It is in plain colours only. In pure Sateen weaves the surface of the cloth consists almost entirely of weft floats.

Sateen is manufactured in many different types and weights and according to quality it may be used as curtain lining or curtain fabric. It does not wear particularly well; seams tend to pull and crack-marks appear where hems are pressed. It is not often used as a dress fabric for these reasons, but is popular as curtains, and as costumes for the stage and fancy dress.

Width
114–120cm (45–48in).

Handling
Easy to sew, a good fabric for beginners. Soft and drapes well.

Thread
Synthetic or mercerized.

Needle
Machine: 90 14. Medium to large stitch.
Hand: 6.

Pressing
Hot iron.

Care
Hot wash. Iron slightly damp.

SATIN
A fabric that is very smooth on the right side (although sometimes

both sides are satin weave). This smoothness is produced by weaving in an interlaced pattern (see page 48). Satin-weave fabrics are made from all yarns, including silk, acetate, nylon, viscose, polyester, cotton.

For handling, look under name of fabric.

SATIN-BACK
Any fabric of any fibre where the reverse side is of satin weave.

See Satin, page 223.

SATIN STRIPE
A fabric of almost any fibre, including cotton, that has a satin-weave shiny stripe alternating with a contrasting stripe of a different weave or thickness of yarn, even of a different colour.

Handle according to weight of fabric and fibre content.

SAXONY
Originally made in the province of Saxony, Germany, the name has come to be used to describe any soft, plain-weave woollen or worsted cloth with a slight nap. High grade yarns are used so the term always implies a good quality cloth. It may be plain or in small checks.

Handle as Flannel, see page 152.

SCHAPPE SILK
A type of silk from which the gum has been removed by fermentation. The fabric produced and called by this name is similar to Spun Silk, page 233.

SCHIFFLI LACE
The name of a machine producing various effects on lightweight fabrics. See page 63.

SCHREINER
A fabric finishing process which smoothes the right side, often impressing a pattern at the same time.

See Finishes, page 69.

SCOTCHGUARD

A registered showerproof finish applied to some fabrics.

See Finishes, page 69.

SCOTCH TWEED

Woollen tweed made in twill weave using a white warp and brightly coloured weft yarns. It has a rough, shaggy appearance, and is made in various weights for suits and overcoats.

For handling, see Harris Tweed, pages 167 and 168.

SCRATCH FELT
Cheap quality woollen fabric made to resemble camel cloth. Poor wearing qualities.

For handling, see Camel Cloth, page 118.

SCRIM
Loosely woven cloth in cotton yarn, similar to voile but a poorer quality fabric. It is very similar to Cheesecloth.

Normally used only for backing other fabrics such as fur.

SEA ISLAND COTTON

The best quality cotton yarn in the world, it is long, soft and smooth and made into top quality cotton fabrics both plain and printed. Production is limited, so it is a very expensive yarn.

SEAL

Black or grey in colour, the hair is shiny and flat with coarse texture; not hard-wearing.

SEALSKIN

Fur of the Alaskan seal, usually dyed black or brown. It is very hard-wearing.

Often used for handbags.

SEERLOOP GINGHAM

Gingham with slack-tension loops of yarn on the surface, often on the white lines only.

See Gingham, page 160.

SEERSUCKER

A fabric with puckered stripes alternating with flat ones of various widths. The stripes may be multi-coloured, or in a plain coloured fabric with a printed floral pattern on it. Early Seersucker, all cotton, was made by physically forcing bubbles into the plain fabric, and so after a few washes the bubbles began to flatten and, if ironed, they would certainly disappear. Now, however, the cloth is made on a twin-beam loom which feeds the yarns at different speeds and the puckers are therefore woven in. Fibre content now normally includes polyester with cotton, but it can be a nylon fabric.

Used for lightweight casual clothes, such as shirts, skirts, beachwear, aprons, and for tablecloths and kitchen curtains. Creases do not show.

Width

114cm (45in).

Handling

Easy to sew and, with the exception of Nylon, Seersucker would be a good choice for beginners. Use soft sew-in interfacing.

Thread

Synthetic.

Needle

Machine: 80 11. Medium slight zigzag stitch.
Hand: 7.

Pressing

Use the toe of a medium hot iron on the wrong side. The whole garment may be pressed if necessary.

Care

Hand or machine wash. Drip dry.

SERGE

Either a twill cloth or a smooth faced plain-weave material, made from worsted or woollen yarn. It is very hard-wearing.

Used for men's suits, but more often for classic coats, school uniforms, etc. It becomes shiny with wear but pressing revitalizes it.

Width
140cm (54in).

Handling
Should only be used by the most experienced dressmakers. Use only tailoring processes. Use firm interfacing.

Thread
Synthetic or 30's cotton.

Needle
Machine: 100 16.
Hand: 6–7.

Pressing
Hot iron and damp cloth and sharp pressure to avoid shine.

Care
Dry clean.

SEW-IN WOVEN INTERFACING

Stiffened Cotton Sew-In
Width
90cm (36in).
An open wavy-weave cotton stiffened to a crisp finish. Suitable for firm fabrics. Not cheap. Washable.

Marquisette Sew-In
Width
88–90cm (35–36in).
An open lattice-weave nylon fabric. Very stiff and unyielding. The sort of thing to use for underlining a bride's skirt. Not cheap. Washable.

Viscose/Cotton Sew-In
Width
100cm (40in).
A lovely soft plain-weave fabric, suitable for mounting rather than interfacing most fabrics. Not cheap. Washable.

Sanforized Cotton Sew-In
Width
90cm (36in).
The trade name for a permanently stiffened cotton interfacing (although the process is also applied to other fabrics). It is a slightly open-weave cotton. Slightly stiff. Washable.

Victoria Sew-In
Width
90cm (36in).
A fine Lawn that is fairly stiff. An excellent fabric to interface medium-weight crisp fabrics. Not cheap. Washable.

Shirt Collar Interfacing Sew-In
Width
88–90cm (35–36in).
Plain, very even weave cotton made from a fairly heavy yarn. It is very heavily stiffened. Expensive but obviously only small amounts are required. Washable.

Permastiff Sew-In
Width
88–90cm (35–36in).
Trade name for a fabric that has been treated with the Permastiff finish. The interfacing is a very stiff fairly thick cotton fabric of medium price. Washable.

Tie Interfacing Sew-In
Width
90cm (36in).
A thick, soft fabric made of viscose fibre in plain open-weave. In cream only. It is used on the bias for ties so its softness makes it very pliable, yet the thickness

will give the tie sufficient padding. Washable.

Pocketing Sew-In

Width

94cm (37in).

A close-weave plain fabric, usually cream and with a glazed finish on the right side. It is strong to withstand wear but soft so that the pocket bag does not show through the garment. Made from viscose (Vincel) fibre. Washable.

SHADOW LACE

The density of the stitch forms the pattern in this type of machine-made lace. There is no outlining thread to make the design stand out.

It is light and flimsy and is used for blouses, evening dresses, etc.

SHARKSKIN

Made from worsted yarn, this is an expensive fabric in fancy or novelty weaves, sometimes mixing colours. It is of fine texture and very hard-wearing. Acetate or Viscose Sharkskin is used for sportswear. It is crisp and washes well. Needs to be ironed carefully to avoid a shine, and is not hard-wearing. Occasionally made in silk.

Handle Worsted Sharkskin as Unfinished Worsted, see page 243.

SHEEPSKIN

Also referred to as Shearling, this is the skin of the sheep or goat with the wool left on. It can be made up with the wool on the outside or the inside. A suede finish is sometimes applied to the skin side. Readily available for sewing. Bulky to handle.

SHEETING

Since the introduction of fitted sheets and duvets, and particularly since coloured and printed sheets became popular, sheeting has been made available to us as piece goods. It can be plain or printed and in all colours. Most of it is 50 per cent cotton, 50 per cent polyester for easy care.

Used for sheets, pillowcases, duvet covers, valances, curtains.

Width

228cm (90in).

Handling

Soft and easy to handle. Machine all seams and hems. Fasten duvet covers with Velcro, or metal or plastic snaps.

Thread

Synthetic.

Needle

Machine: 90 14. Large stitch.
Hand: 7.

Pressing

Hot iron.

Care

Hot wash. May not need ironing if tumble dried. Always wash dark colours separately when new and always wash maroon separately.

SHEPHERD'S CHECK

Description of a traditional Scottish Border design in 6mm squares of black and white. The size of check remains the same regardless of the thickness of the yarn. A twill weave, producing alternate solid black squares and diagonally striped squares.

In wool, it is used for shawls, caps, coats. In worsted, it is used for men's suiting. In cotton, acrylic, polyester fibres, it is a lighter weight washable fabric used for shirts, sports clothes, children's clothes.

Handle according to the weight and fibre.

SHEPHERD'S PLAID

See Shepherd's Check, above.

SHETLAND

Real Shetland wool is the underneath part of the fleece of Shetland sheep, pulled out by hand in springtime. It has a characteristic softness and is made into yarn for soft suitings and knitting yarns. Very expensive. The term should not be applied to any other yarns, but it is often used to describe something of equal softness.

SHIRTING

Any fabric of any fibre that is closely woven and implies absorbent, hard-wearing qualities. The most common are made from cotton, silk, polyester and cotton.

SHODDY

Fibres made from ground-up rags and mixed with other fibres to reduce the cost.

SHOT

The term used to describe the effect created by using one colour in the warp and a totally different colour in the weft. Any fibre may be used, but the most effective are the shiny ones, such as acetate, triacetate, polyester and silk.

SHOT TAFFETA

One of the most luxurious types of Taffeta, as it is made from two colours and can be seen to change colour as the wearer moves.

See also Shot, above.

SHOWERPROOF

A process by which a garment is made resistant to light rain; it is always described as showerproofing not waterproofing.

See Finishes, page 69.

SHOWERPROOF COTTON AND LATEX

A base fabric of cotton, or polyester and cotton, resembling Cheesecloth in appearance and sprayed on one side with Latex to make it showerproof. The layer of Latex is quite thin so the right side of the fabric is wrinkled like Cheesecloth. It is a soft, fairly floppy fabric.

Used for raincoats, jackets, hats, etc.

Width
150cm (60in).

Handling
Does not fray at all. Not difficult to sew, except that, when stitching on the right side, the machine foot may stick on the Latex. Difficult to tack and hand-sew.

Thread
Synthetic.

Needle
Machine: 90–100 14–16. Large stitch.
Hand: 5–6.

Pressing
Medium hot iron on the cotton side only. When pressing seams, cover the fabric with a dry cloth and use a cooler iron.

Care
Hand washable.

SHOWERPROOF POLYESTER AND COTTON

A medium-weight fabric with a showerproof finish, in plain weave and usually in plain colours only.

Used for raincoats, anoraks, etc.

Width
150cm (60in).

Handling
Seams may be inclined to wrinkle, especially across the warp direction. A springy fabric that may be difficult to press adequately. Keep to plain styles and use topstitching as decoration. Use medium sew-in or iron-on interfacing.

Thread
Synthetic.

Needle
Machine: 90 14. Medium to large stitch.
Hand: 7.

Pressing
Medium hot iron and damp cloth, or steam iron.

Care
Probably washable but check the instructions.

SICILIENNE
This was first made in Sicily as a coarse-weave lining fabric of mohair and cotton. It is now a plain-woven fabric with heavy weft ribs, made from silk, cotton and wool mixtures and resembling poplin in appearance. It is very occasionally used as a dress fabric.

Handle according to weight and fibre content.

SILESIA

A lightweight cotton twill fabric with a calendered glaze. It is very closely woven and very hard-wearing. Made in a limited range of colours.

Used as a lining fabric, and in tailoring for the bags of pockets.

Width
90–95cm (36–40in).

Handling
Does not fray, but stitch well as it will have hard wear; for example, work two parallel rows of machining round pocket bags.

Thread
Synthetic or mercerized.

Needle
Machine: 90 14. Medium stitch.
Hand: 7.

Pressing
Hot iron.

Care
Hot wash, iron slightly damp with hot iron, but the entire garment must be considered if the Silesia is used in conjunction with another fabric.

SILK
A natural fibre unreeled from the cocoon of the silkworm. There are two main types: Mulberry Silk, which is made into fine fabrics, such as Georgette; and Tussah, which is a darker silk and not easy to make white, so colours are usually cream and dyed colours. Tussah is used to make heavier fabrics.

See also Silk, page 41.

For handling various fabrics, see under name of fabrics, e.g. Brocade, Douppion, Crêpe de Chine, Satin, etc.

SILK JERSEY

A fine, lightweight knitted fabric, often printed. It drapes beautifully, wears well and always looks superb.

Used for special outfits: dresses, blouses, long dresses.

Width
90cm (36in) or more.

Handling
Like all light jersey, it has a lot of elasticity, so if used on the bias it may stretch too much. Choose styles with fullness and gathering. It is safest to keep to those paper patterns that suggest silk jersey as a suitable material. Use light sew-in interfacing, nylon zips, sewn in by hand, or concealed zips. The fabric lends itself to fine features, such as binding, rouleaux, ball buttons, etc.

Thread
Silk or synthetic.

Needle
Machine: 70–80 9–11. Small to medium stitch. Slight zigzag.
Hand: 9–10.

Pressing
Warm iron or steam iron. The heat may cause the edges to curl up at first but they will flatten upon cooling.

Care
May be dry clean only, but often hand washable.

SILK NOIL
An attractive silk fabric of dress or suit weight, its feature is that it has small pieces of cocoon woven in it and these appear as dark cream flecks.

Handle as Slub Silk, page 232.

SILK SHANTUNG

A medium-weight silk fabric woven with irregular yarns. The fabric has a dull appearance and rough texture and is popular for blouses, shirts and dresses. It is also referred to as Nankeen or Rajah and also sometimes carries the name of the province where the yarn originated.

Width
85, 90, 102cm (33, 36, 40in).

Handling
Choose plain styles. Topstitching looks attractive. Neaten all edges to control fraying. Make hand-worked or machine-made button-holes. Use light sew-in interfacing.

Thread
Silk or synthetic.

Needle
Machine: 70–80 9–11. Medium stitch.
Hand: 8.

Pressing
Warm iron on wrong side. No moisture.

Care
Dry clean. Occasionally may be labelled washable.

SINGLE CANVAS
A popular plain-weave cotton, or cotton and polyester, embroidery canvas of fine construction, with easily distinguished holes between the warp and weft threads.

SINGLE JERSEY

This is often wool, but may contain a little acrylic fibre. It is a knit fabric that is thin and curls at the edges. The right side only has the stocking stitch appearance, the wrong side is the reverse and like hand knitting in effect. Single jersey may be in plain or mixed colours, in random stripes, or with a marked appearance. It is soft and drapy.

Used for soft gathered dresses and suits.

Width
90–150cm (36–60in).

Handling
Will not fray, but edges will curl up when cut, so do not remove pattern until ready to sew. Use soft interfacing, nylon zip, rouleaux loops, drawstrings, etc.

Thread
Synthetic.

Needle
Machine: 80 11. Possibly ball point. Slight zigzag stitch.
Hand: 11.

Pressing
Medium hot iron and damp cloth, or steam iron, on wrong side. Do not move fabric until it is cool or the edges will curl up.

Care
Acrylic: Warm wash. Probably no ironing necessary. Wool: Dry clean.

SISAL
Coarse vegetable fibres manufactured from leaves. They are a

cream colour and are used for matting and rope.

SLEAZY SATIN

A cheap, soft satin with high lustre, usually made from acetate or acetate and viscose. It is a thin fabric suitable for lining.

SLIPPER SATIN

A closely woven satin made from good quality yarns, which make it hard-wearing. It is less glossy than other satins due to the closeness of the weave, and a more elegant fabric because of this.

See Satin, page 223.

SLUB

Little balls of yarn at irregular intervals along a length of yarn, causing the fabric to have a surface interest and broken texture. Slub in silk is an imperfection, but slub yarns are deliberately manufactured in other fibres such as polyester, acetate, viscose. The resulting fabric may be of medium or heavy weight.

Handle according to fibre content and weight.

SLUB SILK

Silk yarn with nubs or balls of fibre at intervals. It is woven into fabrics with an interesting surface texture. The fabric is usually dress-weight and often crisp.

Width

90cm (36in).

Handling

It will fray easily, so neaten all seams. Use light to medium sew-in interfacing, nylon zip and piped or machine-made buttonholes.

Thread

Silk or mercerized.

Needle

Machine: 80 11. Medium stitch.
Hand: 7.

Pressing

Warm iron, no moisture.

Care

Dry clean or hand wash according to label.

SNOW CLOTH

This term is used to describe any heavy outdoor cloth, particularly those with nap or pile.

SOISETTE

The name given to a fine cotton made from mercerized yarns. Its use is confined mainly to good quality nightwear and negligées, due to its softness.

Handle as Cotton Lawn, page 183.

SOLEIL

The name for a very highly finished wool fabric woven in twill broken-rib effect. The weave and finish give the fabric a shiny appearance. The term is also used to describe any shiny, light-reflecting fabrics in any fibres.

SPANISH LACE

The most common Spanish Lace is made of silk in flat designs, usually floral, and held together with a mesh, but the term Spanish

Lace also refers to all lace made in Spain.

SPANZELLE

A polyurethane fibre. Trade name for Courtaulds' synthetic elastomeric fibre which is produced as a multi-filament yarn. It is made in a range of deniers and stretches very well.

Used for foundation garments, swimwear and support stockings.

SPARTERIE

Stiff fabric, used in making hat bases as it can easily be shaped.

SPUN SILK

This is a type of silk yarn, although the fabric itself may be labelled this way. The yarn is made by breaking up short fibres of waste silk and spinning them together, and this yarn is then woven into fabric. Although the fabric should be cheaper than silk as it is made from waste yarn, the processing is lengthy and expensive. The fabric produced may be of any weight.

SPUN VISCOSE

This is really the name of a yarn, but fabrics also carry this title. They are in plain weave and may be plain or printed. These fabrics were once considered poor in quality and performance but the fabric finishing techniques have improved so much that they are now good fashion fabrics. They are soft and drape well and are fairly warm, but they crease in wear and are highly inflammable.

Used for dresses, blouses, shirts, nightwear and children's clothes.

Width

90–114cm (36–45in).

Handling

Easy to sew. A little floppy, but quite good for a beginner. Some fabrics may fray. Choose soft styles, gathers etc. Use soft iron-on interfacing.

Thread

Synthetic.

Needle

Machine: 80 11. Medium stitch.
Hand: 7.

Pressing

Warm iron or steam iron.

Care

Warm wash by hand or machine. Short spin only, or drip dry. Iron slightly damp.

STITCH BONDED FABRIC

See Malimo, page 191.

STRETCH TOWELLING

A knit fabric with short loop pile to give it a thin Terry towelling appearance on the right side. It is produced in plain colours and in patterns and stripes. Made from cotton and polyamide, it has a great deal of stretch.

Very useful for baby clothes, children's clothes, sports outfits, jumpsuits, bath robes, etc.

Width
90cm (36in) or more.

Handling
The garment can be made quite tight fitting so it is usually safe to make a smaller size. The fabric will curl at the edges when cut and the loop pile will fall off, but it will not fray after that. Very easy to sew and a good fabric for beginners. Seams across the body, e.g. shoulder seams, should be reinforced with tape as stretch towelling will continue to stretch in wear. Use cuff ribbing at wrists and ankles. Use nylon zips, narrow machined hems, metal stud fasteners, press studs on tape, etc.

Thread
Synthetic.

Needle
Machine: 80 11. Ball point needle may be required. Slight zigzag stitch.
Hand: 7.

Pressing
Warm iron.

Care
Machine or hand wash. No ironing required.

STUFF
An old eighteenth-century word used to describe any fabric containing worsted yarns.

SUEDE
The correct term is Suede Leather, because it is now usually calfskin treated on the inside to give it a napped or sueded finish. It is smooth and attractive and can be dyed in a variety of fashion colours. Readily available for sewing and can be made into a wide variety of garments.

For handling, see Leather, page 183.

Care
Hang the garment in a steamy atmosphere and while it is damp, brush up the nap with a clothes brush or sponge.

Many suedes are washable. Follow the instructions carefully.

When dry cleaning, it is necessary to take the garment to a specialist dry cleaner.

SUEDE CLOTH

There is a wide variety of simulated suede or suede fabric available. Most types are expensive, although the advantage over real suede is that they do not take on permanent creases or show wear easily, and most of them are washable. The method of manufacture varies.

One less expensive type consists of a viscose base fabric with a flocked polyester pile stuck with adhesive to both right and wrong sides.

Another consists of a knitted base fibre made of cupro, nylon and polyurethane with a surface pile on the right side of polyurethane. This one feels and looks exactly like real suede and is only washable. It is very expensive.

Yet another variation consists of a soft synthetic backing with a pile that is obviously synthetic and makes no pretence to be real suede. It is inexpensive.

The choice of suede cloth depends entirely on the garment it is intended for and the prospective life of it. Suede fabrics are suitable for dresses, jackets for men and women, skirts and children's clothes.

Width
90–114cm (36–45in).

Handling
All synthetic suede fabrics are easy to sew. Cut out accurately, making sure the pile runs in the same direction over the entire garment. It is advisable to use a pattern previously tried and adjusted to fit as unpicking may leave marks in the fabric. The style of the garment may be tailored or soft, depending on the weight of the fabric. Use iron-on interfacing, nylon or metal zips and piped buttonholes or metal capped studs. Use topstitching for decoration.

Thread
Synthetic.

Needle
Machine: 80–90 11–14. Medium stitch. Slight zigzag if jersey backed. A ball point needle may be needed. Use a roller foot on the machine for stitching on the right side.
Hand: 7.

Pressing
Cover the pressing area with a spare piece of fabric with the pile uppermost. Press the garment areas lightly on the wrong side with a warm iron. Seams tend to make ridges show on the right side if too much pressure is applied. A steam iron is effective on some types of fabric.

Care
Be guided by the instructions on the fabric.

SUITING LACE
The term used to describe any type of firm lace which would be suitable and durable for formal garments such as jackets and skirts. The yarns are usually thick matt and firm, such as cotton and viscose. The motifs or designs are deliberately close together to provide stability and to prevent the fabric from being too 'see-through'.

SURAH

A soft twill fabric made from filament yarns, including silk, polyester, acetate, triacetate. It is always a printed, shiny fabric. It is not hard-wearing, and tends to develop slippage at seams and points of strain, and creases easily.

Used for loose dresses, blouses, scarves, ties and as a lining fabric.

Width
90–114cm (36–45in).

Handling
Slippery and will fray readily. To be avoided by beginners. Handle carefully so that unpicking is avoided as the stitches leave holes. Use transparent interfacing and nylon zips. Avoid topstitching as it may cause wrinkling.

Thread
Synthetic.

Needle
Machine: 9–11 70–80. Small to medium stitch.
Hand: 8.

Pressing
Warm iron, light pressure. Take care to press creases only where needed as they are often impossible to remove in synthetic fabrics.

Care
Warm hand wash. Drip dry. Iron slightly damp with warm iron or steam iron.

SWANSDOWN
(1) A heavily napped cotton fabric. Highly inflammable. Used for nightwear.

Handle as Flannel, see page 152.
(2) A narrow fuzzy decoration originally made from the downy breast feathers of the swan, but now more often made from synthetic fibres. Used to trim nightwear, evening gowns.

SYNTHETIC FELT

This is a non-woven fabric (see pages 58 and 201), fairly thin but with an interesting texture. It dyes well and is available in a range of bright clear colours. It has no grain but it does not stretch.

Used for decoration, appliqué, etc., and such things as fancy dress and theatrical costumes.

Width
85cm (32in).

Handling
Cut pieces in any direction. The fabric does not fray at all.

Thread
Synthetic.

Needle
Machine: 80–90 11–14. Medium to large stitch.
Hand: 6.

Pressing
Medium iron or steam iron.

Care
Hand wash in medium hot water, squeeze gently. Drip dry. Press with a warm iron.

T

TAFFETA

A smooth plain-weave fabric made from even yarns of light or medium weight, usually from shiny filament fibres which give the fabric sheen. Taffeta is characteristically crisp and is usually plain coloured but can be printed. Originally a silk fabric, but now more likely to be composed of acetate, triacetate, nylon or blends of these.

It is not hard-wearing so should be confined to evening wear, stiff petticoats when in fashion, lampshades and drapes, and small items such as cummerbunds, artificial flowers, evening bags, stage costumes and linings.

Width
90–114cm (36–45in).

Handling
Most types will fray easily when cut so all raw edges must be neatened. The fabric creases very readily. Garments should be loose fitting — if fitted tightly, the area should be supported by a stronger fabric or the seams will give way. Not an easy fabric to sew.

Thread
Synthetic.

Needle
Machine: 70–80 9–11. Small to medium stitch.
Hand: 8–9.

Pressing
Warm iron. Use the toe of the iron only, as double areas, such as seams, will easily produce marks on the right side which cannot be removed. It is easy to overpress taffeta and make it look overhandled.

Care
Most types will be labelled dry clean only. If a fabric is washable, squeeze it gently in warm water and liquid soapless detergent, then rinse, pat off the surplus water. Iron slightly damp on the wrong side only.

TAMISE
Similar to Marquisette.

For handling, see page 192.

TAPA CLOTH
A non-woven cloth, made in the South Seas, of beaten bark fibres of the mulberry tree. Not often used outside the Pacific Islands.

TAPESTRY

A highly ornamental fabric, woven on a Jacquard loom, which has an embroidered look. Cotton and worsted yarns are used in many colours, usually showing a picture.

A heavy fabric used for upholstery, curtains and bedspreads. Tapestry sometimes comes into fashion for clothes and is then made lighter in weight.

Width
120cm (48in).

Handling
Arrange design carefully to match exactly. The fabric will fray so all hems must be double and all raw edges neatened, preferably bound. For clothing, choose very simple garments such as boleros and skirts.

Thread
Synthetic or 30's cotton.

Needle
Machine: 100 16. Large stitch.
Hand: 5–6.

Pressing
Medium hot iron and damp cloth.

Care
Dry clean.

TARLATAN

An open, plain-weave coarse cotton with a starched finish, resembling coarse net. Highly inflammable.

Used in millinery and for stiffening belts as well as for extra stiff petticoats or bustle effects. Often used for stage costumes.

Width
90cm (36in) or more.

Handling
Cut exactly to size if possible. Edges may be left raw but they can be scratchy and uncomfortable against the skin.

Thread
Synthetic or mercerized.

Needle
Machine: 90 14. Large stitch.
Hand: 6.

Pressing
Medium hot iron.

Care
Wash if the stiffening is referred to as permanent. Iron slightly damp with a medium hot iron. May be starched.

TARTAN

Authentic tartan designs belong to individual Scottish clans, although they are now worn by many other people. The cloth is woollen or worsted in twill weave, each tartan is an elaborately coloured check design. The traditional garment is the pleated kilt, but tartan cloth is also used for trousers, shawls and fashion garments. Elaborately checked fabric is available which is not authentic tartan, often made from acrylic and blends of wool and acrylic or cotton.

The weight of the cloth varies considerably; handle according to the fibre content and thickness, but remember that the checks must always be matched up.

TATTERSALL
Large, loud check woollen cloth, often in black and white with another colour. Often worn on the race course.

Used for overcoats, hats, caps and capes for men. Usually heavy, so handle as for an overcoating fabric, but match up the checks.

TATTING
A lacy work of varying coarseness, depending on the thread used (usually crochet thread). It is worked using a shuttle with thread wound on to it, and using the fingers of the other hand in conjunction with it.

Usually used only for edgings, motifs or table mats.

TEKLAN

Courtaulds' modacrylic fibre. It is strong and hard-wearing but also soft, warm and light and can be bulked. It has good resistance to sunlight, bacteria and chemicals.

Used mainly in woven and knitted dress materials, and household textiles, such as net curtains and furnishing fabrics, and because it is particularly flame-resistant, for children's nightwear.

See Acrylics, page 35.

TENERIFFE LACE

An inexpensive lace typified by a wheel design or spider's web motif. These are often joined to make mats or added to table linen. It is similar to Paraguay Lace.

TERRY TOWELLING

Also sometimes called Turkish Towelling. It is cotton backing with uncut loops on the surface. The best quality towelling has loops on both sides and a firmly woven selvedge. The loops are formed by the extra yarn being fed in at a slack tension; they are easily caught and pulled on cheap towelling, but on better quality fabric they are shorter and closer and more firmly anchored. Terry may be plain or printed.

Used for robes and beach wear as well as towels and curtains.

Width

90–114cm (36–45in).

Handling

Terry varies in thickness, but it is all bulky, so make loose fitting garments with few bulky gathers, etc. Keep fullness to a minimum in curtains. The loops of pile will fall off when the fabric is cut, so it helps to spread newspaper or old sheets on the floor before you start. Use machine fell seams and enclose all raw edges. Use big plastic zips or tie fastenings. Machine all hems.

Thread

Synthetic or mercerized.

Needle

Machine: 100 16.
Hand: 6.

Pressing

Hot iron and light pressure.

Care

Hot wash, spin, shake when nearly dry, iron if necessary. Wash strong colours alone.

TERRY VELVET

A velvet with a looped pile, produced in the same way as Terry Towelling.

TERYLENE

I.C.I.'s polyester fibre, produced from petroleum and its by-products. It can be successfully bulked. It is extremely hard-wearing and mixes well with many other fibres such as cotton, wool and viscose. It does not catch light but it melts.

Used in all types of dress and furnishing fabrics.

See Polyester, page 40.

TICKING

A very strong, closely woven twill fabric. It is stiff and recognized mainly by the fact that it is woven in narrow stripes of a colour and white, but it can be plain. It is usually made of cotton, although sometimes linen is added.

Not an attractive fabric, although it occurs occasionally as a fashion fabric for women's jackets and trousers. Its main use is as hard-wearing covers for mattresses, and for pillows as it is featherproof.

Width
140–160cm (54–60in) or more.

Handling
Very hard to sew; hand sewing is unsuitable except perhaps for initial tacking. Do not leave raw edges inside covers if they are to be detached for washing.

Thread
Cotton.

Needle
Machine: 100–110 16–18. Large stitch.
Hand: 5.

Pressing
Hot iron.

Care
Hot wash, boil. Iron damp.

TIE CLOTH
Any soft or crisp fabric suitable for men's ties or cravats, including tie silk and Faille, Pongee, in twill weave, acetate, polyester or silk fibres.

TISSUE
The term used to describe a light transparent cloth in any fibre. It usually means one that has body and is not soft and floppy.

TISSUE TAFFETA
The finest, lightest taffeta. It is almost transparent and normally only used for underwear or for lining fine garments.

TORCHON LACE
A coarse lace made from cotton or linen thread, often with a shell design. It is inexpensive and not hard-wearing, due to the fact that the threads are loosely twisted and it is quickly made.

Used for mats and decorations on clothes.

TRACK SUIT FABRIC

A synthetic knit with slightly sueded backing made from polyester or polyester with cotton. It is of medium thickness, and in plain bright colours, black and white.

Used for track suits, anoraks, trousers, shorts, and it is an excellent fabric for children's clothes.

Width
150cm (60in).

Handling
Very easy to sew as it has 'give' but does not stretch uncontrollably in sewing. Use narrow finish seams. Fasten with plastic zips or metal studs. Finish wrists with cuff ribbing. A smaller size pattern can be used unless the pattern says 'for knit fabrics only'. Decorate with braid, club colours, etc.

Thread
Synthetic.

Needle
Machine: 80 11. Ball point if necessary. Zigzag stitch.
Hand: 7.

Pressing
Warm iron and light pressure.

Care
Machine or hand wash. Drip dry.

TRANSPARENT VELVET
Lighter in weight than Chiffon Velvet, soft and silky with good draping qualities. Made with a silk viscose or acetate backing and viscose or nylon pile.

TRICEL
An acetate made by Courtaulds Ltd. It is not particularly hard-wearing on its own, but blends well with other fibres such as nylon, polyester and viscose.

Used for a wide variety of clothing and furnishing fabrics.

See Acetate, page 93.

TRICELON
A yarn produced from Courtaulds' Tricel and Celon mixed together. The result is a softer version of Tricel that mixes well with other fibres, or is made on its own for blouses, lingerie and nightwear fabrics.

TRICOT

A lightweight, warp knit fabric characterized by vertical ribs or wales on the right side and slight crosswise ribs on the wrong side. The fabric has 'give' and is comfortable. Almost any fibre can be made into tricot, including silk, polyester, nylon and viscose.

Used for underwear, nightwear and lining fabric. Also used in nylon for sheets.

Width
90–140cm (36–54in).

Handling
Most of these fabrics will curl up when cut, but this can be controlled. Use sharp scissors. Use narrow finish seams and machined or decorative hems.

Thread
Synthetic.

Needle
Machine: 80 11. Slight zigzag stitch. Ball point needle may be needed.
Hand: 7.

Pressing
Warm iron or steam iron.

Care
Machine or hand wash. Drip dry. Ironing unnecessary except where areas or seams are wrinkled.

TRICOTINE
The name implies a knit fabric, but it is in fact a twill-weave dress fabric woven as double twill, giving a pair of diagonal lines on the right side. It may be made from any fibre, including worsted, polyester, acrylic, viscose.

Handle as for Gabardine (see page 158), setting the iron temperature accordingly.

TROPICAL WORSTED

A plain or fancy weave worsted cloth, very light in weight and mainly in light colours, beige and white. An excellent cloth for hot weather as the high-twist worsted yarn makes it cool. It pleats and creases well.

Used for men's suits, women's suits, trousers, etc. Handle as for Gabardine, see page 158.

TUFTED EMBROIDERY

Lace fabric, usually composed mainly of cotton and possibly nylon to create a firm base, with gold, silver or coloured tufts inserted into the right side of the fabric in a pattern.

TUFTED FABRIC

Any fabric made from any yarn or mixture of yarns in which a pile is created by inserting an extra yarn, often thicker than the backing. Some tufts are locked in position, some, e.g. Candlewick, are easily removed.

Handle according to weight and fibre of fabric.

TULLE

Hexagonal mesh net made from silk yarn is called Tulle.

Used for bridal veils etc.

See Net, page 200.

TUSSAH

Also known as Wild Silk, fabrics are thick and usually in plain or hopsack weave. Some are almost like hessian in weight but softer. The yarn has an uneven slub which gives a rough texture to the cloth.

Used for suits, dresses, skirts, shirts.

Width

90–114cm (36–45in).

Handling

Keep gathers and fullness to a minimum. Fabrics make up well into plain tailored styles, shirt collars, etc. Use medium-weight sew-in interfacing. Piped buttonholes. The fabrics will fray easily so neaten all edges. Jackets may be lined. Topstitching in matching thread looks good on these fabrics.

Thread

Silk or mercerized.

Needle

Machine: 80 11. Medium to large stitch.
Hand: 8–9.

Pressing

Medium hot iron and medium pressure, or steam iron.

Care

May be labelled dry clean or hand wash.

TWEED JERSEY

The old traditional term tweed, which implies hairy, has been applied to a modern fabric. This is a thick knit fabric with fancy knobbles and a hairy surface. It is extremely stretchy and would be suitable for patterns labelled 'knit fabrics'. The fibre is likely to be acrylic with some wool and nylon.

Used for soft suits and dresses.

Width
150cm upwards (60in).

Handling
Do not cut any pieces across the width of the fabric as it stretches too much. Neaten all edges if they curl. Dispense with a zip in the skirt; instead, sew up the seams and stitch elastic Petersham to the waist. Use stretch interfacing.

Thread
Synthetic.

Needle
Machine: 80 11. Stitch zigzag.
Hand: 11.

Pressing
Medium hot iron and damp cloth on wrong side only. Light pressure.

Care
Mixed fibres may be hand washable. Wool must be dry cleaned.

TWILL
A type of weave showing a diagonal line on the right side of the fabric. There are various types of twill weave and any fibre can be woven in this way.

See Basic Weaves, page 47.

U

ULSTER
The name is often used to describe a heavy overcoat, but it is in fact the name of a thick cloth napped on the right side. The pile is flattened but still lies in one direction.

Once often used for men's and women's travelling cloaks, but now mainly confined to men's overcoats.

Handle as for heavy overcoating, e.g. Loden Cloth, see page 188.

UNBLEACHED COTTON
See unbleached Calico, page 116.

UNFINISHED WORSTED

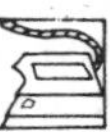

Despite the name, the cloth is finished and is characterized by a slight nap. It is a plain-weave, heavyweight men's suiting and may be plain or check.

Used for men's suits, women's heavy duty trousers.

Width
140cm (54in).

Handling
Cut all pieces in one direction as the cloth is napped. Use heavy interfacing and tailored buttonholes. Should be handled only by the experienced.

Thread
Synthetic or mercerized.

Needle
Machine: 90–100 14–16. Large stitch.
Hand: 7.

Pressing
Hot iron and damp cloth. Take care not to impair nap or mark with iron.

Care
Dry clean.

UNION
The term can mean two things:
(a) A fabric made from the union of two fibres, e.g. cotton and worsted, or cotton and linen.
(b) A striped fabric made from two fibres and then dyed, the fibres taking the dye differently and therefore producing a coloured stripe. This was often produced as a cheap, hard-wearing cotton cloth and made into men's working shirts, worn with white cardboard or celluloid collars and cuffs, which were removed at home.

UTRECHT VELVET
A hard-wearing upholstery velvet. The base cloth is closely covered with the pile which is arranged so that there are no gaps.

V

VALENCIENNES LACE
A hand-made flat type of Bobbin Lace. Real Valenciennes is made only of linen thread, but cotton imitations are very common. The lace is typified by the ground fabric, either round mesh or diamond, and of the same thread as the decorative design.

VAL LACE
An abbreviation of Valenciennes.

VEILING
An open-mesh fabric, usually net, made from silk, acetate, viscose, nylon.

It is made plain or possibly with flocked spots for millinery, and often embroidered with elaborate patterns for bridal veils.

Handle as Net, page 200.

VELOUR
The French for velvet or the Italian for hairy. This is a fabric with short warp pile. There are many types of Synthetic Velour now available for a variety of uses (see Jersey Velour, page 177), but originally Velour was a thick woven overcoating made from top quality wool with a soft close nap on the right side.

An expensive fabric used for men's and women's coats, to be handled only by those who are very experienced. Some women's weight Velours may contain some other fibre but the best ones are all wool. Cut one way and handle as Camel Cloth, see page 118.

VELVET

Velvet, once only silk, may now be cotton, nylon, acetate, viscose, polyester, modal, etc. Velvet is identified as a cloth with a pile of no more than 3mm in length, see also Plush, page 211. The fabric is woven with a warp pile and additional yarn. In production, wires are inserted to lift this yarn and then, when withdrawn, there are loops which are cut or not according to the type of velvet being made. Velvet is one fabric that dyes truly; there are no bad colours in velvet fabrics, all are rich and attractive.

Used for all types of special clothes for men, women and children and there are also special furnishing velvets. Choose tailored or soft styles according to the type of velvet.

Width
90cm (36in) or more.

Handling
Velvet is difficult to handle. It should be avoided completely by the beginner and regarded with respect even by the expert. Always cut it one way, to give a dark, rich effect (with the exception of Panne or Crushed Velvets which can look attractive if pale). When laying out the fabric, fold it with the right side inside and if the pile catches and causes puckers, open it out and cut out singly. Place pattern on wrong side of fabric and chalk round accurately with tailor's chalk. Pile will drop from the cut edges while handling. Tack and machine all seams in the direction of the pile, not against it or puckering results. Try out a seam on spare fabric, altering the stitch size if necessary. If the fabric puckers, try inserting tissue paper between the layers of pile. There are some velvets, mainly all-nylon, that are impossible to machine without puckering and they have to be hand-sewn. Use soft or medium sew-in interfacing and never use any product with adhesive on the back. Choose simple styles with as few seams as possible. Avoid top-stitching. Use concealed zips to avoid stitching showing. If buttonholes are needed, they must be perfectly tailored hand-worked ones. Otherwise alter the form of fastening (Velcro, frogs, clips, etc.).

Thread
Synthetic.

Needle
Machine: 11 80. Medium stitch. Slight zigzag on jersey velvet.
Hand: 8–9.

Pressing
Place a spare piece of velvet on the pressing surface, pile side up. Place seams, etc., pile side down and press very lightly with a medium hot iron and damp muslin.

Care
Most Velvets are dry clean only.

There are many types of velvet, all handled in this way. To identify the type, look under the name included in the following list:
Bagheera; Brocade; Chiffon; Cisele; Embossed; Faconné; Figured; Genoa; Lyons; Mirror; Panne; Terry; Transparent; Utrecht.

VELVETEEN
A fabric, usually cotton, that is made in the same way as Corduroy, but the surface is completely covered by the short-cut pile. It may be plain or printed and it varies in weight. The colours are good and it is equally as attractive as velvet. Its great advantage is that it is not difficult to sew. Follow the same rules for handling as for Velvet, page 244, but there will be few problems with stitching, and none at all with pressing.

VENETIAN

A well-known fabric term used to describe a highly lustrous twill cloth originally made in Venice from silk. When made in satin weave from wool, it is the cloth worn by Arabs visiting Mecca. Venetian for men's suiting is made from worsted yarn, but women's clothes can be made from synthetic varieties, usually polyester.

An expensive fabric in any fibre. Confine its use to suits, skirts, trousers.

Width
114–140cm (45–54in).

Handling
The fabric will fray as it is twill. Cut pieces all one way to avoid shading. Use firm interfacing, metal zips. Takes pleats and trouser creases well.

Thread
Synthetic.

Needle
Machine: 90–100 14–16. Large stitch.
Hand: 6–7.

Pressing
Hot iron and damp cloth, but sharp pressure to avoid iron marks. Tends to be springy, especially in polyester, so the pressing block may have to be used.

Care
Dry clean worsted. Hot wash and drip dry polyester.

VENETIAN LACE
Floral motifs and designs connected with picots or brides. The effect is irregular. Originally a Needlepoint Lace, it is almost Guipure in style.

VICTORIA
Sometimes called Victoria Lawn, this is a stiffened cotton 90cm (36in) wide and used as an interfacing.

VICUNA
A South American animal threatened with extinction. The hair is soft and pale brown and makes the most expensive and luxurious cloth there is. Often mixed with wool to reduce the price.

See also Guanaco, page 165.

VILOFT
The most recent viscose fibre development by Courtaulds and a most versatile fibre. It is soft and absorbent, dyes well, can be knitted or woven into fabrics, from thick towelling to light, lacy fabrics. It also blends well with other fibres. It washes well.

VINCEL
Cellulosic fibre made by Courtaulds. It closely resembles cotton, but is slightly weaker. Vincel (Modal) is soft and absorbent and on its own is made into fabrics for nightwear, but can also be blended with other fibres, such as cotton, for additional body.

See Modal, page 38.

VINYL
Shortened version of polyvinyl chloride. See page 216.

VISCOSE
Cellulosic fibre usually made from wood-pulp. The fibre is soft and absorbent and can be used alone or mixed with other fibres to produce fabrics of all types and weights.

See also Viscose, page 43.

VIYELLA

Trade name for a very old established and popular wool and cotton fabric. It always contains 55 per cent lamb's wool and 45 per cent cotton. It is a fine soft, light twill-weave fabric, first produced in 1893 in Britain and used almost exclusively for children's and baby wear and nightwear. It later became a popular fabric for blouses and shirts and is now, due to improved design and printing, a fabric used for top fashion clothes.

Width
114cm (45in).

Handling
An easy fabric to sew and a good fabric for beginners, provided they choose a print to start with. It is soft and comfortable to stitch and frays very little. Lends itself to plain classic shirts as well as full gathered styles and also quilting and tucks. Neaten all raw edges. Use French seams on blouses and children's clothes. The fabric creases in wear but it recovers overnight. Use soft interfacing.

Thread
Synthetic or mercerized.

Needle
Machine: 80 11. Medium stitch.
Hand: 7.

Pressing
Warm iron or steam iron.

Care
Hand wash or warm machine wash, short spin. Iron slightly damp with a warm to medium iron.

VOILE

Voile is a high twist yarn, see page 31, but the term Voile refers also to a fine, light, plain-weave fabric made in a variety of yarns.

Cotton, and also polyester with cotton, produces a soft, comfortable fabric used for blouses, dresses, children's clothes and sometimes for men's shirts.

Voile is also made from silk, and should then be handled as Jap Silk or Marceline, page 175. Wool Voile is referred to as Challis, page 122.

Width
90–114cm (36–45in).

Handling
Choose full styles and make good use of gathers. Use fine decoration, such as tucks, binding, rouleaux, narrow hems and hand sewing. Use transparent interfacing, nylon zips sewn in by hand. Dresses will need lining.

Thread
Synthetic.

Needle
Machine: 70–80 9–11. Small to medium stitch.
Hand: 8–9.

Pressing
Medium hot iron or steam iron.

Care
Hot wash by hand or machine. Iron slightly damp with medium hot iron. Cotton Voile may be starched.

W

WADDING (1)

Cotton wadding is thick and lightweight. It is sandwiched between two papery layers of non-fluffy, shiny covering which holds it together. The wadding can be split to half depth. Use for quilting, shoulder pads, etc.

Width
90cm (36in).

Handling
Handle carefully as it is not bonded together. Soft and pleasant to handle. Place between two layers of fabric to stitch or, in the case of shoulder pads, arrange with the glazed skin to the outside.

Thread
Synthetic.

Needle
Use needle size according to main fabric.

Pressing
Do not press until inserted in fabric.

Care
Dry clean only (take note for quilting).

WADDING (2)

Polyester wadding is more open and springy and firmer than cotton. It is available in various thicknesses, i.e. 2oz, 4oz, 8oz per metre. Use for shoulder pads, quilting, padding embroidery.

Width
90cm (36in).

Handling
Easy to cut out, difficult to hand-sew until it is inserted between two layers of fabric.

Thread
Synthetic.

Needle
According to main fabric.

Pressing
Warm iron.

Care
Washable. Treat according to outer fabric.

WAFFLE CLOTH
See Honeycomb, page 170.

WASHABLE SUEDE
Particularly useful if colours are pale. Suitable for most garments.

WASH SATIN

A soft, fine inexpensive white, cream or flesh-coloured satin, made from silk or, more usually, acetate or triacetate. It washes and irons well (warm wash; iron with warm iron).

Used for lingerie, as it drapes well.

For handling, see Satin, page 223.

WAXED CAMBRIC

See Downproof Cambric, page 144.

WELSH TAPESTRY

Brightly coloured fabrics in geometric designs that resemble tapestry-work The cloth is double-sided and reversible, plain weave, made from coarse Welsh woollen yarns. The cloth is constructed so that, although the same colours appear on both sides, the arrangement is reversed and gives a different colouring.

Used for capes, coats, blankets, shawls, cushion covers.

Width
140cm (54in) or wider.

Handling
A firm, thick cloth. Avoid bulk by binding edges (which will also make the garment reversible). Avoid facings where possible. Edges may be fringed. Use machine fell seams. As the designs are elaborate and the colours bright and mixed, choose very plain styles and where possible use areas of plain colour. The cloth is very hard-wearing and does not crease. It frays easily so enclose all edges that are not fringed.

Thread
Synthetic or mercerized.

Needle
Machine: 100 16. Large stitch.
Hand: 6.

Pressing
Hot iron, damp cloth and maximum pressure, using pressing block.

Care
The cloth is hand-washable, but so bulky that facilities are unlikely to be available, so it is normally dry-cleaned.

WEST OF ENGLAND

Very high quality woollen cloth, produced in the Cotswold area. The type of cloth varies, e.g. it may be flannel, and it often has a characteristic window-pane check design.

Used for men's suits, trousers, and overcoats, and for women's coats.

Width
140cm (54in).

Handling
To be handled only by those with a great deal of experience. Choose tailored styles. Use firm interfacing, make hand-worked

tailored buttonholes. Garments require lining.

Thread
Synthetic or mercerized.

Needle
Machine: 100 16. Large stitch.
Hand: 6.

Pressing
Hot iron, damp cloth, firm pressure.

Care
Dry clean.

WHIPCORD

A twill weave fabric using bulky yarns to give a raised look to the twill ribs. Although originally always wool or worsted, possibly with cotton filling, it is now made in any fibre, including nylon, polyester, acrylic, viscose, cotton and blends.

According to fibre content and weight, it is used for making tough riding and sports clothes; light sports clothing such as tennis and squash shorts; children's clothes; men's trousers; and car seat covers.

Handle according to the weight and fibre content.

WHITNEY
An overcoating cloth made in wool. It is soft and thick with a face-finish on the right side that produces a wavy line effect. If made from good quality woollen yarn, it is an excellent and hard-wearing cloth.

Handle as thick overcoating, such as Chinchilla Cloth, page 127.

WIGAN
A dull-finish, plain-weave cotton cloth, usually in dark colours but resembling sheeting. Its main use is as a backing or interfacing in men's jackets, and coats, but not easily obtained on the roll.

See Woven Interfacing (page 251) for alternatives.

WILLOW
A stiff fabric woven from esparto grass and cotton, the result is similar to Sparterie.

Used for making the foundations of hats. See Sparterie, page 233.

WINCEYETTE

A plain-weave cotton fabric that has been brushed to give a warm soft feel. It may be plain or printed. It washes well.

Used for nightwear, sheets, pillowcases, baby wear. It is highly inflammable and should never be used for nightdresses for children or elderly people. There is a flame-resist treatment that can be applied to Winceyette but it is destroyed by boiling, by bleach and by ordinary soap. Also it is virtually impossible to buy flame-resistant Winceyette by the metre as most of it is used in ready-to-wear manufacture.

Handle as Brushed Cotton, see page 111.

Care

Hot wash or boil, iron slightly damp with a medium hot iron. If flame-resistant, wash only in soapless detergent.

WOOL

The yarn made from a sheep's fleece; it is hairy and hard-wearing. The fabrics made from wool are warm and easy to manipulate, but good pressing is essential.

See also Sheep's Wool, page 40.

WOOL CRÊPE

Soft, drapy fabric for dresses, usually lightweight but heavier types may be used for ladies' suits. A slack weave fabric with typical crêpe surface. Sometimes the wrong side appears smooth by comparison.

WORSTED

The yarn from a sheep's fleece; it is firm, thin and twisted for added strength. Used for making worsted cloth which is usually light and springy, closely woven and smooth to touch. Requires expert handling.

See also Unfinished Worsted, page 243.

WOVEN INTERFACINGS

These are all grained, even if they are iron-on varieties, so they must be cut to the same grain as the garment section. Choose according to the type and weight of fabric. Use the size of needle and type of thread appropriate to the fabric. Make sure the interfacing is washable if the garment is intended to be washable.

See also Canvas Interfacing, page 120.

Z

ZEPHYR

Originally, a good quality lightweight worsted yarn, but now refers to fine, soft sheer gingham type cottons.

See Gingham, page 160.

ZIBELENE

A heavy coating fabric with a long, shaggy nap laid in one direction. Usually woollen, but there may be other fibres such as acrylic included. Strong colours are normally used and the cloth is often striped.

Used for women's coats, capes, children's coats.

Width

140–150cm (54–60in).

Handling

The cloth looks most effective made into simple but loose fitting capes and coats with features, such as patch pockets and hood, and frog style fastenings. Stripes can be chevroned effectively. No lining is needed unless a fitted coat is made. Use firm interfacing. Cut one way with pile running down.

ZIBELENE

Thread
Synthetic or mercerized.

Needle
Machine: 100 16. Large stitch.
Hand: 6.

Pressing
Hot iron and damp cloth.

Care
Dry clean unless labelled washable.

Part Three

Sewing Equipment

With all crafts it helps to have the correct tools and equipment to hand. The results are better and the whole business of creating something is much more enjoyable, because good tools are invariably more comfortable to use, as well as being more efficient and economical in time and movement.

This list includes all essential items and also a few additional ones that make sewing easier. No outright gimmicks are included; I always feel they are mainly for people who want to sew but resort to gadgets in order to avoid learning the skills involved.

Threads and Haberdashery

In addition to equipment, an assortment of haberdashery and threads soon accumulates. It helps to know which are going to be in constant use and therefore worth keeping in stock. It is also very important to know which threads should be used for which tasks. So often it is not until you begin handling a fabric that you can decide exactly what haberdashery will produce the best results.

EQUIPMENT

Sewing Machine

You may already possess one that you are happy with, but if you are intending to buy a new one do remember that, as with all expensive items of machinery, you only get what you pay for. A cheap, poorly constructed machine with a strange name will not last your lifetime and certainly will not be fit to hand on down the family. It is usually possible to find a shop to give you a considerable cash discount, but beware of a machine advertised at an enormous reduction — it may well be that it was an unsatisfactory model or that it is about to be superseded by a much better one. Avoid buying a second-hand machine privately as there is usually a good reason for the sale. No woman will part with a treasured sewing machine in perfect order.

Buy the best machine that you can afford. Ask your friends about their machines and try them out. Find out which makes are preferred by the teachers at the local schools and colleges.

When you find one you like the sound of, go and try it at your local shop. Check that you can lift it unaided; that threading is simple; that changing the stitches is easy and feet can be changed without the aid of tools. Make sure the machine does what you want it to do: don't be brainwashed by sales talk about the latest embroidery stitch, you may never need to use it. Consider your own needs and think of the direction your sewing is likely to take in the future. For example, if you make a lot of children's clothes, blouses and men's shirts you need a machine that makes good buttonholes at the flick of a lever or knob. If you are shortly to retire and will have more time to make your own clothes, it is very unlikely that you need a machine that performs a wide variety of embroidery stitches.

If you cannot afford the machine you like, make do with your old one until you can afford it.

Extras

Always keep the following within reach as you sit at the machine.

Duster Use for wiping away the coloured dust-like deposit left by thread as it passes through the control points. This is easily seen if your machine is light-coloured and you have been using dark thread, but remember all threads leave the deposit. If left it may discolour the next fabric, but it will also build up and eventually affect the efficient running of the machine.

Oil This must be machine oil sold specially for sewing machines. If the machine is making undue noise, one spot of oil in the spool socket will often cure it. When sewing plastics, one spot of oil on the needle will ensure smoother penetration of the fabric.

Oil the machine once a week if you use it regularly. Put one spot in each oiling point. Wipe the machine all over with the duster and leave overnight. Before using the machine again run it for a while unthreaded with a piece of fabric under the needle to soak up the oil that has run down the needle.

Needles Keep an adequate stock of ordinary machine needles and also some for sewing leather. You may also need ball point needles for synthetic jersey. Have all sizes so that you will not be tempted to use the wrong sized needle.

Change the needle often. Synthetic fibres blunt a needle so quickly that it is unlikely to be still sharp after making one garment. Throw used machine needles away immediately, do not put them back in the drawer.

Thread snips Although your machine will have a shaped metal blade situated near the needle for cutting threads, there are many occasions when you want to trim the thread ends very precisely. Thread snips have small scissor-like blades but no finger-holes. Hold the blades near the tip and close them over the thread. They are quick to use and allow your scissors to remain with your hand-sewing equipment.

Pin-holder Keep a dish or pot or a magnetic pin tube by the machine for depositing pins removed from fabric. It not only keeps them tidy but avoids the danger of their falling into the machine.

Brush and Screwdriver These may well be in the box of additional sewing feet and should therefore be near the machine. If not, keep them somewhere close. The needle-fitting screwdriver is needed every time you change the needle. The brush should be used very frequently to remove the fluff that quickly accumulates round the head of the needle, below the needle plate and round the spool socket area. If not removed, this will soon build up and cause jamming.

HAND-SEWING EQUIPMENT

Much of the success of your work will depend on your ability to hand-sew. Although a lot can be done by machine most people come to enjoy the perfection that hand finishing produces. Even if you want to keep it to the minimum, the first stages of tailor tacking and tacking should be performed by hand on most fabrics. In addition many items of clothing look best if the hem is hand-finished.

Needles

This is the most basic tool — never use the wrong type of needle.

Betweens Sometimes called quilting needles. These are in fact the correct needles for professional hand-sewing. They are short and therefore easier to use than longer ones. Stitches are quicker to make and smaller and more even as a result. Use size 4, 5, or 6 for tacking and tailor tacking, sizes 7, 8, 9, 10 for hand-sewing. Choose the size according to the thickness of the fabric. Do not use needles for too long, they quickly become blunt. Sizes available: 1–12.

Ball point Some synthetic jersey fabrics can be difficult to sew with the sharp pointed between, so keep some ball point needles to use in case of difficulty.

Sharps These are long needles which can be used for piercing several thicknesses of bulky fabric where a between is not long enough. Such occasions may include sewing on buttons and work on furnishings. Sizes available: 1–12.

Crewel These are for embroidery. They are similar to sharps but have a longer eye to take thicker threads or stranded embroidery thread. Sizes available: 1–12.

Tapestry For working tapestry, but also useful for a variety of other sewing purposes because the needle has a large eye and a blunt point that does not split fibres or threads. Sizes available: 18, 20, 22, 24, 26.

Straws Also called milliners' needles, these are long with round eyes and are useful where several layers have to be pierced or where a lot of stitches have to be gathered at once as in smocking. Sizes available: 1–12.

Glovers Also called leather needles, these have the same spear-sharp point as the machine needles. The point cuts leather and plastic without tearing it by forcing a hole in it. Sizes available: 1–8.

Darners Darning needles are very long with large eyes for taking wool. The additional length enables you to span the hole being darned and this makes it impossible to use the needle for any other purpose. Sizes available: 1, 3, 5, 7, 9, 14, 15, 16, 17, 18.

Chenille Although originally intended only for chenille work as they are short and have very large eyes, like tapestry needles they are very useful for other tasks involving thick threads, such as attaching knotted fringe to fabric. Sizes available: 18, 20, 22, 24.

Mattress This is a large curved needle, originally intended for attaching buttons to mattresses, but also very useful for many furnishing processes.

Beading Beading needles are very fine with long eyes. Available only in small sizes 10, 12, 13, they are very long to enable several round or bugle beads or seed pearls to be threaded on at one time. This type of decoration is usually worked on fine materials and the small size of the needle ensures that the weave of the fabric is not disturbed.

Choice of needle size

The choice of needle size, i.e. its thickness, depends on the weave of the fabric and on the thickness of thread being used. The needle pierces a hole in the fabric and the thread follows. If the hole is too big, the thread is loosely held in it, which causes an ugly stitch, and makes it difficult to sew evenly. If the hole made by the needle is too small to take the thread, then thread abrasion occurs and the fabric may be damaged. When machining, a stitch may not even form, and when hand-sewing, the needle may go into the fabric but when the eye reaches it you will have to pull the needle to get the eye and the thread through. The wrong size of hand-sewing needle always makes it an uncomfortable procedure. Always choose a bigger needle when using thread double so that a bigger hole is made.

A general rule is: the closer the weave of the fabric the smaller the needle. The small needle can penetrate between fibres. If the fibres are very durable and close, e.g. fine polyester knit, then a ball point needle — small size — will make penetration easier. Use small needles on fine or sheer fabrics so that smaller less obvious stitches are made. Use a fine needle too on open or lacy fabrics.

STRAIGHT STITCHING

Fabric	Machine needle no.	Hand needle no.	No. of stitches to cm (in)
Fine Fabrics such as:			
Challis	80 (11)	7–8	3–4 (8–10)
Chiffon	70 or 80 (9–11)	8 or 9	3–4 (8–10)

Cotton Jersey	70 or 80 (9–11)	8 or 9	3–4 (8–10)
Cotton Lawn	70 or 80 (9–11)	8 or 9	3–4 (8–10)
Crêpe	70 or 80 (9–11)	8 or 9	3–4 (8–10)
Fine knit	70 or 80 (9–11)	8 or 9	3–4 (8–10)
Georgette	70 or 80 (9–11)	8 or 9	3–4 (8–10)
Net	80 (11)	7	3–4 (8–10)
Nylon	70 or 80 (9–11)	8 or 9	3–4 (8–10)
Seersucker	80 (11)	7	3–4 (8–10)
Surah	70 or 80 (9–11)	8	3–4 (8–10)
Taffeta	70 or 80 (9–11)	8	3–4 (8–10)
Voile	70 or 80 (9–11)	8 or 9	3–4 (8–10)
Fine-Medium Fabrics such as:			
Brocade	90 or 100 (11–16)	7 or 8	4–5 (10–12)
Cotton Piqué	90 (14)	6	4–5 (10–12)
Firm knits	80 or 90 (11–14)	7 or 8	4–5 (10–12)
Linen	80 or 90 (11–14)	7 or 8	4–5 (10–12)
Matelassé	80 (11)	7	4–5 (10–12)
Medium-Heavy Fabrics such as:			
Bonded Fabric	90 (14)	6	3–4 (8–10)
Denim	100 (16)	6	3–4 (8–10)
Fur Fabric	90 or 100 (14–16)	5 or 6	4 (10)
Heavy Satin	80 (11)	7	5–6 (12–14)
P.V.C.	100 (16)	8	3–4 (8–10)
Slub Silk	90 (14)	7 or 8	5–6 (12–14)
Suede and Leather	80 or 90 (11–14)	6 or 7	5–6 (12–14)
Tweed Coating	100 or 110 (16–18)	5 or 6	4–5 (10–12)
Velvet	80 (11)	8 or 9	5 (12)
Worsted Suitings	90 (14)	7 or 8	5 (12)

DARNING BY MACHINE

Fabric	Thread	Machine needle no.	Stitch length
Fine Fabrics such as:			
Cotton Lawns	Anchor Machine Embroidery No. 50	70	Nil Feed down
Polyester/ Cottons	Anchor Machine Embroidery No. 50	70	Nil Feed down
Medium Fabrics			
Cottons	Anchor Machine Embroidery No. 30	80	Nil Feed down
Linens	Anchor Machine Embroidery No. 30	80	Nil Feed down

BUTTONHOLES

Fabric	Thread	Machine needle no. (1)	(2)	Stitch length
Fine Fabrics such as:				
Challis		70	70	Satin stitch
Chiffon		70	70	Satin stitch
Cotton jersey		70	70	Satin stitch
Cotton Lawn		70	80	Satin stitch
Crêpe	Drima (1)	70	80	Satin stitch
Georgette	or	70	70	Satin stitch
Lace	Anchor Machine	70	70	Satin stitch
Net	Embroidery	70	70	Satin stitch
Organdie	No. 50 (2)	70	70	Satin stitch
Seersucker		70	70	Satin stitch
Surah		70	70	Satin stitch
Taffeta		70	70	Satin stitch
Voile		70	70	Satin stitch
Fine-Medium Fabrics such as:				
Brocade		80 or 90	80 or 90	Satin stitch
Linen		80 or 90	80 or 90	Satin stitch
Matelassé	Drima (1)	80 or 90	80 or 90	Satin stitch
Piqué Cotton	or	80 or 90	80 or 90	Satin stitch
Poplin	Anchor Machine	80 or 90	80 or 90	Satin stitch
Satin	Embroidery	80 or 90	80 or 90	Satin stitch
Taffeta	No. 50 (2)	80 or 90	80 or 90	Satin stitch
Fine knits		80 or 90	80 or 90	Satin stitch
Viscose spun		80 or 90	80 or 90	Satin stitch
Medium-Heavy Fabrics such as:				
Bonded Fabric		90	90	Satin stitch
Corduroy		90 or 100	90	Satin stitch
Denim		90 or 100	90	Satin stitch
Dress Wool		90	90	Satin stitch
Flannel		90 or 100	90	Satin stitch
Fur Fabric	Drima (1)	90 or 100	90	Satin stitch
Heavy Satin	or	90	90	Satin stitch
Jersey	Anchor Machine	90	90	Satin stitch
Slub Silk	Embroidery	90	90	Satin stitch
Suede and Leather	No. 30 (2)	90	90	Satin stitch
Tweed Coating		90 or 100	90	Satin stitch
Velvet		90	90	Satin stitch
Worsted Suitings		90	90	Satin stitch

DECORATIVE STITCHING

Fabric	Thread	Machine needle no.
Fine Fabrics such as:		
Challis		70
Chiffon		60
Cotton Jersey		70
Cotton Lawn		70
Crêpe		70
Georgette	Anchor Machine	70
Net	Embroidery No. 50	70
Organdie		60
Seersucker		70
Silk		60
Surah		70
Taffeta		70
Voile		70
Medium Fabrics such as:		
Brocade		80
Cotton Piqué		80
Fine knits	Anchor Machine	80
Gingham	Embroidery No. 30	80
Linen		80
Matelassé		80
Poplin		80

Thimble

This must be the most ill-treated piece of equipment. There seems to be a vogue for manufacturing thimbles for commemorative purposes, and collecting them for display. This is quite acceptable provided functional thimbles are to be found in the work box and seen to be used, but this appears too often to be an old-fashioned notion now.

A thimble must be used if good, even stitches of strength are to be produced and if the sewer is to be comfortable. A bare finger obviously cannot be used to push a steel point through fabric, however soft.

Use a thimble without a top — a tailor's thimble — and all the arguments against the use of a thimble are dissipated. The open-end allows ventilation and therefore comfort in use. The thimble is, in fact, completely forgotten. To form a stitch correctly, the eye of the between needle is lodged against the side of the thimble and the needle is inserted and removed in one action.

A thimble with a top can only be worn for short periods of time, because of its lack of ventilation. Use it only for embroidery — the needle is inserted, the fingers let go in order to push with the top of the thimble, then the hand moves to the under side of the frame to take the needle through. Dissatisfaction with hand-sewing is often caused by trying to wear this type of thimble and then discarding it in desperation.

Scissors

Ideally three pairs are needed for making clothes and for household sewing, with an optional pair of very small scissors for embroidery.

Scissors made from drop-forged steel are best. These are heavier than cheaper types, but good scissors are constructed so that the weight is distributed and does not rest on the wrist or fingers. Although obviously good sharp blades are important, make sure the finger and hand holes are big enough. Embroidery scissors have small finger holes and are therefore very uncomfortable to use for anything other than snipping threads.

Cutting out shears Many people try to make do without these but as with other aspects of the craft, the job becomes easier, quicker and less daunting with the correct tool. Cutting out shears should be as large as possible (the long blade cuts accurately), they are 'side bent', which means the scissor is shaped to allow four fingers in the lower part of the handle and the thumb in the upper part, and yet the blades are level and balanced correctly. When trying them, remember that the scissors rest on the table while in use.

Trimming shears A medium pair of side-bent scissors with blades about 15cm (6in) long are needed for trimming edges of seams after sewing, for layering turnings and other jobs where control is required.

Small scissors These will have two equal holes, the upper one for the thumb and the lower one for the forefinger. The second finger supports the lower arm of the scissors to control it. Make sure your fingers fit the holes comfortably. The blades are short and these scissors should only be used for snipping thread, snipping turnings and cutting buttonholes. Never attempt actually to cut fabric with them, as it will spring out of the short blades and produce a chopped effect. These scissors can also be used for unpicking, and for this it is easier to hold the blades only (in the same way that 'thread snips' are held).

Never abuse any of your scissors by cutting paper or anything other than thread and fabric — use an old pair of scissors instead that will not be harmed. Old, blunt scissors cut paper more accurately than good, sharp ones anyway.

Tape measure

This is an obvious piece of equipment to include and most people have one, but if buying a new one, make sure it has a metric scale on one side. Tapes with both metric and imperial scales on one side are confusing to read. The clearest type is one that has a different colour on each side, and on the metric side a clear mark or change of colour every 10 cm.

Adjustable marker

Although this has been around for some years, surprisingly few people have discovered how useful it can be. It is a short metal rule with a sliding arrow which can be set to a certain measurement, and it is quicker to use than a tape measure. It is good for any job where a particular measurement is to be used several times, for example spacing buttonholes, marking the depth of a hem, width of a belt, etc. As the arrow is firmly set there is no danger of error. Make sure the marker is graded in centimetres when you buy. Some have both metric and imperial scales.

Tailor's chalk

To be effective tailor's chalk must be kept sharp. To sharpen, open your medium scissors wide and holding them by the apex, slide the blade held flat down the edges of the chalk, shaving in gently on both sides until very sharp. An alternative is to buy the chalk in a container. The container protects the chalk from breakage and also has on it a small blade for sharpening the chalk.

Tailor's chalk can be seen on most fabrics if a clear sharp line is drawn. Even on white fabric the chalk will show as a dull mark. Always use the chalk with the entire sharp edge on the fabric and draw firmly. It should not be held like a pencil as only the point can be used this way, producing a vague line and often wrinkling the fabric. Always use a ruler for straight lines. The chalk brushes off easily afterwards so it may be used on the right side of the fabric. Avoid coloured chalk, it is always difficult to remove, and may be impossible to remove on some fabrics.

Make good use of the chalk. The lines can be clearly seen when machining, so mark the stopping points at the ends of darts, draw straight lines and stopping points on pleats, seams, openings of all kinds, mark depths of hems, sleeve lengths, etc., and use anywhere where it is essential to stitch lines of equal lengths. When fitting a garment on someone or fitting chair covers, etc., chalk is useful for marking alterations.

Marking pencil

Tailor's chalk is not convenient to use for marking dots so these and other small marks may be indicated by using a white marking pencil. The pencil has a brush at the other end for removing the marks. Keep the pencil sharp.

It is useful for marking balance marks, seam lines, etc., on the fabric before removing the pattern.

Beeswax

A traditional piece of equipment, but many modern sewers have not discovered the pleasure of its use. It is bought in small cakes. It is also available in containers but this limits its use.

When sewing permanently with double thread, e.g. sewing on buttons, stitching sleeves into armholes, back-stitching for strength, etc., prevent the threads from parting by running the double thread through beeswax after threading through the needle and knotting the ends, then twisting it into a cord by rubbing the palms together across the threads. Another use for beeswax is to run synthetic sewing thread through it to prevent twisting and snarling in hand-sewing. When zip fasteners become stiff to fasten, especially after dry cleaning, run beeswax over the teeth to lubricate.

Bodkin

This is another very old tool. Some people are lucky enough to have inherited a bone or ivory bodkin, but if you haven't one of those, they are now made in plastic. Use it for removing tacking threads after permanent stitching has been finished. The rounded point slips easily under the thread without harming the fabric. It is quicker to use than fingers and much safer than the points of scissors.

Pins

These are not an expensive item and yet too many people buy inferior quality pins that make holes in some fabrics and even eventually go rusty. Buy good steel dressmaker's pins in a cardboard or plastic box. The box is lined with black paper which prevents rust. Keep them in this paper or at least take out and use only a few at a time. Generally three different lengths are available, 16mm long for lingerie and fine fabrics; 25mm long for most general use and 30mm long for thick fabrics, making lampshades, etc. There are also long pins with coloured plastic heads usually bought on a circular card. These are excellent for use on open or lacy fabrics where ordinary pins could be left undetected, and for work on furnishings. They are also slightly easier to pick up, but their excessive length makes them inconvenient to use for general work on garments.

Transparent plastic pins are also available but their use is limited to a narrow range of synthetic fabrics that are difficult to pierce with conventional pins. Plastic pins are thicker, they are soft and bend easily, and they do not have sharp points.

Ruler

Always keep a ruler with your sewing equipment. Use it with tailor's chalk for marking and for checking that lines of tacking are straight. The most useful length rulers are 50cm or 1 metre, and if you can buy these from a specialist shop they will have metal ends and will be rectangular in cross section, making them easier to use than the shaped variety.

Plastic Curve

These shapes were once made in wood and used only by people engaged in pattern drafting. Now they are made from transparent plastic with a number of generally useful markings on them. After altering a paper pattern or making fitting alterations to a garment, use the curve, with pencil or tailor's chalk, to re-mark curves on necklines, armholes, sleeve heads, etc. Make use of the markings on the curve when drawing two identical curves.

Tracing Wheel and Carbon Paper

Using this is a quick way of transferring pattern markings to fabric before removing the paper pattern, but it is only possible to mark one side of the fabric. The coloured carbon marks can be difficult, sometimes impossible, to remove, so for this reason always mark only the wrong side of the fabric. Using a colour of carbon paper that does not contrast too greatly with the fabric, in case the marks come through to the right side, lift pattern, place the paper carbon side to wrong side of fabric, replace pattern and run tracing wheel along pattern lines. Use the paper folded double to mark two layers of fabric at once.

Elastic Threader

This is a flat metal needle with a large triangular eye. Tie or sew elastic, tape, cord, drawstring, etc., to this eye, and thread.

Rouleau Turner

This is another traditional piece of equipment that is being produced again after a lapse of many years. It is a long round needle with a ball shaped end and a large eye. After stitching a piece of rouleau, slip the needle into the tube of fabric, sew the eye to the seam allowances at the top and gently ease through. The advantage of the turner is that, generally, most of the length of rouleau can be pushed on to the needle before you start to pull the fabric, so avoiding the great risk of breaking the stitching.

Fray Stop

This is a colourless liquid bought in a small plastic bottle, which controls fraying of fabric. Eject it sparingly on to badly fraying edges of fabric while working on it. This will make hand-working easier and will prevent fraying woven fabrics from causing jamming in the machine. The liquid remains effective through wear and washing.

Skirt Hem Leveller

Although it is possible, and indeed necessary, to ensure most hems are level by repeated measuring and trying on yourself, nevertheless it is useful to have a hem leveller for accuracy; all types are best operated by one person while a second person wears the hem. Fabrics, such as chiffon and voile, and skirts cut on the bias are very difficult to level as the fabric moves, so best results are gained by using a hem leveller and a friend.

After deciding on the length and marking the point with a pin, stand still, preferably on a table or at the top of the stairs, while the friend moves round making marks at intervals at the same level. The most accurate marker is one that puffs chalk from a nozzle, but be sure the marker has a firm base to it to keep it still while in use. If chalk will be invisible on your fabric, or this type of marker is not available, pins can be inserted.

A marker can be simply constructed by screwing a long ruler or straight piece of wood to a firm wood block.

Threads

Sewing threads are produced with a certain number of twists per centimetre. Without this twist, the thread could not be controlled in sewing because the individual plies would fray and break. Twisting gives the thread uniform strength and also the flexibility that is so vital in sewing threads. Most threads are now produced with a Z twist (see diagram on page 30) because this functions best in modern sewing machines. The direction of twist does not affect the strength of the thread, but if used on a machine for which it is not correct, the results will be unsuitable. A machine which is not functioning perfectly, or which has worn parts, will often not accept a Z twist thread and may fail to form a stitch.

Tacking Thread For tacking and tailor tacking, a soft, fluffy, unfinished thread, bought on large reels, is used, e.g. Atlas. The fluff ensures that the thread grips the fabric, so keeping layers together for fitting, machining, stitching etc.; its softness ensures that it can be easily removed later, often breaking when pulled, without damaging the fabric. Long lengths can be re-used. Use double for tailor tacking, the tufts then stick firmly in the fabric for as long as they are needed.

Never use tacking thread for permanent stitching. Avoid the use of black or coloured tacking thread on white fabrics. The white thread is easily visible on all colours; the texture can be seen even if the fabric is white.

Sewing Threads There are two main types of thread. The first is mercerized cotton, e.g. super sheen, in size 40, fine (very easily available in a wide range of colours); and 30, coarse, for furnishing and heavy fabrics such as coatings and suiting. There is a very fine 50, but its availability is limited.

A mercerized thread has a shiny, silky appearance. As well as creating this characteristic lustre, the process of mercerization slightly increases the strength of the thread, so that a finer thread can be used than would be possible with ordinary cotton. The threads for mercerizing are twisted fairly loosely, and singed to remove the surface hairs. The smoother, shiny thread gives a good appearance on fabric.

The second type of thread is spun polyester, e.g. Drima. The thread for general sewing is fine yet very strong so can be used for sewing all types of fabric and for all items of clothing and furnishing. There is a wide range of colours available, although as these threads disappear into the fabric more than cotton threads, a perfect match is not so essential.

Drima is finer than cotton thread. Use a smaller size machine and hand needle to prevent slipping and wear on the thread. The thread is tow spun. See page 27.

Cotton Also available, in black and white, is matt cotton thread in sizes 10–60. This is not particularly suitable for making clothes but can be used for furnishings and household items.

Silk Thread This is available but its distribution is limited. It is usually in 50-metre lengths on cardboard spools. It is expensive but quite nice to use on special garments made from exceptionally good wool or silk.

Never use sewing threads for tacking, they are too slippery and harsh. When hand-sewing, use short lengths of thread, as it quickly becomes worn with constant passing through fabric, especially the synthetic fibre fabrics. For this reason never use cotton thread for sewing synthetic fibre fabric, as the fibres act abrasively on the thread and quickly wear it through.

Buttonhole Thread This is a thick thread for making hand-worked buttonholes on coats, and also for decorative top stitching on medium- and heavy-weight fabrics. Polyester thread is widely available, silk thread less so.

When hand-sewing, use a needle with an eye large enough to take the thread without pressure, or it will quickly fray. When machining with these threads, use them on the top of the machine and insert a No. 110 or No. 18 machine needle. If possible, use normal sewing thread on the machine spool.

Button Thread This is a thick glacé finished linen or polyester thread used for attaching buttons to coats and for some soft furnishing processes where its strength is required. It is available in a limited range of colours.

Gimp A thick thread with a cotton core and silk or mercerized cotton covering, used for inserting in hand-made coat buttonholes to produce a raised hard-wearing edge. It is available in limited colours, and often only found in tailor's supply shops. A substitute is fine crochet cotton or several strands of embroidery thread. The latter is not thick enough for coat buttonholes but works well in machine-made buttonholes.

Machine Embroidery Thread A finely twisted mercerized cotton thread available in a wide range of colours, e.g. Anchor. Sizes 30, 50 and 60 are most used although finer ones exist. It produces excellent machine-made buttonholes on fine fabrics. On medium weight fabrics, work round the buttonhole twice for a sufficiently firm result. It can also be used for very fine hand-work, e.g. decorative work on a christening gown.

HABERDASHERY

Press Fasteners

Keep a variety of different types in stock. Conventional metal press studs are available in black and white and the most useful sizes are from 00 (small) to 2, although there is a very large one available for furnishings. A small size transparent plastic press stud is made, which is useful for baby clothes and where a single fastener is required, e.g. on the neckline of a blouse, but they are not very durable. Use buttonhole stitch to attach all press studs.

Slightly more bulky press fasteners already attached to tape are useful for furnishings and for some items of clothing. In addition there are decorative fancy-capped metal stud fasteners that are excellent for sports and casual clothes, children's wear and leather and suede, as well as for furnishings.

Hooks

Hooks and eyes and hooks and bars are available in a variety of sizes but the most useful are from 00 (small) to 2; they can be black or silver coloured. Attach with buttonhole stitch. Large soft covered hooks and eyes are also produced. They are sometimes referred to as fur hooks but they can be used successfully to fasten any bulky fabric provided the style is loose fitting and no strain is put on the hook.

Larger metal hooks of various types are available and are used for waistbands and Petersham bands. Choose the type according to the process.

Velcro

This is a nylon woven tape in two parts which fasten when pressed together. One side of the tape is hooked and the other side appears fluffy but is in fact looped. The resulting fastening is strong. Velcro has a great many uses, e.g. for cuffs and waistbands, detachable pieces and decorations, cushion covers and pelmets. It is available in three widths and it can be cut to shape without fear of fraying. It is very durable and is washable. Attach with small hemming stitches using a small size needle to penetrate the Velcro easily, or use a straight or small zigzag machine stitch.

Velcro is available in a wide range of colours, but as it is not used where it will be visible a good colour match is not important. Keep a selection of Velcro to substitute for other fastenings when desired.

Button Moulds

There are several types of metal and plastic button mould that can be covered with fabric. Most have either a stud fastening or a special press stud that fits a hollow in the back of the button. All are easy to cover and attach and it is worth keeping some of all sizes.

Petersham

Apart from its use inside waistbands or by itself in the waists of skirts and trousers, Petersham is used as a stay inside waisted dresses and a length can be used as a fitting aid. Petersham is straight or curved to follow the waist and it is available in several widths. The most satisfactory types are made from polyester fibre as these are not adversely affected by washing. Elastic Petersham is useful where size is liable to vary slightly and boned Petersham can be used for additional rigidity.

Keep the type you prefer for your needs. It is more economical to buy a large amount and cut off exactly what you need. Apart from economy, the advantage of keeping a stock is that you can substitute a Petersham finish for other waist finishes, whenever it seems desirable.

Wundaweb and Bondaweb

It is a great advantage to have both these adhesives. Wundaweb strip adhesive can be used in hems of garments, curtains and other furnishings and small pieces help to prevent fraying where seam allowances are trimmed to the minimum, e.g. sleeve openings, points of collars. Always place between two layers of fabric and press, using a damp muslin and medium-hot iron, until it has thoroughly adhered to both layers of fabric. Bondaweb is a similar adhesive web but is attached to paper and in sheet form. Cut to size for buttonhole pipings, appliqué openings, etc.; press with paper uppermost by the same method as for Wundaweb. When cool, remove the paper and continue sewing. When pressed again, it will melt so it must then be covered with another layer of fabric. Bondaweb slightly stiffens and lessens fraying.

Fold-a-Band

An accurately produced iron-on woven strip, 6cm wide, with a row of slits running along the centre. Place on the wrong side of fabric and press in place using the centre and the edges as a guide to making even-sized cuffs, pocket welts, waistbands, central openings, etc. Use also along the knife edge of pleats. The central slits enable the fabric to be crisply pressed into a fold wherever Fold-a-Band is used.

Elastic

There is a wide variety of types of elastic available and, apart from a selection of all-purpose elastic, a supply of the following specialist types is useful.

Shirring elastic — a thin cord made from viscose and elastomer for winding on to the machine spool, using sewing thread on top; or it can be fed into the machine through the hole in the plate beneath the foot and held in place with a small zigzag stitch. Several rows of shirring are needed for sufficient grip.

Waistband elastic is made from viscose, nylon, rubber and elastomer. It is usually 3cm wide with very firm vertical ribs, but has a soft edge to sew through.

Baby elastic is made from viscose and rubber. It is very narrow and soft and, unlike the firmer ones, it has plenty of 'give' but is not inclined to tighten up in wear.

Zip Fasteners

A selection of metal and nylon zips in the two most useful lengths — 20cm and 55cm — and also the concealed type can be kept. Other special zips, such as open-ended, jeans' zips and heavyweight moulded plastic zips, will have to be purchased according to need.

The following table shows the range available, the lengths and the approximate number of colours in each type.

Application	Type	Lengths available cm	Colours available
All dressmaking purposes	Lightweight Nylon	10, 15, 18, 20, 23 25, 30, 35, 40, 45 50, 55	41
Dresses, Knitwear	Featherweight Coloured Metal	10, 15, 18, 20, 23 25, 30, 35, 40, 45 50, 55	49
Skirts, Slacks	Lightweight Coloured Metal	15, 18, 20	24
Dresses, Skirts and Slacks	Lightweight Concealed Polyester	20, 23, 55	14
Cardigans	Lightweight Coloured Metal Open-end	25, 30, 35, 40, 45 50, 55, 60	15
Jackets	Medium-weight Aluminium Open-end	30, 35, 40, 45, 50 55, 60, 65, 70	15
Cardigans/ Jackets	Medium-weight Polyester Open-end	30, 35, 40, 45, 50 55, 60, 65	19
Jackets	Heavyweight Moulded Nylon	45, 50, 55, 60, 65 70, 75	10
Trousers	Lightweight Nickel Silver	18, 20, 23, 25	15
Jeans	Medium-weight Brass	15, 18, 20	6

Nearest Inch Equivalents to Centimetre Lengths

cm	10	15	18	20	23	25	30	35	40	45	50	55	60	65	70	75
in	4	6	7	8	9	10	12	14	16	18	20	22	24	26	28	30

Quick Reference List

Some of the terms that may be encountered in connection with textiles.

ANNE An obsolete unit of measurement used for silk.
ARMURE Small chain designs brought back to France from the East by the Crusaders. Sometimes used to describe metallic designs.
ARABESQUE Scroll design made with cord, or stitched.
BALANCE The ratio of warp yarns to weft.
BALE A pack of compressed raw fibre.
BEIGE Unbleached wool.
BIAS The cross of fabric, at an angle of 45° to the weft.
BLEEDING Loss of dye.
BOLT A complete roll of fabric as it comes from the manufacturer. The length of the piece varies.
BRIDES The warp and weft threads of lace fabrics, connecting the pattern.
BROCHE Raised designs on the surface of fabric, often introduced with the warp.
CHEESE A cone of yarn.
CHEMICAL SPINNING In producing man-made fibres, polymer solution is forced through holes in a spinneret and several filaments are combined and twisted or spun.
CONVERTERS Those who specialize in finishing cloth after weaving or knitting.
CORE-SPUN YARN Yarn that consists of a central core (elastomer, rubber, another yarn) with a covering of another yarn.
CROCKING Loss of colour through abrasion in wear.
CROSS-DYEING A combination of piece-dyeing and yarn-dyeing.
DENIER The size of filament yarn, e.g. 1 denier expresses 9,000 metres that weigh 1 gram.
DETERGENT . A cleaning agent. Now generally refers to those not containing soap.
DRY-SPINNING Used in man-made fibre production. The basic solid material is dissolved and then spun into warm air.
ELASTICITY The ability of a fibre to return immediately to its former size after stretching.

QUICK REFERENCE LIST

FIBRES Threads of raw material, natural or man-made.

FILAMENT Continuous strands of fibre. All synthetics can be produced in this form, without being broken until required.

FILLING The crosswise or weft yarns in fabric.

FLOATS Additional yarns used to introduce patterns in fabrics, when not being used they pass or float across the back of the fabric.

HANK A skein of yarn, often in the raw state.

LOFT The ability of a fibre of yarn to spring back to its original thickness.

MELT-SPINNING In man-made fibre production the basic material is melted before being spun.

NAP Surface pile or brushed effect that lies in one direction only.

OLEFIN Oil-based fibres.

PICKING Inserting weft or filling yarns.

PILE Flattened or upright tufts on the surface of fabric.

PILLING The tendency of man-made fibres to roll into tiny balls on the surface of the fabric.

RHEA Ramie.

SLIPPAGE Movement of yarn in fabrics occurring at points of strain.

STAPLE Short fibres, natural and man-made. Length varies according to fibre.

SWATCH A sample of fabric, either specially prepared, or cut from the roll.

THERMOPLASTIC A yarn that can be permanently put in any shape or position using heat.

THREAD COUNT The number of warp and weft threads in 1 square inch of fabric before dyeing, shrinkage, etc. Warp is quoted first, followed by weft, e.g. 110 × 100.

TOP DYEING Dyeing on top of other colours.

WALE Rib in woven fabrics or line of stitching in a knit fabric.

WET SPINNING Used in man-made fibre production. The filament from the spinneret is passed into an acid-bath to coagulate.

WOOF Crosswise or weft yarns.

List of Foreign Fibre Names*

Name of fibre	Type	Manufacturer
ACELBA	Acetylated viscose	Société de la Viscose Suisse, Switzerland
ACELE	Cellulose acetate, now known as 'acetate'	du Pont de Nemours & Co, USA
ACETA	Cellulose acetate filament	Farbenfabriken Bayer, Germany
ACETAT RHODIA	Acetate staple	Deutsche Rhodiaceta AG, Germany
ACETATE	Generic name for cellulose acetate	
ACETATE, Type C	Crimpable cellulose acetate	du Pont de Nemours & Co, USA
ACRIBEL	Acrylic	Fabelta, Belgium
ACRILAN	Modified polyacrylonitrile, staple	Monsanto Textiles, USA and N. Ireland
ACRYBEL	Former name for Acribel	Fabelta, Belgium
AGIL	Polyethylene	USA
AGILON	Stretch elastic nylon filament	Deering Milliken Research Corp, USA
AKULON	Nylon 6	A.K.U., Holland
AKVAFLEX	Polyolefines	Norway
ALASTIN	Viscose filament	Fabelta, Belgium
ALASTRA	Viscose filament	Fabelta, Belgium
ALBENE	Cellulose acetate	Deutsche Rhodiaceta AG, Germany and France
ALBUNA	Cellulose acetate dull, filament	Snia Viscosa, Italy
ALGINATE	Calcium alginate filament	Courtaulds Ltd, UK
ALON	High tenacity acetate staple	Toyo Rayon Co, Japan
AMILAN	Nylon 6	Toyo Rayon Co, Japan
AMILAR	Early name for Dacron	du Pont de Nemours & Co, USA
AMPLUM	Viscose bright	Algemene Kunstzijde N.V., Holland
ANTRON	Nylon	du Pont de Nemours & Co, USA
ANTRON 24	Trilobal nylon 66 for upholstery	du Pont de Nemours & Co, USA
ARGENTEA	Viscose filament, bright	Snia Viscosa, Italy
ARNEL	Cellulose triacetate, filament and staple	Celanese Corp of America, USA
ARTILANA	Viscose (protein added)	Artilana Schlutius, Germany
ASAHI	Viscose filament	Asahi Chemical Industry Co, Ltd, Japan

* This list is taken from *Man-Made Fibres* by R. W. Moncrieff, and is reproduced by kind permission of Newnes-Butterworth.

LIST OF FOREIGN FIBRE NAMES

Name of fibre	Type	Manufacturer
ASTRALENE	Stretch (twist) Terylene	Dobsons (Silk Throwsters) Ltd, UK
ASTRALON	Stretch (twist) nylon	Dobsons (Silk Throwsters) Ltd, UK
ATLON	Cellulose acetate	Toyo Rayon Co Ltd, Japan
AUSTRYLON	Nylon 66	Austria
AVILA	Viscose straw, plain ribbon-like	Feldmühle Ltd, Switzerland
AVLIN	Viscose staple	American Viscose Corp, USA
AZLON	Generic name for reconstituted protein fibres	
AZOTON	Cyanoethylated cotton	
BAN-LON	Stretch elastic nylon, filament	J. T. Bancroft & Sons Inc, USA
BAYER-ACRYL	Old name for Dralon	
BELIMAT	Viscose filament, dull	Fabelta, Belgium
BEMBERG	Cuprammonium filament	J. P. Bemberg AG, Germany, American Bemberg Corp, USA
BEMSILKIE	Cuprammonium	Asahi Chemical Industry Co Ltd, Japan
B.H.S.	Modacrylic	Courtaulds Ltd, UK
BIJOHAI	Viscose filament	Teikoku Rayon Co Ltd, Japan
BLACKBIRD	Viscose filament	Nippon Rayon Co Ltd, Japan
BLUE C NYLON	Nylon 66	Monsanto, USA and N. Ireland
BOBOL	Viscose staple	Snia Viscosa, Italy
BODANA	Viscose filament (2½ den) bright and dull natural and spun-dyed	Feldmühle Ltd, Switzerland
BODANELLA	Viscose filament (2 den) dull	Feldmühle Ltd, Switzerland
BODANITA	Viscose filament (2 den) dull, high twist	Feldmühle Ltd, Switzerland
BODANYL	Polycaprolactam filament	Feldmühle Ltd, Switzerland
BOLTAFLEX	Polyvinylidene chloride round and flat monofils	Bolta Products, USA
BOLTATHENE	Polyethylene	Monsanto, USA
BORGOLON	Polyamide	Italy
BREDANESE	Viscose, semi-dull	N.V. Hollandsche Kunstzijde Industries, Breda, Holland
BRENKA	Viscose filament	British Enka Ltd, UK
BRENKONA	Viscose filament, bright	British Enka Ltd, UK
BRIGLO	Viscose filament, bright	American Enka Corps, USA
BRI-NYLON	Nylon 66	British Nylon Spinners Ltd, UK, now I.C.I. Fibres Ltd
BRITENKA	Viscose filament, bright	British Enka Ltd, UK
CADON	Multilobal nylon 66	Monsanto, USA
CALYX	Viscose matt	North British Rayon Co Ltd, UK
CANTONA	Viscose, semi-dull	Algemene Kunstzijde N.V., Holland
CANTRECE	Polyamide	Canada
CARANA	Polyamide	Canada

LIST OF FOREIGN FIBRE NAMES

Name of fibre	Type	Manufacturer
CAROLAN	Cellulose acetate filament and staple	Mitsubishi Acetate Co Ltd, Japan
CASHMILAN	Polyacrylonitrile staple	Asahi Chemical Industry Co Ltd, Japan
CELACLOUD	Acetate filling fibre	Celanese Corp of America, USA
CELAFIBRE	Cellulose acetate staple	British Celanese Ltd, UK
CELAFIL	Cellulose acetate, ruptured	British Celanese Ltd, UK
CELAIRE	Nylon-acetate blend	Celanese Corp of America, USA
CELANESE	Cellulose acetate filament	British Celanese Ltd, UK
CELAPERM	Cellulose acetate, spun-dyed	Celanese Fibers Co, USA
CELARA	Textured cellulose acetate	American Celanese
CELASPUN	Staple fibre, e.g. polypropylene	Celanese, Canada
CELATOW	Acetate tow	Celanese Fibers Co, USA
CELCOS	Cellulose acetate, partly saponified	Celanese Corp of America, USA
CELON	Polycaprolactam	Courtaulds Ltd, UK
CELTA	Hollow filament viscose	Société de la Viscose Suisse, Switzerland
CETRYL	Polypropylene	France
CHADOLON	Polyamide	du Pont de Nemours & Co, USA
CHESLON	Bulked acetate and nylon	UK
CHEVIOT	Viscose filament, bright	North British Rayon Co Ltd, UK
CHEVISOL	Viscose filament, bright	North British Rayon Co Ltd, UK
CHINLON	Nylon 6	China
CHINON	Acrylic-protein graft	Japan
CHROMSPUN	Cellulose acetate spun-dyed, filament and staple	Tennessee Eastman Co, USA
CIFALON	Polyamide	Portugal
CISALFA	Viscose proteinized	Snia Viscosa, Italy
CLÉVYL	Polyvinyl chloride	France
CLORENE	Polyvinylidene chloride (monofil)	Société Rhovyl, France
COLCESA	Viscose filament, bright spun-dyed	Glanzstoff-Courtaulds G.m.b.H., Germany
COLCORD	High tenacity viscose tyre cord	Glanzstoff-Courtaulds G.m.b.H., Germany
COLNOVA	Viscose filament pearl, spun-dyed	Glanzstoff-Courtaulds G.m.b.H., Germany
COLOMAT	Viscose filament matt, spun-dyed	Glanzstoff-Courtaulds G.m.b.H., Germany
COLORAY	Viscose staple, spun-dyed	Courtaulds (Alabama) Inc, USA
COLVA	Viscose staple	Glanzstoff-Courtaulds G.m.b.H., Germany
COLVADUR	High tenacity viscose staple	Glanzstoff-Courtaulds G.m.b.H., Germany
COLVALAN	Crimped viscose staple	Glanzstoff-Courtaulds G.m.b.H., Germany
COMISO	Viscose tow	Beaunit, USA

LIST OF FOREIGN FIBRE NAMES

Name of fibre	Type	Manufacturer
CORVAL	Cross-linked viscose	Courtaulds (Alabama) Inc, USA
COURLENE	Polyethylene filament	Courtaulds Ltd, UK
COURLENE X3	Polyethylene filament	Courtaulds Ltd, UK
COURNOVA	Polypropylene monofils	British Celanese, UK
COURPLETA	Cellulose triacetate, filament and staple	Courtaulds Ltd, UK
COURTELLE	Modified polyacrylonitrile	Courtaulds Ltd, UK
COURTOLON	Bulked nylon 66 yarn	Courtaulds Ltd, UK
CREMONA	Vinylon	Kurashiki Rayon Co Ltd, Japan
CREPESYL	Viscose filament	North British Rayon Co Ltd, UK
CRESLAN	Modified acrylic	American Cyanamid Co, USA
CRESLAN Type 63	Readily dyeable modification of filament Creslan	American Cyanamid Co Ltd
CRILENKA	Acrylic	Spain
CRIMPLENE	Textured polyester yarn	Licensees of I.C.I.
CRINOL	Viscose monofil	Société de la Viscose Suisse, Switzerland
CRINOVYL	Polyvinyl chloride staple	Société Rhovyl, France
CRISPELLA	Viscose, ribbon shaped filaments	Hollandsche Kunstzijde Industries, Holland
CRYLENE	Acrylic	Italy
CRYLOR	Modified polyacrylonitrile filament and staple	Société Rhodiaceta, France
CTA	Polyamide	France
CUMULOFT	Textured nylon 66	Chemstrand (now Monsanto), USA
CUPIONI	Cuprammonium slub yarn	J. P. Bemberg AG, Germany
CUPRACOLOR	Spun-dyed cuprammonium	American Bemberg, USA
CUPRAMA	Cuprammonium staple	Farbenfabriken Bayer AG, Germany
CUPRAMMONIUM	Regenerated cellulose made by cuprammonium process	
CUPRESA	Cuprammonium filament	Farbenfabriken Bayer AG, Germany
CYDSA	Polyamide	Mexico
DACRON	Polyethylene *tere*phthalate filament and staple	du Pont de Nemours & Co, USA
DAIFUKI	Viscose filament	Toyo Rayon Co Ltd, Japan
DANUDUR	High tenacity viscose staple	Süddeutsche Chemiefaser AG, Germany
DANUFIL	Staple viscose, natural and spun-dyed	Süddeutsche Chemiefaser AG, Germany
DANUFLOR	Staple viscose for worsted system	Süddeutsche Chemiefaser AG, Germany
DARELLE	Flame retardant	UK
DARLAN	Polyvinylidene dicyanide staple	B. F. Goodrich Chem Co, USA (see Darvan)
DARVAN	New name for Darlan	Celanese Fibers Co, USA
DARYL	Triacetate filament	Fabelta, Belgium
DAWBARN	Polyolefine	Dawbarn Bros Inc, USA
DAYAN	Nylon 6	Perlofil S.A., Spain

LIST OF FOREIGN FIBRE NAMES

Name of fibre	Type	Manufacturer
DECORA	Viscose filament spun-dyed	Société de la Viscose Suisse, Switzerland
DELFION	Nylon 6	Soc. Bombini, Italy
DELUSTRA	Viscose filament, dull	Courtaulds Ltd, UK
DEXON	Polyglycollide	American Cyanamid
DIAFIL	Viscose filament	Teikoku Rayon Co Ltd, Japan
DICEL	Cellulose acetate filament	British Celanese Ltd, UK
DIMAFIL	Polyamide Nylon 6	Plasticizers Ltd., Drighlington
DIOLEN	Polyethylene *tere*phthalate	Vereinigte Glanzstoff-Fabriken AG, Germany
DLP	Polyolefines	Dawbarn Bros. Inc, USA
DOLAN	Modified polyacrylonitrile staple	Süddeutsche Zellwolle, Germany
DORIX	Polyamide	Belgium
DORLASTAN	Polyurethane	West Germany
DORLON	Polyurethane (Perlon U) monofils	Farbenfabriken Bayer AG, Germany
DRAHT	Polyethylene	West Germany
DRALON	Modified polyacrylonitrile staple	Farbenfabriken Bayer AG, Germany
DRAWINELLA	Cellulose acetate staple	A. Wacker G.m.b.H., Germany
DRYLENE	Polyethylene monofil	Plasticizers Ltd, Drighlington
DULKONA	Viscose filament matt	British Enka Ltd, UK
DUL-TONE	Viscose dull	Industrial Rayon Corp, USA
DURACOL	Indicative of Spun-dyed, e.g. DURACOL-FIBRO	Courtaulds Ltd, UK
DURAFIL	High tenacity viscose staple	Courtaulds Ltd, UK
DURAFLOX	High tenacity viscose staple	Spinnfaser AG, Germany
DURASPON	Polyurethane	USA
DURETA	Cuprammonium filament	J. P. Bemberg AG, Germany
DYNEL	Copolymer of vinyl chloride/ acrylonitrile staple	Carbide & Carbon Chemicals Corp, USA
ENCRON	Polyester	American Enka
ENGLO	Viscose filament dull	American Enka Corp, USA
ENKA	General name for products of Algemene Kunstzijde N.V., Holland	
ENKALENE	Polyethylene *tere*phthalate	Algemene Kunstzijde N.V., Holland
ENKALON	Nylon 6	American Enka Corp, USA, and British Enkalon Ltd, N. Ireland
ENKASWING	Polyurethane	Netherlands
ENKATRON	Multilobal nylon 6	American Enka Corp, USA
ENKA-5000	Viscose tyre yarn	American Enka Corp, USA
ENKONA	Viscose	Algemene Kunstzijde N.V., Holland
ENVILON	Polyvinyl chloride filament	Toyo Chemical Co Ltd, Japan
ESSEVI	Viscose filament	Snia Viscosa, Italy
ESTANE	Polyurethane spandex	B. F. Goodrich Chemical Co, USA
ESTERA	Cellulose acetate staple	Dai Nippon Celluloid Co Ltd, Japan

LIST OF FOREIGN FIBRE NAMES

Name of fibre	Type	Manufacturer
Estron	Cellulose acetate filament	Tennessee Eastman Co, USA
Ethofil	Experimental cyanoethylated cellulose	Dow Chemical Co, USA
Ethylon	Polyethylene	Kureha Kasei Co Ltd, Japan
Euroacryl	Acrylic	Italy
Evlan	Modified cellulose staple for carpet yarn	Courtaulds Ltd, UK
Evlan M	Similar to Evlan but with better abrasion resistance	Courtaulds Ltd, UK
Exlan	Polyacrylonitrile staple	Japan Exlan Co Ltd, Japan
Fabelcord	High tenacity viscose filament	Fabelta, Belgium
Fabelnyl	Polyamide	Fabelta, Belgium
Featheray	Hollow filament viscose	Hartford Rayon Corp, USA
Fiber G	Early name for Cordura	du Pont de Nemours & Co, USA
Fiber V	Early name for Dacron	du Pont de Nemours & Co, USA
Fiber Y	Early name for Qiana	du Pont de Nemours & Co, USA
Fiberfrax	Aluminium silicate refractory fibrous material	Carborundum Co, USA
Fiberglas	Glass filament and staple	Owens-Corning Fiberglas Corp, USA
Fibrana	Viscose staple	Spain
Fibranne	Viscose staple (generic French name)	
Fibravyl	Polyvinyl chloride staple	Société Rhovyl, France
Fibreglass	Glass	Fibreglass Ltd, UK
Fibre K	Polypivalolactone (being developed)	Shell, UK
Fibrelta	Viscose staple	Fabelta, Belgium
Fibrenka	Viscose staple	Algemene Kunstzijde Unie N.V., Holland
Fibro	Viscose staple	Courtaulds Ltd, UK
Fibroceta	Cellulose acetate staple	Courtaulds Ltd, UK
Fibrolane A	Casein staple	Courtaulds Ltd, UK
Fibrolane BX	Casein staple	Courtaulds Ltd, UK
Fibrolane BC	Casein staple chromium combined	Courtaulds Ltd, UK
Fidion	Polyester	Anic, Italy
Filmtex	Polyolefines	Norway
Flattoyo	Viscose ribbon straw (for wallpaper)	Toyo Rayon Co Ltd, Japan
Flimba	Viscose staple, spun-dyed	Société de la Viscose Suisse, Switzerland
Flisca	Viscose staple	Société de la Viscose Suisse, Switzerland
Flixor	Polyamide	Switzerland
Flock	Viscose very short staple (also a generic name for this material)	Société de la Viscose Suisse, Switzerland
Floterope	Polypropylene	USA
Flox	Viscose staple	Spinnfaser AG, Germany

LIST OF FOREIGN FIBRE NAMES

Name of fibre	Type	Manufacturer
Fluflene	Stretch Terylene filament	Wm. Frost & Sons Ltd, UK
Fluflon	Stretch nylon filament	Wm. Frost & Sons Ltd, UK
Forlion	Nylon 6	Soc. Orsi Mangeli, Italy
Fortinese	Stretch spun cellulose acetate	Celanese Corp of America, USA
Fortisan	Cellulose (acetate stretched and saponified) filament	Celanese Fibers Corp, USA
Fortisan 36	High tenacity cellulose, heavy denier	Celanese Corp of America, USA
Fortrel	Polyester	Fiber Industries Inc (Celanese), USA
Frankelon	Polyamide	Italy
Frankilene	Polyester	Fratelli Franchi, Italy
FT(ARCT)	Stretch nylon (false twist)	Deering Milliken Research Corp, USA
Ftorlon	Polypropylene	USSR
Fulflex	Polyurethane	USA
Furon	Polyamide	Poland
Garflon	Polyamide	India
Garnyl	Polyamide	India
Gerrix	Glass	Gerresheimer Glasshüttenwerke, Germany
Glanzstoff	Viscose	Vereinigte Glanzstoff-Fabriken AG, Germany
Glanzstoff-Perlon	Nylon 6 staple	Vereinigte Glanzstoff-Fabriken AG, Germany
Glaswolle	Glass	K. G. Schuller & Co, Germany
Glospan	Polyurethane snap-back	Globe Mnfg. Co, USA, and Globe Elastic Thread Co Ltd, UK
Gossamer	Polyester sewing thread	Coats, Patons, UK
Grafil	Carbon fibre	Courtaulds Ltd
Grilene	Polyester-polyether	Grilon S.A., Switzerland
Grillon	Polycaprolactam	Nippon Rayon Co Ltd, Japan
Grilon	Polycaprolactam	Grilon S.A., Switzerland
Gusei-Ichigo	Polyvinyl alcohol	Japan
Hautrage	Acrylic	Belgium
Heatherdine	Stretch nylon 66 with ruptured filaments	G. H. Heath & Co, UK
Helanca	Stretch elastic nylon filament and Terylene	Heberlein & Co, AG, Switzerland
Helcon	Polyamide	Italy
Helion	Polyamide	Italy, Malta
Helpon	Polyamide	USA
Herculan	Polypropylene staple	Hercules Powder Co, USA
Hi-Bulk Acrilan	Acrilan which crimps on near boiling	Chemstrand Corp (now Monsanto), USA
Hi-Crimp Vicara	Crimped zein protein	Virginia Carolina Chem Corp, USA
High Bulk Orlon	Orlon Type 42 which crimps on near boiling	du Pont de Nemours & Co, USA
High Bulk Tricel	Bulked Tricel	Courtaulds Ltd, UK

LIST OF FOREIGN FIBRE NAMES

Name of fibre	Type	Manufacturer
Hightel	Polynosic viscose staple	Teikoku Rayon Co Ltd, Japan
Hilon	Polyamide	Italy
Hi-Narco	Viscose for tyres	North American Rayon Corp, USA
Hipolan	Polynosic rayon	Japan
Hiralon	Polyethylene	Japan
H-Nylon	Polyamide	New Zealand
Hostalen	Polypropylene	Germany
Hsien-Chin	Polyethylene	Taiwan
Hsien-Thin	Polyethylene	Taiwan
Hualon	Polyester	Taiwan
Igg-Vestan	Polyvinylidene chloride	Internationale Galalith G.m.b.H., Germany
IRC, Type 6	Polycaprolactam staple	Industrial Rayon Corp, USA
Iridex	Viscose spun-dyed filament	Kirklees Ltd, UK
Iridye	Viscose yarn-dyed	Kirklees Ltd, UK
Isovyl	Polyvinyl chloride	Société Rhovyl, France
Istrakin	Polypropylene	Spain
Ivorea	Viscose filament dull	Snia Viscosa, Italy
Jayanka	Polyamide	India
Jaykaylon	Polyamide	India
Jedmat	Viscose filament matt	North British Rayon Co Ltd, UK
Jedsol	Viscose filament matt	North British Rayon Co Ltd, UK
Jedsyl	Viscose filament bright	North British Rayon Co Ltd, UK
K-6	Early name for Chinon	Toyobo, Japan
Kalimer	Polyester	Resina Sud, Italy
Kanebian	Vinylon	Kanegafuchi Spinning Co Ltd, Japan
Kanekalon	Acrylonitrile/vinyl ester copolymer (modacrylic staple)	Kanegafuchi Chem Co Ltd, and Kanekalon Co Ltd, Japan
Kanelion	High tenacity rayon staple	Kanegafuchi Spinning Co Ltd, Japan
Kasei Ester	Polyester	Japan
Kasilga	Viscose filament	Kunstsilkefabrikken, Norway
Kelheim H	Hollow filament viscose	Süddeutsche Zellwolle AG, Germany
Khlorin	Polyvinyl chloride	USSR
Kikansei	Viscose filament	Toyo Spinning Co Ltd, Japan
Kirksyl	Viscose filament	Kirklees Ltd, UK
Kodel	Polyester	Eastman Chemical Products, USA
Kosei-Silk	Fibre spun from waste silk protein	Fuji Spinning Co Ltd, Japan
Krehalon	Polyvinylidene chloride	Kuahi Kasei, Japan
Krehalon S	Polyvinyl chloride	Kureha Kasei, Japan
K.R.P.	Viscose staple	Kokohu Rayon & Pulp Co Ltd Japan
Krylion	Acrylic	Italy

LIST OF FOREIGN FIBRE NAMES

Name of fibre	Type	Manufacturer
KUO-HWA	Polyamide	Taiwan
KURALAY	Polyester	Japan
KURALON	Polyvinyl alcohol (Vinylon) staple	Kurashiki Rayon Co Ltd, Japan
LAMÉ	Metallic	Standard Yarn Mills, USA
LAMITA	Viscose tow spun-dyed	Société de la Viscose Suisse, Switzerland
LAMO	Viscose tow	Société de la Viscose Suisse, Switzerland
LANABETA	Viscose proteinized	Snia Viscosa, Italy
LANALPHA	Viscose proteinized	Snia Viscosa, Italy
LANCOLA	Dope-dyed textured acetate yarn	Lansil Ltd, Lancaster, UK
LANESE	Cellulose acetate staple	Celanese Corp of America, USA
LANON	Polyester	V.E.B. Thuringisches Kunstfaserwerk, Germany
LANSIL	Cellulose acetate filament	Lansil Ltd, UK
LANTUCK NR	Non-woven fabric	West Point Mfg Co, USA
LAVETEN	Polyethylene	Sweden
LAVSAN	Polyester	USSR
LEACRIL	Italian Acrilan	A.C.S.A., Italy
LEASTER	Polyester	Châtillon, Italy
LEAVIL	Polyvinyl chloride	Italy
LENCRIL	Acrylic	Spain
LETIN	Polyvinyl alcohol	USSR
LILION	Polycaprolactam	Snia Viscosa, Italy
LIRELLE	Polyester	Courtaulds, Carrickfergus, UK
LONZONA	Acetate filament	Lonzona G.m.b.H., Germany
LUMITE	Polyvinylidene chloride	Chicopee Mfg Corp, USA
LUMIYARN	Metallized polyester filament	Toyo Chemical Co Ltd, Japan
LUREX	'Butyrate' metallic filament	Dobeckmun Co, USA
LUREX MF	'Mylar' metallic filament	Dobeckmun Co, USA
LUSTRAFIL	Viscose filament	Lustrafil Ltd, UK
LUXEL	Polyester	Argentine
LYCRA	Snap-back	du Pont, USA, and Maydown, Northern Ireland
MADAME BUTTERFLY	Viscose filament	Toyo Rayon Co Ltd, Japan
MARIMUSUME	Viscose staple	Nippon Rayon Co Ltd, Japan
MARLEX	Polyethylene	Phillips Petroleum Co, USA
MATAPONT	Viscose straw	Société de la Viscose Suisse, Switzerland
MATESA	Cuprammonium filament	American Bemberg Corp, USA
MENDEL	Bicomponent polyester and nylon	Teijin, Japan
MERAKLON	Polypropylene	Montecatini, Italy
MERAKRIN	Polypropylene	Italy
MERON	Bulky nylon	USSR
MERYL B8	Viscose	Comptoir des Textiles Artificiels, France
METALIAN	Anti-static yarn	Teijin, Japan

LIST OF FOREIGN FIBRE NAMES

Name of fibre	Type	Manufacturer
METLON	Butyrate metallic	Metlon Corp, USA
METLON-with-MYLAR	Metallic in Mylar	Metlon Corp, USA
MEUBALESE	Cellulose acetate slub filament	British Celanese Ltd, UK
MEWLON	Polyvinyl alcohol filament and staple (Vinylon)	Dai Nippon Spinning Co Ltd, Japan
MIHARAHYO	Viscose filament	Teikoku Rayon Co Ltd, Japan
MIKRON	Polyvinyl alcohol	
MINALON	Cellulose acetate filament and staple	Shin Nippon Chisso Hiryo Co Ltd, Japan
MIRALON	Bulking process for nylon	
MISRNYLON	Polyamide	Egypt
MISROPHANE	Viscose film	Société M.I.S.R. pour la Rayonne, Egypt
MOBILON	Polyurethane	Japan
MODMOR	Carbon fibre	Courtaulds Ltd
MONOLENE	Polypropylene	Canada
MONOPRO	Polypropylene	Canada
MOPLEN	Polypropylene	Montecatini, Italy
MOVYL	Polyvinyl chloride	Montecatini, Italy
MOYNEL	Polynosic viscose rayon staple same as S.C. 28	Courtaulds (Alabama) Inc, USA
MULTIFLEX	Polypropylene	Denmark
MULTILENE	Polyolefines	Canada
MYLAR	Polyester film	du Pont de Nemours & Co, USA
N-53	Modified polyacrylonitrile	Kunstzijde-spinnerij, Nyma, Holland
NAILON	Nylon 66	Rhodiatoce S.p.A., Italy
NARCO	Viscose filament	North American Rayon Corp, USA
NEFA-PERLON	Polycaprolactam	Glanzstoff Fabriken AG, Germany
NEOCHROME	Courtelle spun-dyed	Courtaulds Ltd, UK
NEVA	Polyamide	West Germany
NILOM	Polyamide	India
NIP	Polyvinyl chloride filament	Nichay Plastics Co, Japan
NIPLON	Nylon 66	Dai Nippon Spinning Co Ltd, Japan
NIRESTER	Polyester	India
NIRLON	Nylon 6	Indian Rayon Corp, India
NITLON	Acrylic	Japan
NITRILON	Uncertain, possibly polyvinylidene dicyanide	USSR
NIVION	Polyamide	Italy
NOMEX	Aromatic polyamide	du Pont, USA
NORTHYLENE	Polyethylene	Norddeutsche Seekabelwerke AG, Germany
NOVACETA	Cellulose acetate	S.A. Novaceta, Italy
NRC NYLON	Nylon 6	Nippon Rayon Co, Japan
NUFIL	Polypropylene film tape	I.C.I. Ltd
NUMA	Polyurethane	USA
NUPRON	Viscose	Industrial Rayon Corp, USA

LIST OF FOREIGN FIBRE NAMES

Name of fibre	Type	Manufacturer
NUREL	Polyamide	Spain
NYLENKA	Polycaprolactam filament and staple	American Enka Corp, USA
NYLFIL	Polyamide	Mexico
NYLFRANCE	Nylon 66	Rhodiacetta, France
NYLHAIR	Polyamide	Spain
NYLOFT	Polyamide Nylon 6	I.R.C., USA
NYLON	Generic name for fibre-forming polyamides	du Pont de Nemours & Co, USA; British Nylon Spinners, UK; Chemstrand Corp, USA, and others
NYLON 4	Polypyrrolidone	General Aniline & Film Corp, USA
NYLON 6	Polycaprolactam (Perlon and many other names)	British Celanese Ltd, UK; Farbenfabriken Bayer AG, Germany, and many others
NYLON 66	Polyhexamethylene adipamide filament, and staple and tow	du Pont de Nemours & Co, USA; British Nylon Spinners, UK, and others
NYLON Type 91	Whiter (fluorescent) nylon 66	du Pont de Nemours & Co, USA
NYLON Type 250	Deep dye nylon 66	du Pont de Nemours & Co, USA
NYLON 1 B-610	Rubber-like nylon	du Pont de Nemours & Co, USA
NYLON 610	Polyhexamethylene sebacamide filament	du Pont de Nemours & Co, USA
NYLON R	Nylon 11	
NYLPAK	Polyamide	Pakistan
NYLSUISSE	Nylon 66	Société de la Viscose Suisse, Switzerland
NYMACRYL	Acrylic	Kunstzijde-spinnerji, Nyma, Holland
NYMACRYON	Acrylic	Kunstzijde-spinnerij, Nyma, Holland
NYMCRYLON	Acrylic	Netherlands
NYMKRON	Acrylic	Netherlands
NYMPLEX	Polyethylene	Netherlands, Denmark
NYPEL	Polyamide	USA
OKSON	Polyester (modified)	USSR
OLANE	Polypropylene filament and staple	Avi-Sun, USA
OLETENE	Polyethylene	France
OMNIALON	Polyamide	Italy
OMNI-NYLON	Polyamide	Mexico
OPACETA	Cellulose acetate filament matt	Courtaulds Ltd, UK
OPELON	Snap-back	Toyo Rayon Co, Japan
OPELON	Polyurethane	Japan
OPLEXMATT	Viscose filament matt	Harbens Ltd, UK
ORLON, Type 39	Modified acrylic heavy denier for woollen spinning	du Pont de Nemours & Co, USA

LIST OF FOREIGN FIBRE NAMES

Name of fibre	Type	Manufacturer
ORLON, Type 42	Modified acrylic staple and tow	du Pont de Nemours & Co, USA
ORLON, Type 81	Polyacrylonitrile filament	du Pont de Nemours & Co, USA
ORLON-CANTRECE	Filament polyacrylonitrile	du Pont de Nemours & Co, USA
ORLON SAYELLE	Bicomponent acrylic with built-in crimp	du Pont de Nemours & Co, USA
ORTALION	Polyamide	Bemberg, Italy
PAN	Modified polyacrylonitrile filament	Farbenfabriken Bayer AG, Casella Farbwerke Mainkur AG, Germany
PARAMAFIL	Viscose staple	Nitto Spinning Co Ltd, Japan
PARAMOUNT	Viscose bright warp	North British Rayon Co, UK
PCU	Polyvinyl chloride	Badische Anilin & Soda Fabrik, Germany
PERFIL	Polyethylene	Australia
PERLENKA	Nylon 6	A.K.U., Holland
PERLGLO	Viscose filament, semi-dull	American Enka Corp, USA
PERLOFIL	Polycaprolactam	Spain
PERLON	Polycaprolactam filament and staple	Farbwerke Hoechst AG, Deutsche Rhodiaceta AG, & Phrixwerke AG, Germany
PERLON 6	Another name for Perlon	
PERLON-HOECHST	Nylon 6 filament and staple	Farbwerke Hoechst AG, Germany
PERLON T	Nylon 66	I.G. Farbenindustrie, Germany
PERLON U	Polyurethane	Germany
PERMALON	Polyvinylidene chloride	Pierce Plastics Inc, USA
PERRO	Blend of 1 part viscose staple, 2 parts Peruvian cotton, same strength wet as dry	
PHRILAN	Crimped viscose staple	Phrixwerke AG, Germany
PHRILON	Polycaprolactam	Phrixwerke AG, Germany
PHRIX-PERLON	Nylon 6 staple	Phrixwerke AG, Germany
PHRIX-REYON	Viscose	Phrixwerke AG, Germany
PHRIX STW	Viscose staple	Phrixwerke AG, Germany
PIRFLEX	Polyurethane	UK
PLATILON	Polyethylene	Toyo Chemical Co Ltd, Japan
PLUTON	Organic heat-resistant fibre	Minnesota Mining & Mfg Co, USA
POLIAFIL	Polyamide	USA
POLITAL	Polyethylene	West Germany
POLITEN-OMNI	Polyethylene	Mexico
POLYÄTHYLEN	Polyethylene	West Germany
POLYCAISSIS	Polypropylene	West Germany
POLYCORD	Polyamide	Italy
POLYETHYLENE	Generic name for fibres made by polymerizing ethylene, e.g. Courlene, Wynene	
POLYFIBRES	Polyamide	France
POLYFILENE	Polypropylene	Netherlands

LIST OF FOREIGN FIBRE NAMES

Name of fibre	Type	Manufacturer
POLYMER R	Nylon 11	Rehoboth Research Lab, Israel
POLYPIVALO-LACTONE	Polyester new development	Shell, UK and Kanegafuchi, Japan
POLYSPLIT	Polyethylene	Sweden
POLYSPLIT	Polypropylene	Sweden
POLYTHENE	Polyethylene	
POLYTIE	Polypropylene	Canada
POLYTWINE	Polypropylene	Canada
POWLON	Acrylic	Japan
PRELANA	Modified acrylic	Eastern Germany
PREMIER	Viscose	Industrial Rayon Corp, USA
PUSAN	Polyester	Korea
PVC-BORSTEN HOECHST	P.V.C. bristle	Farbwerke Hoechst AG, Germany
PYLEN	Polyethylene	Toyo Rayon Co Ltd, Japan
PYLON	Polypropylene	Pakistan
QIANA	Polyamide	du Pont de Nemours & Co, USA
RADILON	Polyamide	Italy
RAILAN	Viscose proteinized	Snia Viscosa, Italy
RAINBOW	Viscose staple	Teikoku Rayon Co Ltd, Japan
RAYCELON	A twinned yarn made from 5 parts viscose rayon and 3 parts Celon	Courtaulds Ltd
RAYFLEX	High tenacity viscose filament	American Viscose Corp, USA
RAYOLANDA	Modified viscose	Courtaulds Ltd, UK
RAYONNE	Generic French name for filament viscose	
REDON	Modified polyacrylonitrile crimped staple	Austria
REEVON	Polyethylene	Reeves Bros Inc, USA
RETRACTYL	Polyvinyl chloride staple	Société Rhovyl, France
REYMET	Metal foil-film laminate cut	Reynolds Metals Co, USA
RHIAKNOT	Acetate fancy yarn	Deutsche Rhodiaceta AG, Germany
RHODASTIC	Polyurethane	France
RHODELIA	Acetate textured yarn	Deutsche Rhodiaceta AG, Germany
RHODIA	General name for products of Société Rhodiaceta, France	
RHODIA FASER	Cellulose acetate staple	Deutsche Rhodiaceta AG, Germany
RHODIAFIL	Cellulose acetate filament	Deutsche Rhodiaceta AG, Germany
RHODIALIN	Cellulose acetate	Deutsche Rhodiaceta AG, Germany
RHODIANIL	Nylon 66	Brazil
RHONEL	Cellulose triacetate	France
RHOVENYL	Fibravyl/nylon blend	Société Rhovyl, France
RHOVYL	Polyvinyl chloride filament	Société Rhovyl, France

LIST OF FOREIGN FIBRE NAMES

Name of fibre	Type	Manufacturer
Rhovyl Moss	Helanca type Rhovyl	Société Rhovyl, France
Rhovyline	Fibravyl blends with other fibres	Société Rhovyl, France
Rhovylon	Thermovyl/nylon blend	Société Rhovyl, France
Rilsan	Nylon 11	Organico S.A., France; and Snia Viscosa, Italy
Rofil	Polyethylene	UK
Ronbel	Graft polymer of acrylonitrile and viscose; wool-like staple	Kanegafuchi Spinning Co Ltd, Japan
Rotwyla	Viscose rayon	Rottweiler Kunstseidenfabrik AG, Germany
Rovana	Ribbon shaped Saran monofil	Dow Chemical Co, USA
Royalene	Polyolefines	US Rubber Co, USA
Saaba	Stretch nylon (false twist)	Leesona Corp, USA
Safa	Polyamide	Spain
Sanderit	Polycaprolactam monofil	Fr. Sander-Nachf., Germany
Sanflon	Polyamide	India
Saran	Polyvinylidene chloride	Saran Yarns Co, USA (Polymer made by Dow Chemical Co, USA)
Sarfa	Viscose filament twisted	Feldmühle Ltd, Switzerland
Sarille	Crimped viscose staple	Courtaulds Ltd
Sarlane	Polyurethane	Belgium
Sastiga	Viscose filament (4 den) bright and dull, natural and spun-dyed	Feldmühle Ltd, Switzerland
SC 28	Polynosic rayon staple	Courtaulds Ltd, UK
Scaldura	Polynosic viscose	Fabelta, Belgium
Seraceta	Cellulose acetate filament	Courtaulds Ltd, UK
Seria	Polyester	Italy
Seris	Polyester	Châtillon, Italy
Shalon	Polystyrene	USA
Shalon	Polyethylene	USA
Shinko	Viscose staple	Mitsubishi Rayon Co Ltd, Japan
Shiro Diafil	Viscose filament, dull	Teikoku Rayon Co Ltd, Japan
Silene	Cellulose acetate	Novaceta S.p.A., Italy
Sircril	Acrylic	Italy
Siron	Polyester	Italiana Resine, Italy
Skenandoa	Viscose	Skenandoa Rayon Corp, USA
Skybloom	High crimp rayon staple	American Enka Corp, USA
Slovina	Viscose proteinized	Bata Slovenska, Czechoslovakia
SM 27	Polynosic rayon staple	Courtaulds (Alabama) Inc, USA
Sniafil	Viscose filament	Snia Viscosa, Italy
Softalon	Polyamide	West Germany
Solvron	Water-soluble polyvinyl alcohol	
Spandelle	Snap-back fibre	Firestone, USA
Spandex	Generic term for polyurethane snap-back fibres	

LIST OF FOREIGN FIBRE NAMES

Name of fibre	Type	Manufacturer
SPANNY	Acrylic	Italy
SPANZELLE	Snap-back fibre	Courtaulds, UK
SPIRALOK	Polypropylene	Canada
SPUNIZED	Stretch nylon	Spunize Co of America, USA
STARNEL	Scandinavian name for Arnel	
STILON	Same as Steelon	Italy
STYROFLEX	Polystyrene	Norddeutsche Seekabelwerke AG, Germany
SUIKO	Viscose staple	Toyo Rayon Co Ltd, Japan
SUPER AMILAN	Nylon 66 monofil	Toyo Rayon Co Ltd, Japan
SUPER CORDENKA	High tenacity viscose filament	A.K.U., Holland
SUPER NARCO	High tenacity viscose filament	North American Rayon Corp, USA
SUPER RAYFLEX	High tenacity viscose filament	American Viscose Corp, USA
SUPER TENAX	High tenacity viscose filament	Toyo Rayon Co Ltd, Japan
SUPER TOYOTENAX	High tenacity viscose filament	Toyo Rayon Co Ltd, Japan
SUPER VISTRON	High tenacity viscose filament	Nippon Rayon Co Ltd, Japan
SUPERBREDA	Viscose filament	Hollandsche Kunstzijde Industries, Holland
SUPERENKA	Viscose filament	American Enka Corp, USA
SUPERLOFT	Stretch nylon (false twist)	Leesona Corp, USA
SUPRACOL	Spun-dyed viscose staple	Aktieselskapel Borregaard, Norway
SUPRAL	Viscose staple, cotton type	Aktieselskapel Borregaard, Norway
SUPRALAN	Viscose staple, wool type	Aktieselskapel Borregaard, Norway
SYNFOAM	Stretch nylon	
SYNTHOFIL	Polyvinyl alcohol	Wacker-Chemie G.m.b.H, Germany
SYNTHYL	Polyamide	Greece
T-1700	Polyester elastic fibre (similar to spandex)	Tennessee Eastman Co, USA
TACRYL	Polyacrylonitrile	Sweden
TAIRILAN	Acrylic	Taiwan
TAIRILIN	Polyester	Taiwan
TANIKALON	Polyethylene	Japan
TASLAN	Texturing process applied to nylon, viscose, etc.	Licensed by du Pont de Nemours & Co, USA
TECA	Cellulose acetate staple	Tennessee Eastman Co, USA
TEFLON	Polytetrafluoroethylene filament and staple	du Pont de Nemours & Co, USA
TEIJIN	Viscose filament	Teikoku Rayon Co Ltd, Japan
TEIJIN ACETATE	Cellulose acetate filament	Teikoku Rayon Co Ltd, Japan
TEIJIN CORD	High tenacity viscose filament	Teikoku Rayon Co Ltd, Japan
TEKLAN	Modacrylic	Courtaulds Ltd, UK
TEMPRA	High tenacity viscose filament	American Enka Corp, USA

LIST OF FOREIGN FIBRE NAMES

Name of fibre	Type	Manufacturer
TENASCO	High tenacity viscose filament	Courtaulds Ltd, UK
TENAX	High tenacity viscose filament	A.K.U., Holland
TENDAN	Viscose filament	Nippon Rayon Co Ltd, Japan
TENKYO	Viscose filament	Teikoku Rayon Co Ltd, Japan
TERENE	Polyester	India
TERGAL	Polyethylene *tere*phthalate	Société Rhodiaceta, France
TERIBER	Polyester	Barcelona, Spain, also Farbwerke Hoechst, West Germany
TERITAL	Polyethylene *tere*phthalate	Montecatini, Societa Generale per l'Industria Mineraria e Chimica, Rhodiatoce, Italy
TERLENKA	Polyethylene *tere*phthalate	Algemene Kunstzijde Unie N.V., Holland and British Enkalon Ltd
TERSUISSE	Polyester	Switzerland
TERYLENE	Polyethylene *tere*phthalate filament and staple	I.C.I. Ltd, UK
TETORON	Polyester	Toyo Rayon Co Ltd, Japan
TEVIRON	Polyvinyl chloride	Teikoku Rayon Co Ltd, Japan
TEWE	Polypropylene	Austria
TEXNYL	Nylon 6 for apparel	A/B Svenskt Konstsilke, Sweden
TEXTRALIZED	Ban-Lon stretch nylon	J. Bancroft & Co, USA
THERMOVYL	Polyvinyl chloride staple	Société Rhovyl, France
THIOLAN	Polyvinyl alcohol	Eastern Germany
THORNEL	Graphite high modulus	Union Carbide Corp, USA
TIOLAN	Casein	Spinstoff G.m.b.H., Germany
TIPTOLENE	Polypropylene	Netherlands
TOHALON	High tenacity acetate staple	Toyo Rayon Co Ltd, Japan
TOPEL	Cross-linked viscose rayon	Courtaulds (Alabama) Inc, USA
TORAYLON	Acrylic	Japan
TOVIS	Viscose crimped staple and tow	Toyo Rayon Co Ltd, Japan
TOYOBO	Viscose staple	Toyo Rayon Co Ltd, Japan
TOYOFLON	Polytetrafluoroethylene	Toyo Rayon Co Ltd, Japan
TOYOLAN	70 Viscose/30 Amilan blend	Toyo Rayon Co Ltd, Japan
TOYOTENAX	High tenacity viscose	Toyo Rayon Co Ltd, Japan
TRALBÉ	Polyester	France
TRAVIS	European name for Darvan	Celanese-Farbwerke Hoechst, Germany
TR-DRAHT	Polyester	West Germany
TRELON	Polycaprolactam	V.E.B. Thuringisches, Germany
TREVIRA	Polyethylene *tere*phthalate	Farbwerke Hoechst AG, Germany
TRI-A-FASER	Triacetate staple	Deutsche Rhodiaceta, Germany
TRIALBENE	Cellulose triacetate	Rhodiaceta, France
TRICEL	Cellulose triacetate filament and staple	British Celanese Ltd, UK
TRICELON	Bicomponent cellulose triacetate and nylon 6	Courtaulds Ltd, UK

LIST OF FOREIGN FIBRE NAMES

Name of fibre	Type	Manufacturer
TRICELON	A twinned yarn made from Tricel and Celon	Courtaulds Ltd, UK
TRI-DYE	Polyamide	USA
TRILAN	Cellulose triacetate	Canadian Celanese, Canada
TRINYL	Polyamide	Spain
TRITOR	Monofil polypropylene	Plasticizers Ltd
TROFIL	Polyethylene	West Germany
TRYLKO	Polyester sewing thread	English Sewing Ltd
TUDENZA	Viscose fine-filament	Courtaulds Ltd, UK
TUFCEL	Polynosic viscose staple	Toyobo, Japan
TUFTON	Polyethylene	Canada
TURLON	Polyamide	Turkey
TUSSON	Cuprammonium slub yarn	J. P. Bemberg AG, Germany, and American Bemberg Corp, USA
TYCORA	Textured yarn of several kinds	Textured Yarn Co, USA
TYGAN	Polyvinylidene chloride	Fothergill & Harvey Ltd, UK
TYRENKA	Viscose high tenacity filament	British Enka Ltd, UK
TYREX	High tenacity viscose for tyres	Members of Tyrex Inc.
TYRON	Viscose high tenacity filament	Industrial Rayon Corp, USA
ULON	Polyamide	Taiwan
ULSAN	Polyamide	Korea
ULSTRON	Polypropylene filament	I.C.I. Ltd, UK
ULTRAPAN	Acrylic	West Germany
ULTREMA	Viscose filament	Société de la Viscose Suisse, Switzerland
UNEL	Polyamide	Canada
UNIROYAL	Polypropylene	Uniroyal Fibres
URYLON	Polyurea	Toyo Koatsu, Japan
USTEX	Modified cotton	United States Rubber Co, USA
VECTRA	Polyethylene	USA
VELICREN	Acrylic	Italy
VELON	Polyvinylidene chloride	Firestone Industrial Products, USA
VENUS	Viscose staple	Fuji Spinning Co Ltd, Japan
VEREL	Modified acrylic staple	Tennessee Eastman Co, USA
VERI DULL	Viscose dull	Skenandoa Rayon Corp, USA
VESTAN	Another name for Kodel	Eastman Chemical, USA
VESTOLAN	Polyethylene	West Germany
VIBREM	Slubbed viscose filament	Snia Viscosa, Italy
VILOFT	Viscose	Courtaulds Ltd, UK
VINAL 5F	Vinylon	Kurashiki Rayon Co Ltd, Japan
VINAL FO	High tenacity polyvinyl alcohol	Kurashiki Rayon Co, Japan, and Air Reduction Co, USA
VINALON	Polyvinyl alcohol	Korea
VINCEL	Polynosic rayon	Courtaulds Ltd, UK
VINITRON	95 Khlorin/5 cellulose acetate co-spun	USSR

LIST OF FOREIGN FIBRE NAMES

Name of fibre	Type	Manufacturer
VINOL	Polyvinyl alcohol	USSR
VINYLON	Polyvinyl alcohol filament and staple	Kurashiki Rayon Co Ltd, Japan
VINYON CF	Co-polymer of vinyl chloride/vinyl acetate filament	American Viscose Corp, USA
VINYON HH	Co-polymer of vinyl chloride/vinyl acetate staple	American Viscose Corp, USA
VISADA	Viscose	Breda, Holland
VISCOR	High tenacity viscose filament	Société de la Viscose Suisse, Switzerland
VISCOSE	Generic name for regenerated cellulose made by 'viscose' process	
VISTRA XT	Viscose, wool-like staple	I.G. Farbenindustrie, Germany
VISTRALEN	Viscose, wool-like	I.G. Farbenindustrie, Germany
VISTRON	High tenacity viscose	Nippon Rayon Co Ltd, Japan
VITEL	Polyester resin from which Vycron is made	
VITROCELLE	Viscose, film	Ets. Dalle Frères et Lecomte, France
VITRON	Glass	L.O.F. Glass Fibers Inc, USA
VONNEL	Polyacrylonitrile staple	Mitsubishi Vonnel Co, Japan
VOPLEX	Polyvinyl chloride	USA
VYCRON	Polyester	Beaunit Mills, USA
VYRENE	Snap-back	US Rubber Co, Dunlop Rubber Co
W-63	Another name for Lirelle	Courtaulds, North America Inc.
WIKILANA	Viscose, fish protein added	Mecheels-Hiltner, Germany
WISTEL	Polyester	Snia Viscosa, Italy
WOOLIE AMILAN	Stretch elastic nylon 66	Toyo Rayon Co Ltd, Japan
WOOLON	Polyvinyl alcohol	
WYNENE 1	Polyethylene monofil	National Plastic Products Co, USA
XTRA DULL	Viscose dull	North American Rayon Corp, USA
Z54	Polynosic rayon	France and Belgium
ZANTREL	Polynosic rayon	USA
ZARYL	Polynosic staple viscose	Fabelta, Belgium
ZEFKROME	Spun-dyed acrylic	Dow-Badische, USA
ZEFRAN	Nitrile co-polymer staple and tow	Dow Chemical Co, USA
ZEHLA	Staple viscose	Spinnstoff-fabrik Zehlendrof AG, Germany
ZEHLA-PERLON	Nylon 6 filament and staple	Spinnstoff-fabrik Zehlendrof AG, Germany
ZELLWOLLE	Generic German name for viscose staple	
ZETEK	Darvan	B. F. Goodrich, USA

Index